LATIN AMERICAN
SPANISH
PHRASEBOOK

Latin American Spanish phrasebook
   3rd edition

Published by
   Lonely Planet Publications
   Head Office: PO Box 617, Hawthorn, Vic 3122, Australia
   Branches: 150 Linden Street, Oakland CA 94607, USA
                10a Spring Place, London NW5 3BH, UK
                1 rue de Dahomey, 75011 Paris, France

Printed by
Colorcraft Ltd, Hong Kong

Cover Illustration
   I Can't Get No Salsafaction by Penelope Richardson

Published
   March 1998

National Library of Australia Cataloguing in Publication Data

Steward, Sally
   Latin American Spanish phrasebook
   3rd ed.
   Includes index.
   ISBN 0 86442 558 9.

   1. Spanish language – Conversation and phrase books – English. 2.
   Spanish language – Dialects – Latin America. I. Steward, Sally. II.
   Title. (Series : Lonely Planet language survival kit).

   468.3421

   © Lonely Planet Publications Pty Ltd, 1998
   Cover Illustration © Lonely Planet

From the Publisher

Sally Steward edited this book, and Peter D'Onghia and Quentin Frayne proofread and put it all together. Illustrations for the book and cover are by Penelope Richardson, and layout is by Fabrice Rocher.

This Book

This edition was put together at Lonely Planet publications with the assistance of Maria Robson, whose Argentinian background provided us with ideas about meat and tango; Sergio Mariscal, whose Colombian expertise in dancing helped tremendously; and Professor Ronulfo Morera and Alejandra Barahona from the Universidad Veritas in Costa Rica, and the team at Encuentros Comunicacion y Cultura in Morelos, Mexico, all of whom supplied us with details on colloquial usage.

The original edition was written by Anna Cody, who has lived for many years in Central and South America. Contributors to the first two editions include Krzysztof Dydynski, author of the Lonely Planet guide to *Colombia*; Beatrice Glattauer, Angela Melendro and Maria Roca; and the authors of various Lonely Planet guides to Latin American countries.

Thanks to Izaskun Arretxe and Allison Jones, whose groundbreaking work on the *Spanish* phrasebook paved the way for this edition, to Nick Tapp for advice on trekking, and to Anke Munderloh of *Outdoor* magazine, for her enthusiasm for travel in Latin America.

CONTENTS

INTRODUCTION

The large number of people speaking Spanish in Latin America makes Spanish one of the most widely spoken languages in the world. Widespread colonisation by Spain in the 16th and 17th centuries ensured Spanish became the predominant language throughout 19 countries on the American continent and in the Caribbean. You will also find this book useful in the southern states of the USA, where Spanish is widely spoken.

Latin American Spanish developed originally from the Spanish of Spain, in particular southern Spain. This is because many settlers of Latin America either came from Andalusia or waited there for months before leaving. It is thought that Andalusian speech patterns emigrated with them. Most of these peculiarities concern pronunciation. This is the area where the 'c' is not lisped, as it is in most of Spain, and this along with some other local variations formed a basis for the evolution of the language. The language now differs from the Spanish of Spain, to a similar extent as US English does from UK English, and it varies throughout the regions it encompasses. This diversity is due to the influences on the language in each country of Latin America. A strong impact, especially on the vocabulary of flora, fauna and cultural habits, came from the languages of the indigenous population, and later from European immigrants, particulary in Argentina and Uruguay.

The Latin American Spanish in this phrasebook includes essential variations between countries. As you travel from one country to another you will notice that the most obvious difference is in the accents rather than the words used.

Generally, Latin Americans are as fascinated by you and your background as you are with their culture and lives. It is therefore not unusual to be plied with questions once the initial shyness has disappeared. Any effort to reply in Spanish is greatly appreciated and encouraged with a great deal of smiling and laughing.

INTRODUCTION

GETTING STARTED

So you will always have something to say, you should memorise a few basic words of Latin American Spanish. 'Yes' is Sí and 'No' is No – that's easy. A general 'Hello' is Hola (pronounced without the 'h' and a general 'How are you?' is ¿Cómo está? (See page 45 for more greetings.) Por favor means 'Please'. It's a good idea to tack this word onto any request you make. 'Thank you' is Gracias. Page 47 has some useful extra phrases for making conversation while pages 36–38 list the most common verbs. If you get into any difficulties in being understood, see page 49. Page 233 has any phrases you might need in case of emergencies.

Good luck with your attempts to speak the language or, as they say in Latin American Spanish, Buena suerte!

ARTHUR OR MARTHA?

Spanish has two noun forms, known as masculine and feminine. In this book we have placed the feminine form first, the masculine second. While there is no difference between the two forms in terms of priority, language books have consistently placed the masculine first. We wanted to counteract that preference. Ideally we'd have mixed orders, but as this would be confusing to readers new to the language we have stuck with the feminine first throughout.

ABBREVIATIONS USED IN THIS BOOK

col	colloquial usage	m	masculine
f	feminine	sg	singular
inf	informal	pl	plural
lit	literally	v	verb

Countries

These are the countries and areas where Spanish is the predominant language, and the abbreviations are those used through this book to indicate differences.

Argentina	Arg	Mexico	Mex
Bolivia	Bol	Nicaragua	Nic
Central America	CAm	Panama	Pan
Chile	Chi	Paraguay	Par
Colombia	Col	Peru	Per
Costa Rica	Cos	Puerto Rico	Pue
Cuba	Cub	River Plate Region	Rpl
Dominican Republic	Dom	(border Arg/Uru)	
Ecuador	Ecu	South America	SAm
El Salvador	Sal	Spain	Sp
Guatemala	Gua	Uruguay	Uru
Honduras	Hon	Venezuela	Ven
Latin America	LAm		

HOW TO USE THIS PHRASEBOOK
You *Can* Speak Another Language

It's true – anyone can speak another language. Don't worry if you haven't studied languages before, or that you studied a language at school for years and can't remember any of it. It doesn't even matter if you failed English grammar. After all, that's never affected your ability to speak English! And this is the key to picking up a language in another country. You don't need to sit down and memorise endless grammatical details and you don't need to memorise long lists of vocabulary. You just need to start speaking. Once you start, you'll be amazed how many prompts you'll get to help you build on those first words. You'll hear people speaking, pick up sounds from TV, catch a word or two that you think you know from the local radio, see something on a billboard – all these things help to build your understanding.

Plunge In

There's just one thing you need to start speaking another language – courage. Your biggest hurdle is overcoming the fear of saying aloud what may seem to you to be just a bunch of sounds. There are a number of ways to do this.

Firstly, think of some Spanish words or phrases you are familiar with. Such as hasta la vista and ¿que será, será? (remember that one!?). These are phrases you are already able to say fluently – and you'll even get a response. From these basic beginnings, provided you can get past the 'courage to speak' barrier, you can start making sentences. You probably know cuándo means 'when' (cuando is Spanish, quando is Italian and Portuguese – they all sound much the same). So, let's imagine you think the bus will arrive tomorrow. You could ask ¿cuándo será? – 'when will that be?' Don't worry that you're not getting a whole sentence right first time. People will understand if you stick to the key words of the sentence. And you'll find that once you're in the country it won't take long to remember the complete sentence.

The best way to start overcoming your fear is to memorise a few key words. These are the words you know you'll be saying again and again, like 'hello', 'thankyou' and 'how much?'. Here's an important hint though: right from the beginning, learn at least one phrase that will be useful but not essential. Such as 'good morning' or 'good afternoon', 'see you later' or even a conversational piece like 'lovely day, isn't it?' or 'it's cold today' (people everywhere love to talk about the weather). Having this extra phrase (just start with one, if you like, and learn to say it really well) will enable you to move away from the basics, and when you get a reply and a smile, it'll also boost your confidence. You'll find that people you speak to will like it too, as they'll understand that at least you've tried to learn more of the language than just the usual essential words.

Ways to Remember

There are several ways to learn a language. Most people find they learn from a variety of these, although people usually have a preferred way to remember. Some like to see the written word and remember the sound from what they see. Some like to just hear it spoken in context (if this is you, try talking to yourself in

Spanish, but do it in the car or somewhere private, to give yourself confidence, and so others don't wonder about your sanity!). Others, especially the more mathematically inclined, like to analyse the grammar of a language, and piece together words according to the rules of grammar. The very visually inclined like to associate the written word and even sounds with some visual stimulus, such as from illustrations, TV and general things they see in the street. As you learn, you'll discover what works best for you – be aware of what made you really remember a particular word, and if it sticks in your mind, keep using that method.

Kicking Off

Chances are you'll want to learn some of the language before you go. So you won't be hearing it around you. The first thing to do is to memorise those essential phrases and words. Check out the basics (page 45) and don't forget that extra phrase (see Plunge In!). Try the sections on making conversation or greeting people for a phrase you'd like to use. Write some of these words down on a separate piece of paper and stick them up around the place. On the fridge, by the bed, on your computer, as a bookmark – somewhere where you'll see them often. Try putting some words in context – the 'How much is it?' note, for instance, could go in your wallet.

Building the Picture

We include a chapter on grammar in our books for two main reasons.

Firstly, some people have an aptitude for grammar and find understanding it a key tool to their learning. If you're such a person, then the grammar chapter in a phrasebook will help you build a picture of the language, as it works through all the basics.

The second reason for the grammar chapter is that it gives answers to questions you might raise as you hear or memorise some key phrases. You may find a particular word is always used when there is a question – check out the grammar heading on questions and it should explain why. This way you don't have to read the grammar chapter from start to finish, nor do you need to memorise a grammatical point. It will simply present itself to you in the course of your learning. Key grammatical points are repeated through the book.

Any Questions?

Try to learn the main question words (see page 43). As you read through different situations, you'll see these words used in the example sentences, and this will help you remember them. So if you want to hire a bicycle, turn to the Bicycle section in Getting Around (use the Contents or Index pages to find it quickly). You've already tried to memorise the word for 'where' and you'll see the word for 'bicycle'. When you come across the sentence 'Where can I hire a bicycle?', you'll recognise the key words and this will help you remember the whole phrase. If there's no category for your need, try the dictionary (the question words are repeated there too, with examples), and memorise the phrases 'Please write that down' and 'How do you say ...?' (page 49).

I've Got a Flat Tyre

Doesn't seem like the phrase you're going to need? Well, in fact it could be very useful. As are all the phrases in this book, provided you have the courage to mix and match them. We have given specific examples within each section. But the key words remain the same even when the situation changes. So while you may not be planning on any cycling during your trip, the first part of the phrase 'I've got ...' could refer to anything else, and there are plenty of words in the dictionary that, we hope, will fit your needs. So whether it's 'a ticket', 'a visa' or 'a condom', you'll be able to put the words together to convey your meaning.

Finally

Don't be concerned if you feel you can't memorise words. On the inside front and back covers are the most essential words and phrases you'll need. You could also try tagging a few pages for other key phrases, or use the notes pages to write your own reminders.

PRONUNCIATION

Pronunciation of Spanish is not difficult. There is a clear and consistent relationship between pronunciation and spelling, and English speakers will find that many Spanish sounds are similar to their English counterparts. If you stick to the following rules you should have very few problems being understood.

VOWELS

Unlike English, each of the vowels in Spanish has a uniform pronunciation which does not vary. For example, the Spanish a has one pronunciation rather than the numerous pronunciations we find in English, such as the 'a's in 'cake', 'art' and 'all'. Vowels are pronounced clearly, even in unstressed positions or at the end of a word.

a   as the 'u' in 'nut', or a shorter sound than the 'a' in 'art'
e   as the 'e' in 'met'
i   similar to the 'i' sound in 'marine' but not so drawn out
    or strong; between that sound and the 'i' in 'flip'
o   similar to the 'o' in 'hot'
u   as the 'oo' in 'fool'

PRONUNCIATION HINTS

Some of the key sounds to remember are:

c   a hard 'c' as in 'cat' when followed by 'a', 'o', 'u' or a
    consonant; as an 's' before 'e' or 'i'
ñ   which is pretty easy to remember as the 'ny' sound
d   is much softer than in English, almost a 'th' as in 'the'

and finally ... remember that the vowels are short, not
    rounded as in British English, and not slanted as in
    American English.

CONSONANTS

Some Spanish consonants are the same as their English counter-parts. Pronunciation of other consonants varies according to which vowel follows, and also according to what part of Latin America you are in. The Spanish alphabet also contains three consonants which are not found in the English alphabet: ch, ll and ñ.

b   generally a much softer 'b' than the English one: some-where between an English 'b' and 'v' – try saying this with your lips slightly closed, (the English 'b' is pro-nounced with closed lips) and your top teeth on your bottom lip (the English 'v' is pronounced this way, though with open lips). When initial, or preceded by a nasal sound, the sound is as the 'b' in 'book'.

c   a hard 'c' as in 'cat' when followed by 'a', 'o', 'u' or a consonant; as an 's' before 'e' or 'i'

ch   as the 'ch' in 'choose'

d   in an initial position, as the 'd' in 'dog'; elsewhere as the 'th' in 'then'

g   in an initial position, as the 'g' in 'gate' before 'a', 'o' and 'u'; everywhere else, the Spanish 'g' is much softer than the English one. When followed by 'ue' or 'ui' the 'u' is silent, unless it has a diaeresis (ü) in which case it is pronounced. Before 'e' or 'i' it is a harsh, breathy sound, similar to the 'h' in 'hit'.

h   always silent

j   as the 'h' in 'haste'

ll   between the 'ly' sound in 'million' and the 'y' in 'yes'; in Argentina, Uruguay, Chile and some parts of Ecuador it is pronounced as the 'g' in 'deluge', or the 's' in 'measure'

ñ   this is a nasal sound like the 'ny' sound in 'onion' or 'canyon'

q   as the 'k' in 'kick'; as in English the 'q' is always followed by a silent 'u'. It is only combined with 'e' as in 'que' and 'i' as in 'qui'.

r   a rolled 'r' sound; a longer and stronger sound when it is
    a double 'rr' or when a word begins with 'r'
s   as the 's' in 'send'; pronunciation varies from country to
    country. In the Central American countries and coastal
    regions of Venezuela and Colombia it is not pronounced
    when at the end of a word. An 's' in the middle of a
    word in Mexico is sometimes not pronounced at all, and
    in Chile it can be lisped slightly.
v   the same sound as the Spanish 'b'
x   as the 'x' in 'taxi', when between two vowels; as the 's' in
    'say' when the 'x' precedes a consonant
z   as the 's' in 'sin'

Semiconsonant

y   a semiconsonant; pronounced as the Spanish 'i' when at
    the end of a word or when it stands alone as a conjunc-
    tion. As a consonant, it's somewhere between 'y' in
    'yonder' and 'g' in 'beige', depending on the region. In
    Argentina, Chile and Uruguay it sounds similar to the 's'
    in 'measure'.

STRESS

There are three general rules regarding stress:

• For words ending in a vowel, 'n' or 's' the stress goes on the
  second-to-last syllable.

| friend | amigo | the stress is on 'mi' |
| shoes | zapatos | the stress is on 'pa' |

• For words ending in a consonant other than 'n' or 's' the
  stress is on the final syllable.

| love | amor | the stress is on 'mor' |
| city | ciudad | the stress is on 'dad' |

- Any deviation from these rules is indicated by an accent:

here	aquí	the stress is on 'qui'
station	estación	the stress is on 'on'
tree	árbol	the stress is on 'ar'
camera	cámara	the stress is on 'ca'

PRONUNCIATION

This chapter is designed to give you an idea of how Spanish phrases are put together, providing you with the basic rules to help you to construct your own sentences.

WORD ORDER

Generally, the word order of sentences is similar to English word order (subject-verb-object).

Ana drinks beer.   Ana bebe cerveza.

ARTICLES

In English and Spanish there are two articles: the definite article ('the' in English) and the indefinite article ('a'). Spanish, however, has feminine and masculine forms as well as singular and plural forms for each.

Feminine

| the house | la casa | the houses | las casas |
| a house | una casa | some houses | **unas casas** |

Masculine

| the book | el libro | the books | los libros |
| a book | un libro | some books | unos libros |

DID YOU KNOW ...

There are some ways to tell if a word should have a feminine or masculine form, even if it doesn't end in the usual -a or -o. For instance, words derived from ancient Greek are often feminine, such as those ending in -dad (la eternidad) and in -cion (la nación).

NOUNS

In Spanish, nouns always have a feminine or masculine form. Fortunately, there are some rules governing this though, as with all rules, there are always exceptions.

Feminine

- Nouns descriptive of females:

the woman	la mujer
the girl	la chica
the teacher	la profesora

- Generally, nouns ending in -a:

the house	la casa
the mountain	la montaña
the food	la comida

- Nouns ending in -ción, -sión and -dad:

the song	la canción
the university	la universidad
the address	la dirección
the occasion	la ocasión

Masculine

- Nouns descriptive of men:

the man	el hombre
the boy	el chico
the teacher	el profesor

- Generally, nouns ending in -o and -or:

the book	el libro
the glass	el vaso
the engine	el motor

- Days of the week, months, rivers, mountains, sea and oceans:

| Monday | el lunes |
| the Mediterranean | el Mediterráneo |

GRAMMAR

PLURALS

In general, you can simply add an -s to nouns to form the plural:

bed	cama
beds	camas

If the noun ends in a consonant, the plural is made by adding -es:

flower	flor
flowers	flores

DIMINUTIVES

The use of diminutive suffixes is common in Latin American Spanish. These are additions to nouns and adjectives to express smallness or affection; for example, when expressing the smallness and cuteness of a puppy. The most common of these suffixes are -ita/o, -cita/o and, to a lesser extent, -illa/o and -cilla/o.

café	coffee	cafecito
amor	love	amorcito
animal	animal	animalito
perro	dog	perrito

Note: When looking up a word in the dictionary, be aware of such things as diminutives, which are not listed. If the word you've heard ends in -ita/o; -cita/o; -illa/o or -cilla/o, try looking for the base word. For instance, to find perrito, try perro.

GRAMMAR

DID YOU KNOW ... The word gringo, used by Latin Americans to refer to a person from an English-speaking country, originated in the conflict between Mexicans and Americans soldiers in the border between the two countries and comes directly from English: 'green go!'.

MISTAKES TO WATCH FOR – ENGLISH SPEAKERS

It's useful to know what the most common mistakes are for English and Spanish speakers as each attempts to speak and understand the other language. By checking this list from time to time, you can remind yourself of possible mistakes to avoid.

- Unlike English, Spanish nouns can be either masculine or feminine. English-speakers often have difficulty remembering the gender of a particular word.

  So ... say el coche ✔   not la coche ✗
          la gente ✔   not el gente ✗

- Although there are basic rules governing the use of gender (see page **), the inevitable exceptions can be a real source of confusion. Check the dictionary for the correct article.

  So ... say la mano ✔   not el mano ✗
          el mapa ✔   not la mapa ✗

- In English, adjectives are placed *before* the noun (eg the big dog), so it's easy to forget that Spanish generally places them *after* the noun.

          el perro bravo ✔   not el bravo perro ✗
          la casa blanca ✔   not la blanca casa ✗

- The existence of two verbs in Spanish for the English 'to be' is a real headache for English-speakers, who frequently confuse them. Follow the basic rules outlined in the Grammar section, page 34.

          Ella es joven ✔   not Ella está joven ✗
          Isabel está contenta ✔   not Isabel es contenta ✗

GRAMMAR

- In Spanish, to say you like something, you say 'something is pleasing to you', using the verb gustar ('to please/taste') and the pronouns me, te, le, os, nos, les to indicate who it is pleasing to (see page 39).

  Me gusta Bolivia. ✔   not Me gusto Bolivia. ✗
  Nos gustan las patatas. ✔ not Nos gustamos las
                                      patatas. ✗

- The subjunctive is frequently used in Spanish, unlike English, and is therefore often ignored or misused. You won't be misunderstood if you don't use the subjunctive, but it does help to get it right. See page 31 for more details.

  Quiero que vengas   not Quiero que vienes
    conmigo al cine. ✔   al cine. ✗

- In English there is only one verb for 'to know' whilst Spanish has saber ('to have knowledge of, be aware of, be able to do something') and conocer ('to be acquainted with people and places'). See page 32 for more details.

  ¿Conoces a mi   not ¿Sabes a mi
    hermano? ✔   hermano? ✗
  ¿Saben leer? ✔   not ¿Conocen leer? ✗

- Prepositions 'in, on, at, to, by' etc are used quite differently in English and Spanish and it is quite common for English-speakers to use the wrong one. For complete details, you'll have to get hold of a comprehensive grammar book, though listening to what native speakers say is generally the best way to pick these usages up.

  mañana voy a ir de   not mañana voy a ir de
    viaje a Santiago ✔   viaje en Santiago ✗

PRONOUNS
Subject Pronouns

The English singular 'you' has three forms in Spanish - tú and vos, which are generally used in familiar and informal situations and usted, which is a more formal term. Tú is by far the most commonly used today and you should generally avoid the use of usted unless you find yourself in a highly formal situation or wish to show your respect to someone much older than yourself. As a more general rule, you should respond in the same form that you are addressed in.

In Latin American Spanish the term vosotras/os (you, pl) has almost disappeared, and ustedes is now commonly used in both formal and informal situations.

In this chapter all forms are included. Throughout the rest of the book we've stuck mainly to the informal tú, with the exception of certain categories where the formal usted is more appropriate (eg At Customs, Booking Accommodation).

GRAMMAR

I	yo	we	nosotras/os
you	tú * (sg, inf)	you	vosotras/os (pl, inf)
you	usted (sg, pol)	you	ustedes (pl, pol)
she/it	ella	they	ellas/ellos
he/it	él		

* vos in Arg, Bol, CAm, Chi, Uru

You'll find that the subject pronoun is usually omitted in Spanish, because the subject is understood from the verb conjugation and the corresponding ending.

| I'm travelling to Europe. | Viajo a Europa. |
| We speak some Spanish. | Hablamos un poco de castellano. |

If there is a chance of ambiguity the subject pronoun should be included.

Object Pronouns

Direct object pronouns are used in Spanish to refer to people as 'him', 'them', etc.

me	me	us	nos
you (sg, inf)	te	you (pl, inf)	os
her, it, you (pol)	la	them, you (pol)	las/los
him, it, you (pol)	lo		

I don't know him.	No lo conozco.
Can you see me?	¿Me ves?

Indirect objects are used to describe 'to him', 'to them', etc.

I'm talking to her.	Le hablo.
I'm writing them a letter.	Les escribo una carta.

to me	me	to us	nos
to you (sg, inf)	te	to you (pl, inf)	os
to her, him,	le	to them,	les
to you (pol)	le	to you (pl, pol)	les

GRAMMAR

WAITER!

The word ¡Permiso! is useful for getting past people.
To catch someone's attention, try ¡Disculpe! or
¡Perdón!

MISTAKES TO WATCH FOR – SPANISH SPEAKERS

- Spanish speakers tend to find the pronunciation of some English words particularly difficult. For example, words beginning with 's' are often pronounced with an initial 'e'.

    'estarting *instead of* starting'

- Distinguishing between a 'b' and 'v' also presents a problem and they are often both pronounced as a 'b'.

    'best *instead of* vest'

- Because Spanish speakers rarely use 'he/she' before a verb, they sometimes confuse the two in English, as well as the pronouns 'him/her'.

    'Do you know my brother Txabi? She is coming tonight.'

- Just like English speakers, Latin Americans often confuse the order of the adjective and noun.

    'a tomato red'

- In Spanish the partitive ('a half', 'a bit', etc) generally goes after the noun instead of before and thus is often misused in English.

    'one hour and a half' *instead of* 'one and a half hours'

- The Spanish verb hacer can be translated as both 'to do' and 'to make', which is why Spanish speakers commonly confuse the two in English.

    'Make me a favor: shut up!'

- Another difference in the use of prepositions in Spanish and English is highlighted by this common error.

    'What for are you using this phrasebook?' *instead of* 'What are you using this phrasebook for?'

GRAMMAR

- Spanish uses hay, hubo and había, all singular words, to express 'there is; there are' 'there was; there were' (see page 33). Because of this, Spanish speakers will often say 'there is/was' when 'there was/were' is needed.

   'There was onions in the basket.'

- Spanish speakers may use two forms of the past tense together in questions and negative statements. This is because such sentences in Spanish don't use an auxiliary verb (eg 'Did you say?' would be 'You said?': ¿Dijiste?)

   'I didn't washed my hair yesterday.'
   'Did you slept alone last night?'

- Many English verbs change their meaning according to the preposition that is used with them, a good example being 'to look', which has many different meanings when used with 'around, after, at, away, back on, down on, for, forward to, into, out, over, through' and 'up to'.

   'I'm looking at the window.' *instead of*
   'I'm looking through the window.'

- A common mistake which Spanish speakers make in English is to use the third person singular of the verb ('he, she, it …') incorrectly, using the form of the first or second person ('I, you, we …') or the third person plural ('they …').

   'She eat paella.'
   'My mother have a beautiful bike.'

- 'People' is always used as a plural word whilst its Spanish counterpart, gente is singular.

   'People is very strange in Granada.' *instead of*
   'People are very strange in Granada.'

GRAMMAR

VERBS

There are three different categories of verb in Spanish – those ending in -ar, -er and -ir. Tenses are formed by adding various endings to the verb stem, and these endings vary according to whether the verb is an -ar, -er or -ir verb. There are quite a few exceptions to the rules when forming these endings. However the following standard forms are useful to know:

	-ar	-er	-ir
Infinitive	comprar	comer	vivir
	(to buy)	(to eat)	(to live)
Stem	compr-	com-	viv-

Present Tense

	-ar	-er	-ir
I	compro	como	vivo
you (inf)	compras	comes	vives
she/he/it/you (pol)	compra	come	vive
we	compramos	comemos	vivimos
you (pl, inf)	compráis	coméis	vivís
they/you (pl, pol)	compran	comen	viven

Future Tense

This is the easiest tense to form as the endings are the same regardless of whether the verb ends with -ar, -er or -ir. You simply add the endings to the infinitive of the verb:

	-ar	-er	-ir
I	compraré	comeré	viviré
you (inf)	comprarás	comerás	vivirás
she/he/it/you (pol)	comprará	comerá	vivirá
we	compraremos	comeremos	viviremos
you (pl inf)	compraréis	comeréis	viviréis
they/you (pl, pol)	comprarán	comerán	vivirán

Going to ...

As in English, a more common way of creating the future tense, particularly when you are discussing the immediate future, is to use the verb ir ('to go') in the present tense, followed by the preposition **a** ('to/at') and the verb infinitive.

I go/am going to ...	voy
you go/are going to ... (inf)	vas
he/she/it/you go/are going to ... (pol)	va
we go/are going to ...	vamos
you go/are going to ... (pl, inf)	vais
they/you go/are going to ... (pl, pol)	van

I am going to eat later.   Voy a comer más tarde.
It's going to rain this   Va a llover esta tarde.
afternoon.

Past Tense

There are three ways of referring to the past:

1) The preterite, or **simple past tense**, is used to express completed past actions, which usually only happened once.

	-ar	-er	-ir
I	compré	comí	viví
you (inf)	compraste	comiste	viviste
he/she/it/you (pol)	compró	comió	vivió
we	compramos	comimos	vivimos
you (pl, inf)	comprasteis	comisteis	vivisteis
they/you (pl, pol)	compraron	comieron	vivieron

I bought a shirt yesterday.   Compré una camisa ayer.
It rained last Wednesday.   Llovió el miércoles pasado.

GRAMMAR

2) The **imperfect** is used for past actions which went on for some time, happened repeatedly, or were going on when a completed action (simple past) took place. So, in the sentence 'I was reading when John knocked at the door', 'I was reading' is the imperfect as it was going on during the time that 'John knocked'. The imperfect is expressed in English as 'I was buying', 'I bought' (on several occasions) or 'I used to buy'.

	-ar	-er	-ir
I	compraba	comía	vivía
you (inf)	comprabas	comías	vivías
he/she/it/you (pol)	compraba	comía	vivía
we	comprábamos	comíamos	vivíamos
you (pl, inf)	comprabais	comíais	vivíais
they/you (pl, pol)	compraban	comían	vivían

We were living together in Scotland.	Vivíamos juntos en Escocia.
They ate all day.	Comían todo el día.
You (pl, inf) bought vegetables every week.	Comprabais verduras todas las semanas.

3) The **present perfect** is used for a completed past action which implies a strong connection with the present. It is formed with the verb **haber** ('to have') plus the past participle.

An example of the present perfect in English is 'I have bought' – the verb 'have' plus the past participle of 'to buy'. Generally, to create the past participle for -ar verbs you add -**ado** to the stem; for -**er** and -**ir** verbs the past participle is the stem plus -**ido**. For exceptions, refer to the vocabulary.

comprar 'to buy'	becomes	comprado 'bought'
comer 'to eat'	becomes	comido 'ate'
vivir 'to live'	becomes	vivido 'lived'

The Subjunctive Tense

The subjunctive is frequently used in Spanish, unlike English, and is therefore often ignored or misused. You won't be misunderstood if you don't use the subjunctive but it is worth trying to learn the basics. The subjunctive form is used in Spanish to denote irreality, doubt or desire.

	-ar	-er	-ir
I	compre	coma	viva
you (inf)	compres	comas	vivas
she/he/it/you (pol)	compre	coma	viva
we	compremos	comamos	vivamos
you (pl, inf)	compréis	comáis	viváis
they/you (pl, pol)	compren	coman	vivan

I don't want that to happen.	No quiero que suceda esto.
I hope he comes.	Espero que venga.
I doubt we'll eat early tonight.	Dudo que cenemos pronto esta noche.

The Gerund

The gerund is that verb which, in English, is portrayed by the addition of '-ing' to the verb stem. In Spanish, the equivalent is -ando for the -ar verbs, and -endo for both the -er and -ir verbs, and they are used with the verb estar.

We're watching TV.	Estamos mirando la tele.
I'm waiting for my friend.	Estoy esperando a mi amiga.
It's raining.	Está lloviendo.

However, in Spanish it is often common to simply use the present tense for the same meaning. Thus 'It's raining' can also be llueve 'We're going' is usually just Vamos; 'I'm going', Voy.

GRAMMAR

TO KNOW

In Spanish there are two words for 'to know', saber (to have knowledge of, be aware of, be able to) and conocer (to be acquainted with people or places).

Do you know my brother?	¿Conoces a mi hermano?
Do you know Italy?	¿Conoces Italia?
Can you read?	¿Sabes leer?
Have you heard the latest about Amanda?	¿Sabes lo último de Amanda?

KEY VERBS

to be	ser; estar
to bring	traer
to come	venir
to come; arrive	llegar
to cost	costar; valer
to depart (leave)	partir; salir de
to do	hacer
to go	ir; partir
to have	tener; haber
to know (someone)	conocer
to know (something)	saber
to like	gustarle; apreciar
to live (life)	vivir
to live (somewhere)	vivir; ocupar
to make	hacer; fabricar
to meet	encontrar; conocer
to need	necesitar
to prefer	preferir
to return	volver; regresar
to say	decir
to stay (remain)	quedarse
to stay (somewhere)	alojarse; hospedarse
to take	llevar
to understand	entender; omprender
to want	querer; desear

GRAMMAR

TO HAVE

The verb 'to have' has two forms in Spanish, haber and tener.

Haber

As we have seen, haber is used as an auxiliary verb to form the present perfect tense.

Haber	
I have	he
you have (inf)	has
she/he/it has, you have (pol)	ha
we have	hemos
you have (pl, inf)	habéis
they/you have (pl, pol)	han

We have bought tickets.	Hemos comprado billetes.
I have eaten too much.	He comido demasiado.
I have lived in France.	He vivido en Francia.

To find out the past participles of other verbs, see the following page.

Hay

One word you'll often hear is the impersonal form of haber: hay. This is used to mean 'there is/are', and in questions meaning 'are/is there?' or 'do you have …/have you …?'

Do you have any rooms?	¿Hay habitaciones?
Do you have fresh bread?	¿Hay pan de hoy?
We don't have any/ There isn't any.	No (no) hay.

GRAMMAR

Tener

This form of 'to have' can be used to express both possession and compulsion (having to do something – see page 39).

Tener	
I have	tengo
you have (inf)	tienes*
she/he/it/has, you have (pol)	tiene
we have	tenemos
you have (pl, inf)	tenéis
they/you have (pl, pol)	tienen

* tenés in Arg, Uru, CAm

A small number of phrases consisting of 'to be + adjective' in English, are expressed in Spanish by 'to have' (tener) + noun (see also estar, page 35).

to be hungry	tener hambre (lit: to have hunger)
to be thirsty	tener sed (lit: to have thirst)
to be afraid	tener miedo (lit: to have fear)
to be right (correct)	tener razón (lit: to have reason)

TO BE

The verb 'to be' has two forms in Spanish, ser and estar. To know exactly when to use which verb takes practice but here are some basic rules to help you.

Ser

Ser	
I am	soy
you are (inf)	eres *
she/he/it is, you are (pol)	es
we are	somos
you are (pl, inf)	sois
they/you are (pl, pol)	son

* sos in Arg, Uru and CAm

GRAMMAR

The verb ser is used in situations that have a degree of permanence about them:

- characteristics of persons or things

  | Maria is pretty. | María es bonita. |
  | The book is yellow. | El libro es amarillo. |

- occupations and nationality

I am a student.	Soy estudiante.
They are Australian.	Son australianas/os.
You are a journalist.	Vos sos periodista. (Arg)

- telling the time and location of events

It's one o'clock.	Es la una.
It's 3.30.	Son las tres y media.
The party is at my house.	La fiesta es en mi casa.

Estar

Estar	
I am	estoy
you are (inf)	estás
she/he/it is, you are (pol)	está
we are	estamos
you are (pl, inf)	estáis
they/you are (pl, pol)	están

The verb estar connotes temporary characteristics, or those which are the result of an action:

| The food is cold. | La comida está fría. |
| The coffee is too sweet. | El café está demasiado dulce. |

- it is used with the location of persons or things

  | I am in Cádiz. | Estoy en Cádiz. |
  | The city is far away. | La ciudad está lejos. |

- it is used to indicate mood

  | They (f) are happy. | Están contentas. |
  | She/He is sad. | Está triste. |

GRAMMAR

GRAMMAR

KEY VERBS
Regular Verbs

The following three verb forms are regular forms. Most other verbs follow the same conjugations. The three forms are those ending in -ar, -er and -ir.

comprar (to buy)   *past participle:* (haber) comprado

	present	simple past	imperfect	future
I	compro	compré	compraba	compraré
you (inf)	compras	compraste	comprabas	comprarás
he/she/it/you	compra	compró	compraba	comprará
we	compramos	compramos	comprábamos	compraremos
you (pl, inf)	compráis	comprasteis	comprabais	compraréis
they/you	compran	compraron	compraban	comprarán

comer (to eat)   *past participle:* (haber) comido

	present	simple past	imperfect	future
I	como	comí	comía	comeré
you (inf)	comes	comiste	comías	comerás
he/she/it/you	come	comió	comía	comerá
we	comemos	comimos	comíamos	comeremos
you (pl, inf)	coméis	comisteis	comíais	comeréis
they/you	comen	comieron	comían	comerán

vivir (to live)   *past participle:* (haber) vivido

	present	simple past	imperfect	future
I	vivo	viví	vivía	viviré
you (inf)	vives	viviste	vivías	vivirás
he/she/it/you	vive	vivió	vivía	vivirá
we	vivimos	vivimos	vivíamos	viviremos
you (pl, inf)	vivís	vivisteis	vivíais	viviréis
they/you	viven	vivieron	vivían	vivirán

Useful Irregular Verbs

estar (to be)   *past participle:* (haber) estado

	present	simple past	imperfect	future
I	estoy	estuve	estaba	estaré
you (inf)	estás	estuviste	estabas	estarás
he/she/it/you	está	estuvo	estaba	estará
we	estamos	estuvimos	estabamos	estaremos
you (pl, inf)	estáis	estuvisteis	estabais	estaréis
they/you	están	estuvieron	estaban	estarán

ir (to go)

past participle: (haber) ido

	present	simple past	imperfect	future
I	voy	fui	iba	iré
you (inf)	vas	fuiste	ibas	irás
he/she/it/you	va	fue	iba	irá
we	vamos	fuimos	íbamos	iremos
you (pl, inf)	vais	fuisteis	ibais	iréis
they/you	van	fueron	iban	irán

haber (to have)

past participle: (haber) habido

	present	simple past	imperfect	future
I	he	hube	había	habré
you (inf)	has	hubiste	habías	habrás
he/she/it/you	ha	hubo	había	habrá
we	hemos	hubimos	habíamos	habremos
you (pl, inf)	habéis	hubisteis	habíais	habréis
they/you	han	hubieron	habían	habrán

poder (to be able)

past participle: (haber) podido

	present	simple past	imperfect	future
I	puedo	pude	podía	podré
you (inf)	puedes	pudiste	podías	podrás
he/she/it/you	puede	pudo	podía	podrá
we	podemos	pudimos	podíamos	podremos
you (pl, inf)	podéis	pudisteis	podíais	podréis
they/you	pueden	pudieron	podían	podrán

ser (to be)

past participle: (haber) sido

	present	simple past	imperfect	future
I	soy	fui	era	seré
you (inf)	eres	fuiste	eras	serás
he/she/it/you	es	fue	era	será
we	somos	fuimos	éramos	seremos
you (pl, inf)	sois	fuisteis	erais	seréis
they/you	son	fueron	eran	serán

tener (to have)

past participle: (haber) tenido

	present	simple past	imperfect	future
I	tengo	tuve	tenía	tendré
you (inf)	tienes	tuviste	tenías	tendrás
he/she/it/you	tiene	tuvo	tenía	tendrá
we	tenemos	tuvimos	teníamos	tendremos
you (pl, inf)	tenéis	tuvisteis	teníais	tendréis
they/you	tienen	tuvieron	tenían	tendrán

GRAMMAR

traer (to bring)
past participle: (haber) traído

	present	simple past	imperfect	future
I	traigo	traje	traía	traeré
you (inf)	traes	trajiste	traías	traerás
he/she/it/you	trae	trajo	traía	traerá
we	traemos	trajimos	traíamos	traeremos
you (pl, inf)	traéis	trajisteis	traíais	traeréis
they/you	traen	trajeron	traían	traerán

dar (to give)
past participle: (haber) dado

	present	simple past	imperfect	future
I	doy	di	daba	daré
you (inf)	das	diste	dabas	darás
he/she/it/you	da	dio	daba	dará
we	damos	dimos	dábamos	daremos
you (pl, inf)	dais	disteis	dabais	daréis
they/you	dan	dieron	daban	darán

saber (to know)
past participle: (haber) sabido

	present	simple past	imperfect	future
I	sé	supe	sabía	sabré
you (inf)	sabes	supiste	sabías	sabrás
he/she/it/you	sabe	supo	sabía	sabrá
we	sabemos	supimos	sabíamos	sabremos
you (pl, inf)	sabéis	supisteis	sabíais	sabréis
they/you	saben	supieron	sabían	sabrán

hacer (to make/do)
past participle: (haber) hecho

	present	simple past	imperfect	future
I	hago	hice	hacía	haré
you (inf)	haces	hiciste	hacías	harás
he/she/it/you	hace	hizo	hacía	hará
we	hacemos	hicimos	hacíamos	haremos
you (pl, inf)	hacéis	hicisteis	hacíais	haréis
they/you	hacen	hicieron	hacían	harán

querer (to want)
past participle: (haber) querido

	present	simple past	imperfect	future
I	quiero	quise	quería	querré
you (inf)	quieres	quisiste	querías	querrás
he/she/it/you	quiere	quiso	quería	querrá
we	queremos	quisimos	queríamos	querremos
you (pl, inf)	queréis	quisisteis	queríais	querréis
they/you	quieren	quisieron	querían	querrán

MODALS
Must/Have To/Need To

In order to express having to do something, you can use the verb tener followed by que and then the infinitive of the verb.

I have to change some money.	Tengo que cambiar dinero.

Can/To Be Able

There are several ways to express 'can/to be able'. The verb poder can be used, while you may also hear es posible [que], 'it is possible [that]'.

Can (may) I take a photo?	¿Puedo sacar una foto?
Can you show it to me on the map?	¿Me lo puede mostrar en el mapa?
Can you do it?	¿Puedes hacerlo?; ¿Es posible hacerlo?

To Like

In Spanish, in order to say you like something, you say 'something pleases you'. You use the verb gustar ('to please/taste') with the indirect object pronouns (see page 25).

I like beer.	Me gusta la cerveza. ('beer pleases me')
We like it.	Nos gusta. ('it pleases us')
They like ice cream.	Les gusta el helado. ('the ice cream pleases them')
I like action films.	Me gustan las películas de acción. ('action films please me')
I like you (inf).	Me gustas. ('you please me')
You like me (inf).	Te gusto. ('I please you')

ADJECTIVES

Adjectives in Spanish agree in gender and number with the nouns they relate to, so they have different endings depending upon whether the noun is masculine, feminine, singular or plural. Unlike English, they almost always come after the noun.

a pretty house	una casa bonita
some pretty houses	unas casas bonitas
a white hat	un sombrero blanco
some white hats	unos sombreros blancos

Adjectives of quantity such as 'much', 'a lot of', 'little/few', 'too much'; cardinal and ordinal numbers, and possessive adjectives always precede the noun.

a lot of tourists	muchos turistas
first class	primera clase
my car	mi carro/auto

Comparatives

more … than
  más … que
less … than
  menos …que
as … as
  tan … como
	richer than	más rico que
		(lit: more rich than)

	less rich than	menos rico que
	easier than	más fácil que
	less easy than	menos fácil que
	as easy as	tan fácil como
	as beautiful as	tan bonito como
	better	mejor
	worse	peor

Superlatives

the most …
  el más …
the least …
  el menos …
	the richest	el más rico

	the least rich	el menos rico
	the easiest	el más fácil
	the least easy	el menos fácil
	the best	el mejor
	the worst	el peor

FALSE FRIENDS

to say ...	*use ...*	*don't use ...*	*which means ...*
to attend	asistir	atender	to help
to board (the ship)	embarcarse	bordar	to embroider
(bus) conductor	cobrador/a	conductor/a	driver
to be constipated	estar estreñida/o	estar constipada/o	to have a cold
date	la fecha	el dato	information/data
embarrassed	avergonzada/o	embarazada	pregnant
exit	la salida	el éxito	success
injury	la ofensa	la injuria	insult
large	grande	larga/o	long
library	la biblioteca	la librería	bookshop
parents	los padres	los parientes	relatives
to quit	dejar	quitar	to take away
to realize	darse cuenta de	realizar	to carry out
sensible	juiciosa/o	sensible	sensitive

AVERGONZADO = EMBARRASSED

Estoy embarazada

POSSESSION

Possession may be indicated in several ways. The most common way is by using possessive adjectives which agree in number and gender with the noun they describe. They are always placed before the noun.

Possessive Adjectives		
	m/f singular	m/f plural
my	mi	mis
your (inf)	tu	tus
his/her/its/your (polite)	su	sus
our	nuestra/o	nuestras/os
your (pl, inf)	vuestra/o	vuestras/os
their/your (pl, polite)	su	sus

my country	mi país
your (inf) hands	tus manos

Another way to indicate possession is by using possessive pronouns, which also agree in number and gender with the noun and are placed after it.

Possessive Pronouns		
	m/f singular	m/f plural
mine	mía/o	mías/os
yours (inf)	tuya/o	tuyas/os
hers/his/yours (polite)	suya/o	suyas/os
ours	nuestra/o	nuestras/os
yours (pl inf)	vuestra/o	vuestras/os
theirs/yours (pl, polite)	suya/o	suyas/os

The house is mine.	La casa es mía.
These passports are ours.	Estos pasaportes son nuestros.

GRAMMAR

QUESTIONS

As in English, all questions in Spanish require a rise in intonation at the end of the sentence. In written Spanish a question is introduced by an inverted question mark – this is a clear indication to change your intonation.

You're (pl) leaving early tomorrow? ¿Se van mañana temprano?

Question Words		
Where?	¿Dónde?	Where is the bank? ¿Dónde está el banco?
Why?	¿Por qué?	Why is the museum closed? ¿Por qué está cerrado el museo?
When?	¿Cuándo?	When does the carnival begin? ¿Cuándo empieza el carnaval?
What?	¿Qué?	What is he saying? ¿Qué está diciendo?
How?	¿Cómo?	How do I get to there? ¿Cómo puedo llegar/ir allá?
Who? (sg)	¿Quién?	Who is it? ¿Quién es?
Who? (pl)	¿Quiénes?	Who are they? ¿Quiénes son?
Which?/ What? (sg)	¿Cuál?	Which is the best beach? ¿Cuál es la mejor playa?
Which/ What? (pl)	¿Cuáles?	Which restaurants are the cheapest? ¿Cuáles restaurantes son los más baratos?

GRAMMAR

NEGATIVES

To form the negative in a sentence, place no before the verb:

We don't want to go to the museum today.	No queremos ir al museo hoy.
I don't know what the time is.	No sé qué hora es.

Contrary to English, you can use double negatives in Spanish:

I don't have anything.	No tengo nada. (lit: I don't have nothing)

MEETING PEOPLE

YOU SHOULD KNOW

If you don't remember any other Spanish words, these will be the ones that always stay in your mind – the essential greetings and politenesses that exist in any language.

¡HOLA!

Hello.	¡Hola!
Goodbye.	¡Adiós!
Yes/No.	Sí/No.
Excuse me.	Perdón.
	Con permiso. (CAm)
Please.	Por favor.
Thank you.	Gracias.
Many thanks.	Muchas gracias.

May I?/Do you mind?
  ¿Puedo?; ¿Me permite?
Sorry. (excuse me, forgive me)

Lo siento; Discúlpeme;
  Perdón; Perdóneme.

That's fine. You're welcome.

De nada.
Con mucho gusto. (CAm)

GREETINGS

Good morning.

Buenos días.
(You may hear Buén día in some regions)

Good afternoon. (until about 8pm) Buenas tardes.
Good evening/night. Buenas noches.

These three greetings are frequently shortened to buenos or buenas, particularly in Central America and the Andean countries.

How are you?	¿Qué tal?; ¿Cómo está?
Well, thanks.	Bien, gracias.
Not too bad.	Más o menos.
	Regular. (Col)
Not so good.	Pues, no muy bien.
See you later.	Hasta luego.
See you tomorrow.	Hasta mañana.
Bye.	Chao/Chaucito.
	Tambien. (Mex)

FORMS OF ADDRESS

Mrs	Señora; Doña (rare)
Mr	Señor; Don (rare)
Miss	Señorita

Note that it has become less and less common for women to be addressed as señorita. It's more common now to use señora for all women, regardless of age or marital status. However, some 'señoritas' (ie non-married women) take offence when addressed as 'señora', particularly older women.

companion	compañera/o
friend	amiga/o
mate	hermano

isss!

The letters s and z are pronounced 's'. But in Central America and the coastal regions of Venezuela and Colombia, s is pronounced as a j when at the end of a word.

In Mexico, s is sometimes not pronounced when in the middle of a word.

FIRST ENCOUNTERS

What's your name?	¿Cómo te llamas? (inf)
	¿Cómo se llama usted? (pol)
My name's ...	Me llamo ...

I'm a friend of (Maria).	Soy amiga/o de (María).
I'd like to introduce you to ...	Quisiera presentarte a ...
His/Her name is ...	Se llama ...
(I'm) pleased to meet you.	Mucho gusto; Encantadao.
I'm here ...	Estoy aquí ...
on holiday	de vacaciones
business	en viaje de negocios
studying	estudiando
Where are you staying?	¿Dónde te alojas?
	¿Dónde te hospedas? (Mex)
How long have you been here?	¿Cuánto tiempo llevas aquí?
I've been here (three days).	Llevo aquí (tres días).
How long are you here for?	¿Cuánto tiempo te vas a quedar?
We're here for (two weeks).	Nos quedaremos (dos semanas).
This is my first visit to (Chile).	Es la primera vez que visito (Chile).
I like (Argentina) very much.	Me encanta (Argentina).
Are you on your own?	¿Vines sola/o?
I'm with my partner.	He venido con mi compañera/o.
How did you get here?	¿Cómo has venido?
It was nice talking to you.	Me encanto charlar contigo.
I have to get going now.	Ahora tengo que irme.
I had a great day/evening.	Me la he pasado en grande.
Hope to see you again soon.	Espero verte pronto.
We must do this again sometime.	¡Esto tenemos que repetirlo!
Next time it's on me.	La próxima la pago yo.
I'll give you a call.	Ya te llamaré.
See you soon.	Hasta pronto.

NATIONALITIES

Unfortunately we can't list all countries here, however you'll find that many country names in Spanish are similar to English. Remember though that even if a word looks like the English equivalent, it will have Spanish pronunciation. For instance, Japan: *hah-pon*). Listed here are some that differ more considerbly.

Where are you from?	¿De dónde eres?
Are you from around here?	¿Eres de por aquí?

I'm from ...

Soy de ...

England	Inglaterra
Germany	Alemania
Holland/The Netherlands	Holanda/los Paises Bajos
New Zealand	Nueva Zelanda
Scotland	Escocia
Sweden	Suecia
Switzerland	Suiza
the USA	los Estados Unidos
Wales	el País de Gales

Have you ever been to my country?	¿Has estado alguna vez en mi país?
What is your home town/region like?	¿Cómo es tu ciudad/región?

I come from .../live in ...

Vengo de ...;Vivo en ...

the city	la ciudad
the countryside	el campo
the mountains	las montañas
the seaside	la costa
the suburbs of ...	las afueras de ...
a village	un pueblo

CULTURAL DIFFERENCES

How do you do this in (your) country?	¿Cómo se hace esto en (su/tu) país?
Is this a local or national custom?	¿Esto es una costumbre local o nacional?

MEETING PEOPLE

I don't want to offend you.	No quiero ofenderlo. (pol)
	No quiero ofenderlos. (CAm, Arg)
I'm sorry, it's not the custom in my country.	Lo siento, pero esto no es costumbre en mi país.
I'm not accustomed to this.	No estoy acostumbrada/o a esto.
I don't mind watching, but I'd prefer not to participate.	No me importa verlo, pero prefiero no participar.
In my country we ...	En mi país ...

LANGUAGE DIFFICULTIES

Do you speak English?	¿Habla inglés?
Does anyone speak English?	¿Hay alguien que hable inglés?
I don't speak Spanish.	No hablo español/ castellano.
I speak a little Spanish.	Hablo un poco de español/castellano.
I'm learning.	Estoy aprendiendo.
Excuse my Spanish!	¡Perdona mi castellano!
I (don't) understand.	(No) Entiendo.
Do you understand?	¿Me entiendes?
Could you speak more slowly please?	Más despacio, por favor.
Could you repeat that?	¿Puedes repetir?
Could you write that down please?	¿Puedes escribirlo, por favor?
How do you say...?	¿Cómo se dice ...?
What is this called in Spanish?	¿Cómo se dice esto en español?
What does ... mean?	¿Qué significa ...?
How do you pronounce this word?	¿Cómo se pronuncia esta palabra?
Pardon?; What?	¿Cómo?

MEETING PEOPLE

My culture/religion doesn't allow me to ...	Mi cultura/religión no me permite ...
practise this	estas prácticas
eat/drink this	esta comida/bebida
	comer/beber esto (CAm)

AGE

How old are you?	¿Cuántos años tienes?
I am ... years old.	Tengo ... años.
Oh! You don't look it!	¡Vaya! ¡Pues no lo parece!

See Numbers, page 231 for your particular age.

OCCUPATIONS

Where do you work?	¿En qué trabajas?
What is your profession?	¿Cuál es su profesión?

I'm (a/an ...)	Soy ...
artist	artista
business person	hombre/mujer de negocios
doctor	doctora/doctor, médico
driver	chofer
engineer	ingeniera/o
factory worker	obrera/o
homemaker	ama/o de casa
journalist	periodista
lawyer	abogada/o
mechanic	mecánica/o
musician	música/o
nurse	enfermera/o
office worker	oficinista; empleada/o
pastor/priest	pastor/sacerdote
scientist	científica/o
secretary	secretaria/o
self-employed	trabajadora/trabajador independiente

student	estudiante
teacher	profesora/profesor
waiter	mesera/o
	mozo (Arg)
writer	escritora/escritor

I'm ...	Estoy ...
retired	desempleada/o
unemployed	sin empleo; desempleada

Do you enjoy your work?	¿Te gusta tu trabajo?
How long have you been in your job?	¿Desde cuándo trabajas allí?
What are you studying?	¿Qué estudias?

I'm studying ...	Estudio ...
art	arte
business	administración de negocios
education	educación
engineering	ingeniería
humanities	humanidades
languages	idiomas
law	derecho
medicine	medicina
science	ciencias
social sciences	ciencias sociales
Spanish	español

RELIGION

What is your religion?	¿Cuál es tu religión?

I'm ...	Soy ...
Buddhist	budista
Catholic	católica/o
Christian	cristiana/o
Hindu	hindú
Jewish	judía/o
Muslim	musulmana/musulmán

I'm Catholic, but not practising. — Soy católica/o no practicante.

I think I believe in God, or something like God. — Me parece que creo en Dios, o en algo similar.

I believe in destiny/fate. — Creo en el destino.

I'm not religious. — No soy religiosa/o.

I'm agnostic. — Soy agnóstica/o.

I'm an atheist. — Soy atea/o.

FEELINGS

I'm sorry (condolence). — Lo siento mucho.

I'm grateful. — Le agradezco mucho.

I'm ...	Tengo ...
Are you ...?	¿Tienes ...?
afraid	miedo
cold	frío
hot	calor
hungry	hambre
in a hurry	prisa
keen to ...	ganas de ...
right	razón
sleepy	sueño
thirsty	sed

I'm ...	Estoy ...
Are you ...?	¿Estás ...?
angry	enojada/o
happy	feliz
sad	triste
tired	cansada/o
well	bien
worried	preocupada/o

> ### THEY MAY SAY ...
>
> You may hear people saying that they are nerviosa/o. This doesn't always translate directly as 'nervous' but more often as what we may call 'nervy'.
>
> The word ansiosa/o means 'worried' or 'anxious' but it is used so commonly that it often doesn't carry the weight of the equivalent word in English.

GETTING AROUND

The best thing that can be said for transport in Latin America is that it is cheap. Most people don't have cars and so they are using the same buses, trains and colectivos (shared taxis) that you are. It is certainly the best way to really see a country and its people, and by the end of a 10-hour train trip you'll probably know the occupants of your carriage intimately.

FINDING YOUR WAY

Excuse me, can you help me please?	¿Perdone, puede ayudarme por favor?
I'm looking for ...	Busco ...
How do I get to ...?	¿Cómo se va a ...?
Where is ...?	¿Dónde está ...?

the bus station	la estación de autobús/autocares
	la estación de autobuses (Mex)
	la terminal terrestre/de pasajeros (Ven, Col)
	la terminal de ómnibus (Arg)
the bus stop	la para/da de autobús
the city centre	el centro de la ciudad
the port	el puerto
the subway	la parada de metro
the taxi stand	la parada de taxis
the train station	la estación del tren/del ferrocarril
the ticket office	la taquilla; la boletería

Is it far from/near here?	¿Está lejos/cerca de aquí?
Where are we now?	¿Dónde estamos ahora?
What's the best way to get there?	¿Cómo se puede ir?
Can I walk there?	¿Se puede ir andando/caminando?

| Can you show me (on the map)? | ¿Me lo puede mostrar/indicar/ señalar (en el mapa)? |
| Is there another way to get there? | ¿Hay otra forma de ir allí/allá? |

DIRECTIONS

Most people are willing to help when you ask directions. You should be wary of directions you are given, however, as a lot of people, in their efforts to be helpful, won't admit to not knowing and might misdirect you.

Turn left ...	Doble a la izquierda ...
	Dé vuelta a la izquierda ... (Mex)
Turn right ...	Vine a la derecha ...
	Dé vuelta a la derecha ... (Mex)
Cross the road ...	Cruce la calle ...
at the next corner	en la próxima esquina
at the traffic lights	en el semáforo
at the roundabout	en la rotonda; glorieta (Mex)
Go straight ahead.	Siga derecho/directo.
Straight ahead.	Adelante.
It's two streets down.	Está a dos calles de aquí.
It's two blocks down.	Está a dos cuadras hacia allá.

after	después de		near	cerca
behind	detrás de		next to	al lado de
between	entre		opposite	frente a
in front of	enfrente de/ delante de		far	lejos

DID YOU KNOW ... For those Amerindians of Central America who spoke Nahuatl, an avocado resembled a testicle so much that they used the same word to refer to both: ahuacatl.

avenue	avenida
	jirón
	paseo (Per)
	rambla (Rpl)
boulevard	bulevar
	calzada (Mex)
square	plaza
street	calle/paseo
downhill	para abajo
uphill	para arriba
east	este
north	norte
south	sur
west	oeste

THEY MAY SAY ...	
De acuerdo.	Okay.
Claro.	Sure.
Vámonos.	Let's go.
¡Ojo!	Careful!
Espera.	Wait.
Espera un segundo.	Just a minute.
¿Estás lista/o?	Are you ready?
Estoy lista/o.	I'm ready.

BUYING TICKETS

Excuse me, where's the ticket office?	¿Perdón, dónde está la taquilla/boletería?
Where can I buy a ticket?	¿Dónde puedo comprar un boleto?
Do you have a timetable please?	¿Tiene un horario?
I want to go to ...	Quiero ir a ...
How much is the fare to ...?	¿Cuánto vale/cuesto el pasaje/boletoa a ...?
What's the cheapest fare to ...?	¿Cuál es el pasaje más barato para ...?
How long does the trip take?	¿Cuánto se demora en llegar?
Is it a direct trip?	¿Es un viaje directo?
Is it full?	¿Está completo?
Do I need to book?	¿Tengo que reservar?
I'd like to book a seat to ...?	Quisiera reservar un pasaje (Mex)/campo(CAm)/ asiento (Arg) para ...

GETTING AROUND

I'd like ...	Quisiera ...
a ticket	un boleto; pasaje
a one-way ticket	un boleto de ida
a return ticket	un boleto de ida y vuelta
two tickets	dos boletos
a/an ... fare	una tarifa ...
adult	de adulto
child's	de niño
student	de estudiante
pensioner	de pensionado
	jubilado (Arg)

I'd like a window seat, please. — Quisiera un asiento de ventanilla, por favor.

(No) smoking, please. — Quisiera un asiento de (no) fumadores.

I require a ... meal.	Deseo una comida ....
kosher	kosher
vegetarian	vegetariana

I'd like to ... my reservation. — Quisiera ... mi reserva/reservación.

cancel	cancelar
change	cambiar
confirm	confirmar
first class	primera clase
second class	segunda clase
economy class	clase económica/turista

It's full. — Está completo.
Is it completely full? — ¿Está completamente lleno?
Can I go on the standby list? — ¿Puede ponerme en la lista de espera?

Useful Words & Phrases

What time does the ... leave/arrive?	¿A qué hora sale/llega la/el ...?
plane	avión
boat	barco; buque (large boat) bote (small boat; CAm)
bus (city/local)	autobús; bus
bus (intercity)/coach	flota; bus; micro (Arg)
train	tren
tram	tranvía

AT CUSTOMS

SIGNS	
ADUANA	CUSTOMS
ARTÍCULOS LIBRES DE IMPUESTOS	DUTY-FREE GOODS
INMIGRACIÓN	IMMIGRATION CONTROL
CONTROL DE PASAPORTE/S	PASSPORT CONTROL

I have nothing to declare.	No tengo nada que declarar.
This is all my luggage.	Este es todo mi equipaje.
May I go through?	¿Puedo pasar?
Do I have to declare this?	¿Tengo que declarar esto?
I would like to declare (five bottles of rum).	Quisiera declarar (cinco botellas de ron).
May I call my embassy/ consulate?	¿Puedo llamar a la embajada/ al consulado de mi país?

AIR

Sometimes it's a lot quicker and not much more expensive to take internal flights rather than trains or buses. At certain times you may have no choice – the only way to get from Panama into South America, unless you walk the Darien Gap or catch a boat, is to fly.

Is there a flight to ...?	¿Hay un vuelo para a ...?
When is the next flight to ...?	¿Cuándo sale el próximo vuelo para ...?
How long does the flight take?	¿Cuánto tiempo dura el vuelo?
Is it a nonstop flight?	¿Es un vuelo directo?
What's the flight number?	¿Cuál es el número del vuelo?
What time do I have to check in?	¿A qué hora tengo que facturar mi equipaje?
Is there a bus to the airport?	¿Hay algún autobús para el aeropuerto?

arrivals
     llegadas
baggage
     equipaje
departures
     partidas/salidas
exchange
     cambio
flight
     vuelo
gate
     puerta
international
     internacional
passport
     pasaporte
plane
     avión
transit lounge
     tránsito

No tengo nada que declarar.

ADUANA

Is there a departure tax here?	¿Hay que pagar impuestos en este aeropuerto?
Is it delayed?	¿Está atrasado/demorado?
How long will it be delayed?	¿Cuánto tiempo se retrasará?
I'd like to check-in my luggage.	Quisiera facturar/registrar mi equipaje.
What's the charge for each excess kilo?	¿Cuánto vale cada quilo de más?
My luggage hasn't arrived.	Mis maletas no aparecen.

airport tax	impuesto/tasa del aeropuerto
baggage claim	recogida de equipajes
boarding pass	tarjeta de embarque
check-in	facturación de equipajes
domestic (flight)	vuelo domésticos; nacionales (Mex); de cabotaje (Arg)

BUS & COACH

Buses are used extensively by locals and this is where you'll really feel 'at one' with the people. You may need to book ahead for long-distance bus travel. Buses become booked up quickly during local holiday periods.

City buses are usually crowded. The locals will push – so should you. Buses are coded by numbers, colours and routes posted on the front. Prices are generally fixed, regardless of distance. You should also be aware that as buses are so crowded they are ideal playgrounds for robbers.

Some of the more modern cities, such as Santiago, Mexico City and Caracas, have metro systems which are very efficient and reliable. Another common form of transport is the colectivos; shared taxis which go on a fixed route and can sometimes be as cheap as the bus.

bus (city/local)	autobús/bus
	buseta; chiva (Col)
	camión; colectivo; pesero (Mex)
	micro (Bol, Chi)

GETTING AROUND

bus (intercity)/coach	flota; bus; micro (Arg)
Where is the bus stop?	¿Dónde está la parada de autobús?
How often do buses pass by?	¿Cada cuánto pasa el autobús?
Which bus goes to ...?	¿Qué autobús va a ...?
What time is the ... coach/bus?	¿A qué hora sale el ... autobús?
first	primer
next	próximo
last	último

Do you3 stop at ...?	¿Tiene parada en ...?
(Two) tickets, please.	(Dos) boletos, por favor.
Could you let me know when we get to ...?	¿Puede avisarme cuando lleguemos a ...?
Can one smoke in this bus?	¿Se puede fumar en este autobús?
Excuse me.	(Con) Permiso. (when making your way to the door)
I want to get off!	¡Quiero bajarme!; ¡Bajan por favor! (Mex)

Does this bus go to ...?	¿Este autobús va a ...?
the beach	la playa
the city centre	el centro de la ciudad
the station	la estación

TRAIN

Where's the nearest train station?	¿Dónde queda la estación de tren más cercana?
Is it a ... train?	¿Es un tren ...?
direct	directo
express	expreso; directo (Mex)
local	regional
long distance	de largo recorrido; intermunicipal (Col, intercity) distancia

Is this the right platform for ...?	¿El tren para ... sale de este andén?
I'm sorry, I can't find my ticket/train/platform.	Lo siento, pero no encuentro mi boleto/tren/andén.
The train leaves from platform ...	El tren sale del andén número ...
Do I have to change trains?	¿Tengo que cambiar de tren?
What station is this?	¿Qué estación es ésta?
What's the next station?	¿Cuál es la próxima estación?
Passengers must change trains/platforms.	Los pasajeros deben cambiar de tren/andén.
Is that seat taken?	¿Está ocupado este asiento?
Do you mind if I smoke/put the window down?	¿Le importa si fumo/si bajo la ventanilla?
Excuse me. (when making your way to the door)	Permiso.

dining car	coche/carro comedor
local	local
long distance	de largo recorrido; distancias intermunicipal (Col)
platform number	número de andén
sleeping car	coche/carro cama
ticket collector	revisor; cobrador; checador
train	tren

METRO

Which line takes me to ...?	¿Qué línea cojo/tomo para ...?
What is the next station?	¿Cuál es la próxima estación?
Where do I change for ...?	¿Dónde hago el transbordo para ...?

SIGNS	
POR AQUÍ A ...	THIS WAY TO ...
SALIDA	WAY OUT

GETTING AROUND

change (coins)	cambio
destination	destino
line	línea
ticket machine	máquina de tiquetes/boletos

Petty crime is common on the underground systems. When travelling on a train, keep your money in a safe place and try not to stand near the doors. These phrases may help you:

Leave me alone!	¡Déjeme en paz!
Stop, thief!	¡Socorro, ladrón!

TAXI

Found in every city, taxis are usually cheap. In most cities you must fix a price before travelling and this may involve some bargaining. Some taxis may have meters in which case you must be sure the meter is turned on and set at the minimum tariff when you set off.

Please take me to ...	Por favor, lléveme ...
this address	a esta dirección
the airport	al aeropuerto
the city centre	al centro de la ciudad
the railway station	a la estación de tren
Are you free?	¿Está libre?
How much is it to go to ...?	¿Cuánto cuesta/vale ir a ...?
Does that include luggage?	¿Incluye el equipaje?
For two people?	¿Para dos personas?
It's too much!	¡Es demasiado!
Can you take five people?	¿Puede llevar cinco personas?
Do you have change of 5000 pesos?	¿Tiene cambio de cinco mil pesos?
Please slow down.	Por favor vaya más despacio.
Please hurry.	Por favor, dese prisa.
The next corner, please.	En la próxima esquina, por favor.

Continue!	¡Siga!
The next street to the left/ right.	En la próxima calle a la izquierda/derecha.
Here is fine, thank you.	Aquí está bien, gracias.
Stop here!	¡Pare aquí!
Please wait here.	Por favor, espere aquí.
How much do I owe you?	¿Cuánto le debo?

CAR

Hiring a car is an expensive service in most Latin American countries. However, whether you're in your own or a rental car, this section covers some essentials for you.

car	carro; auto; coche
Where can I hire a car?	¿Dónde puedo alquilar un coche?
How much is it daily/weekly?	¿Cuánto cuesta por día/por semana?
Does that include insurance/ mileage?	¿Incluye el seguro/ kilometraje?
Where's the next petrol station?	¿Hay alguna gasolinera por aquí?
Please fill the tank.	Por favor, lléneme el tanque.
Where is the next gas station?	¿Dónde queda la gasolinera más cercana?

DID YOU KNOW ...   The Aztec guaxolotl is a delicious treat whether called guajolote by the Mexicans, chompipe by the Central Americans or pavo by the South Americans. The English took it to their land and decided to call it 'turkey'.

I want ... litres of petrol (gas).	Quiero ... litros de gasolina; nafta. (Arg)
I want (2000 pesos) worth of petrol.	Quiero (cien pesos) de gasolina.
Please check the oil, water and air.	Por favor, revise el nivel del aceite, del agua y el aire.
How long can I park here?	¿Cuánto tiempo puedo aparcar aquí?
Does this road lead to ...?	¿Se va a ... por esta carretera?

air	aire
battery	batería/ acumulador
brakes	frenos
clutch	cloche/embrague
driver's licence	permiso/licencia de conducir
engine	motor

SIGNS

CEDA EL PASO	GIVE WAY
DESVÍO; DESVIACIÓN	DETOUR
ACCESO PROHIBIDO	NO ENTRY
DISMINUYA SU VELOCIDAD	SLOWDOWN
NO REBASE	DO NOT OVERTAKE
OBRAS	ROADWORKS
PEATONES	PEDESTRIANS
PELIGRO	DANGER
PRECAUCIÓN	CAUTION
PROHIBIDO ESTACIONAR	NO PARKING
SALIDA	EXIT
SENTIDO ÚNICO	ONE WAY
STOP/PARE	STOP
ACCESO PERMANENTE	24-HOUR ACCESS

garage	taller
indicator	intermitente direccional
leaded; regular	gasolina normal; con plomo
lights	faros luces
main road	carretera
map	mapa
mobile breath tester	control de alcoholemia
motorway (with tolls)	autopista
oil	aceite
petrol (gas)	gasolina;
	bencina (Chi)
	nafta (Rpl)
petrol/gas station	gasolinera
	grifo (Per)
	estación de servicio (Rpl)
	bomba (Col, CAm)
puncture	pinchazo; agujero
	ponchadura (Mex)
radiator	radiador
ring-road	carretera de circunvalación/cinturón
road map	mapa de carreteras
seatbelt	cinturón de seguridad
self-service	autoservicio
speed limit	límite de velocidad
super	súper
toll free motorway	autovía
	autopista (Arg)
tyres	neumáticos/llantas
unleaded	sin plomo
windscreen	parabrisas

Car Problems

I need a mechanic.	Necesito un mecánico.
What make is it?	¿(De) qué marca es?

I've had a breakdown at ...	He tenido una avería en ...
The battery is flat.	La batería está descargada.
The radiator is leaking.	El radiador tiene una fuga.
I have a flat tyre.	Tengo una llanta ponchada.
It's overheating.	Está recalentándose.
It's not working.	No funciona.
I've lost my car keys.	He perdido las llaves de mi coche.
I've run out of petrol.	Me he quedado sin gasolina.

BOAT

Sometimes this is the only form of transport available and, although slow, can be a great experience.

What time does the next ferry depart?	¿A qué hora sale el próximo barco?
Where do we get on the boat?	¿Dónde subimos al barco?
boat	barco/buque (larger boat) bote (smaller boat CAm) lancha/chalupa (motorboat)
canoe/motorless boat	canoa/panga
port	puerto
raft	balsa
wharf/pier	muelle; embarcadero malecón (Per, CAm)

DID YOU KNOW ...   There is no specific word for toes, instead, they are know as los dedos del pie, (the fingers of the foot).

BICYCLE

Do you like cycling?	¿Te gusta andar en bicicleta?
Do you cycle?	¿Sabes andar en bicicleta?
Can you recommend a good place for a bike ride?	¿Me puedes recomendar algún sitio bonito para pasear en bicicleta?
Is it within cycling distance?	¿Se puede llegar en bicicleta?
Is it safe to cycle around here?	¿Es seguro andar en bicicleta aquí?
Where can I find secondhand bicycles for sale?	¿Dónde venden bicicletas de segunda mano?
Where can I hire a bicycle?	¿Dónde se alquilan bicicletas?
How much is it to hire a bicycle for ...?	¿Cuánto vale alquilar una bicicleta durante ...?
an hour	una hora
the morning/afternoon	toda la mañana/tarde
the day	todo el día
Can you lend me a padlock?	¿Me puede prestar un candado?
Can you raise/lower the seat?	¿Me puede subir/bajar el asiento?
Is it compulsory to wear a helmet?	¿Es obligatorio llevar casco?
Where can I leave the bicycle?	¿Dónde puedo aparcar la bicicleta?
Can I leave the bike here?	¿Puedo aparcar la bici aquí?
Where are bike repairs done?	¿Dónde arreglan bicicletas?
I've got a flat tyre.	Tengo una llanta pinchada.
I came off my bike.	Me he caído de la bici.

bike	bici; bicicleta
brakes	frenos
to cycle	andar en bicicleta

gear stick	cambio de marchas
	cambios (Col)
handlebars	manillares/manivela/munubrios
helmet	casco
to hire	alquilar
inner tube	cámara neumático
lights	luces
mountain bike	mountain bike; bicicleta de montaña
padlock	candado
pump	bomba/inflador
puncture	pinchazo/ponchadura
racing bike	bicicleta de carreras
saddle	asiento
wheel	rueda

ACCOMMODATION

The range of accommodation available to travellers in Latin America is immense. The cheapest places to stay are hospedajes or pensiones. As you venture out into the country areas, accommodation becomes more primitive, sometimes little more than grass huts with beaten dirt floors.

Hot water, let alone running water, cannot be assumed and it is therefore a very good idea to see the bathroom before accepting a room. Even if hot water is guaranteed, don't expect it, as most hotel proprietors know what a drawcard it is for travellers, especially in the Andean countries.

SIGNS

ALBERGUE JUVENIL	YOUTH HOSTEL
REFUGIO DE MONTAÑA	MOUNTAIN LODGE
PENSIÓN;	GUESTHOUSE
CASA DE HUÉSPEDES	
HOSTAL;	BUDGET HOTEL
RESIDENCIA	
PENSIÓN	BOARDING HOUSE
POSADA; HOSTERÍA	INN

Is there a place to stay here?	¿Hay un hotel por aquí?
Where is (a) ...?	¿Dónde hay ...?
boarding house	una pensión;
	una residencia;
	un hospedaje
guesthouse	una casa de huéspedes
hotel	un hotel
inn	una posada
	una hostería (Arg, Chi)
youth hostel	un albergue juvenil

I'm looking for a …	Busco un …
cheap hotel	hotel barato
good hotel	buen hotel
guesthouse	una casa de huéspedes
nearby hotel	hotel cercano

What is the address?	¿Cuál es la dirección?
Could you write the address, please?	¿Puede escribir la dirección, por favor?

For details on camping, see page 169.

BOOKING AHEAD

There are three words commonly used for the English word 'room': cuarto, habitación and pieza. Note that cuarto is masculine while habitación and pieza are feminine.

I'd like to book a room please.	Quisiera reservar un cuarto.
Do you have any rooms available?	¿Tiene habitaciones libres/ disponibles?
For (three) nights.	Para/Por (tres) noches.
How much is it per night/ per person?	¿Cuánto cuesta por noche/ persona?
I will be arriving at (two o'clock).	Llegaré a (las dos).
My name is …	Me llamo …
Is there hot water all day?	¿Hay agua caliente todo el día?
Does it include breakfast?	¿Incluye el desayuno?

CHECKING IN

I've made a reservation.	He hecho una reservacíon.
I'd like …	Quisiera …
a single room	un cuarto sencillo/ individual

a double room	un cuarto doble
to share a dorm	compartir un dormitorio

I want a room with a ...	Quiero una habitación con ...
bathroom	baño privado
double bed	cama matrimonial
shower	ducha
	regadera (Mex)
twin beds	dos camas
view of the sea/mountain	vistas al mar/a la montaña
window	ventana

ACCOMMODATION

THEY MAY SAY ...

Lo siento, no tenemos nada libre.	Sorry, we're full.
¿Cuánto tiempo se queda?	How long will you be staying?
¿Cuántas noches?	How many nights?
¿Tiene carnet de identidad?/ ¿Tiene pasaporte?	Do you have identification?
Su tarjeta de socio, por favor.	Your membership card, please.

It must be ...	Tiene que ser ...
quiet	silenciosa/tranquila
light	luminosa/iluminada

Can I see it?	¿Puedo verla?
Can I see the bathroom?	¿Puedo ver el baño?
Are there any others?	¿Hay otras?
Are there any cheaper rooms?	¿Hay cuartos más baratos?
I there a reduction for students/children?	¿Hay algún precio especial para estudiantes/niños?

ACCOMMODATION

Do you charge for the baby?	¿Los bebés también pagan?
Do I have to hire the bedlinen or is it included?	¿Tengo derecho a ropa de cama o tengo que alquilarla?
It's fine, I'll take it.	Bien, la alquilo.
Can I pay by credit card?	¿Puedo pagar con tarjeta de crédito?

Do you require a deposit?	¿Hay que pagar/dejar un depósito?
I'm going to stay for ...	Me voy a quedar ...
one day	un día
two days	dos días
one week	una semana
I'm not sure how long I'm staying.	No sé cuánto tiempo me voy a quedar.
date	fecha
date of birth	fecha de nacimiento
name	nombre
surname	apellido
signature	firma

ACCOMMODATION

REQUESTS & QUERIES

Do you have a safe?	¿Tiene una caja fuerte?
Where is the bathroom?	¿Dónde está el baño?
Can I use the kitchen?	¿Puedo usar la cocina?
Can I use the telephone?	¿Puedo usar el teléfono?
Is there a lift?	¿Hay ascensor?
	¿Hay elevator? (Mex)
I've locked myself out of my room.	Cerré la puerta y se me olvidaron las llaves dentro.
Do you change money here?	¿Se cambia dinero en este hotel?
Should I leave my key at reception?	¿Tengo que dejar la llave en la recepción?
Is there a message board?	¿Tienen tablero de anuncios?
	¿Tienen pizarra de anuncios? (CAm)
Can I leave a message?	¿Puedo dejar un mensaje?
Is there a message for me?	¿Hay algún mensaje para mí?
Can I get my letters sent here?	¿Puedo recibir cartas aquí?

The key for room (30) please.	La llave de la habitación (trinta), por favor.
Please wake me up at (seven) o'clock.	Por favor, despiérteme a las (siete).
The room needs to be cleaned.	Hay que limpiar la habitación.
Please change the sheets.	Por favor, cambie las sábanas.
Can you give me an extra blanket, please? I'm cold.	¿Puede darme otra manta/cobia, por favor? Tengo frío.
Is there somewhere to wash clothes?	¿Hay algún lugar donde pueda lavar la ropa?

DID YOU KNOW ...

Many of the cheaper places to stay have electric showers. These have a single cold water shower head hooked up to an electric heating element. Don't touch the heating unit, or anything metal, while in the shower or you may get a mild but unpleasant shock.

COMPLAINTS

It's ...	Es ...
too small	demasiado pequeña
noisy	ruidosa
too dark	demasiado oscura
expensive	cara
cold	fría
I can't open/close the window.	No puedo abrir/cerrar la ventana.
I don't like this room.	No me gusta esta habitación.
The toilet won't flush.	La cadena del inodoro/baño no funciona.

Can I change to another dormitory?	¿Puede cambiarme a otro dormitorio/habitación?

CHECKING OUT

When do I/we have to check out?	¿A qué hora hay que dejar la habitación?
I am/We are leaving now.	Me voy/Nos vamos ahora.
I would like to pay the bill.	Quiero pagar la cuenta.
Can I leave my backpack at reception until tonight?	¿Puedo dejar mi mochila en la recepción hasta esta noche?
Please call a taxi for me.	¿Puede llamar un taxi, por favor?

I'll return ...	Voy a volver ...
tomorrow	mañana
in a few days	en unos días

RENTING

flat	piso
	departamento (Mex)
	apartamento (Col, CAm)

I'm here about your ad for a room to rent.	He venido por la habitación que anuncian para alquilar.
Do you have any flats to rent?	¿Tiene pisos en alquiler?
I'm looking for a flat to rent for (three) months.	Estoy buscando un piso para alquilar durante (tres) meses.

I'm looking for something close to the ...	Busco algo cerca ...
city centre	del centro de la ciudad
beach	de la playa
railway station	de la estación

ACCOMMODATION

Is there anything cheaper?	¿Hay algo/alguno más barato?
Could I see it?	¿Puedo verla/o?
How much is it per week/month?	¿Cuánto vale por semana/mes?
Do you require a deposit?	¿Tengo que dejar un depósito?
I'd like to rent the room for one month.	Me gustaría alquilar la habitación durante un mes.

LOOKING FOR ...

I'm looking for ...	Estoy buscando ...
the art gallery	el museo; la galería de arte
a bank	un banco
a cinema	un cine
the city centre	el centro de la ciudad
the consulate	el consulado
the ... embassy	la embajada ...
my hotel	mi hotel
the main square	la plaza mayor; el zócalo (Mex)
the market	el mercado
the museum	el museo
the police	la policía
the post office	correos/el correo
a public telephone	un teléfono público
a public toilet	servicios; baños públicos
the telephone centre	la oficina de teléfonos de larga distancia; la central telefónica
the tourist information office	la oficina de turismo

What time does it open?	¿A qué hora abren?
What time does it close?	¿A qué hora cierran?

AT THE BANK

Where can I change money?	¿Dónde puedo cambiar dinero?
Can I exchange money here?	¿Se cambia dinero aquí?
Can I use my credit card to withdraw some money?	¿Puedo usar mi tarjeta de crédito para sacar dinero?

AROUND TOWN

I want to exchange some
    money/travellers' cheques.
What is the exchange rate?
How many pesos per (dollar)?
Please write it down.
What is your commission?
Can I have smaller notes?

Quiero cambiar dinero/
    cheques de viaje.
¿Cuál es el tipo de cambio?
¿A cuánto está el (dólar)?
¿Puede escribirlo, por favor?
¿Cuál es su comisión?
¿Me lo puede dar en billetes
    más pequeños?

The automatic teller has swallowed my credit card.	El cajero automático se ha tragado mi tarjeta de crédito.
Can I have money transferred here from my bank?	¿Pueden transferirme dinero de mi banco a éste?
How long will it take to arrive?	¿Cuánto tiempo tardará en llegar?
Has my money arrived yet?	¿Ya ha llegado mi dinero?
Can I transfer money overseas?	¿Puedo enviar dinero al extranjero?
Where do I sign?	¿Dónde firmo?

ATM (Automatic Teller Machine)	el cajero automático
bank notes	los billetes/recibos (de banco)
cashier	la caja
coins	las monedas
credit card	la tarjeta de crédito
exchange	el cambio
identification	la identificación
loose change	menudo/suelto; el sencillo el cambio (Arg) la feria (Mex)
signature	la firma

AROUND TOWN

AT THE POST OFFICE

I'd like to send ...	Quisiera enviar ...
a letter	una carta
a postcard	una postal
a parcel	un paquete una encomienda (Arg)
a telegram	un telegrama

| I'd like some stamps. | Quisiera unas estampillas. Quisiera unos timbres. (Mex) |

How much is the postage?	¿Cuánto vale el franqueo?; ¿Cuanto cuestan los timbres? (Mex)
How much does it cost to send this to (London)?	¿Cuánto cuesta enviar esto a (Londres)?
Where is the poste restante section?	¿Dónde está la lista de correos?
Is there any mail for me?	¿Hay alguna carta para mí?

SIGNS

ABIERTO/CERRADO	OPEN/CLOSED
ADUANA	CUSTOMS
CALIENTE/FRÍO	HOT/COLD
ENTRADA	ENTRANCE
ENTRADA GRATIS	FREE ADMISSION
FACTURACIÓN DE EQUIPAJE; CHECK-IN	CHECK-IN COUNTER
INFORMACIÓN	INFORMATION
NO TOCAR	DO NOT TOUCH
NO (USAR EL) FLASH	DO NOT USE FLASH
PROHIBIDO	PROHIBITED
PROHIBIDO COMER	NO EATING
PROHIBIDO EL PASO	NO ENTRY
PROHIBIDO FUMAR	NO SMOKING
PROHIBIDO PISAR LA CÉSPED	KEEP OFF THE GRASS
PROHIBIDO TOMAR FOTOS	NO PHOTOGRAPHY
RESERVADO	RESERVED
SALIDA	EXIT
SALIDA DE EMERGENCIA	EMERGENCY EXIT
SERVICIOS;BAÑOS	TOILETS
TELÉFONO	TELEPHONE

AROUND TOWN

aerogram	un aerograma
air mail	por vía aérea
envelope	un sobre
express mail	el correo urgente
mail box	el buzón
parcel	un paquete
pen	el bolígrafo
postcode	el código postal
registered mail	el correo certificado
surface mail	por vía terrestre; marítima

TELECOMMUNICATIONS

In some countries you use local coins, in others you'll need tokens, fichas , which are sold by street vendors. Long-distance calls are usually made from a telephone centre and you may need to pay a deposit before you make your call.

I want to make a call.	Quiero hacer una llamada.
I want to ring (Australia).	Quiero llamar a (Australia).
I want to speak for (three) minutes.	Quiero hablar (tres) minutos.
How much does a three-minute call cost?	¿Cuánto cuesta/vale una llamada de tres minutos?
How much does each extra minute cost?	¿Cuánto cuesta cada minuto adicional?
The number is …	El número es …
What's the area code for ...?	¿Cuál es el prefijo de ... ?
I want to make a reverse-charges phone call.	Quiero hacer una llamada a cobro revertido.
It's engaged.	Está comunicando/llamando/ ocupado.
I've been cut off.	Me han cortado (la comunicación).
How can I get Internet access?	¿Cómo puedo acceder a Internet?
Is there a local Internet café?	¿Hay algún servicio local de Internet?

I need to check my email.	Tengo que revisar mi correo electrónico.
Is there a cheap rate for ...?	¿Hay alguna tarifa más barata ...?
evenings	para las llamadas nocturnas
weekends	durante los fines de semana

area/city code	prefijo/clave
	código (CAm)
	caracteristica (Arg)
	lada (Mex)
answering machine	el contestador automático
dial tone	el tono
home page	home page; la página
operator	la operadora;el operador
phone book	la guía telefónica
phone box	la cabina telefónica
phonecard	la tarjeta de teléfono
telephone	el teléfono
telephone office	la oficina de teléfonos de larga distancia; la central telefónica

Making a Call

Hello! (making a call)	¡Hola!
Hello! (answering a call)	¿Diga?
Can I speak to (Angel)?	¿Está (Angel)?
Who's calling?	¿De parte de quién?
It's (Susana).	De (Susana).
Just a minute, I'll put (him) on.	Un momento, ahora se pone.
I'm sorry (she)'s not here.	Lo siento, pero ahora no está.
What time will (he) be back?	¿A qué hora volverá?
Can I take a message?	¿Quieres dejar un mensaje?
Yes, please tell (her) I called.	Sí, por favor, dile que he llamado.
No, thanks, I'll call back later.	No gracias, a llamaré más tarde.

ON THE STREETS

What is this?	¿Qué es esto?
What is happening?	¿Qué pasa?
What happened?	¿Qué pasó?
What is s/he doing?	¿Qué está haciendo?
What do you charge?	¿Cuánto cobra?
How much is it?	¿Cuánto vale?
Can I have one please?	Quisiera una/o, por favor.
festival	festival
newspaper kiosk	quiosco
recycling bin	contenedor de reciclaje
street	calle
street demonstration	manifestación
suburb	barrio
tobacco kiosk	quiosco de tabaco;
	tienda de cigarros (Mex)
artist	artista
beggar	mendiga/o
busker	artista callejera/o
clown	payasa/o
fortune teller	adivina/o
magician	maga/o
performing artist	artista callejero
portrait sketcher	retratista; caricaturista
street-seller	vendedora/vendedor
	callejera/o
crafts	artesanía
earrings	aretes
paintings	cuadros
posters	afiches/ carteles/cuadros
scarves	pañuelos y bufandas
T-shirts	camisetas

AROUND TOWN

SIGHTSEEING

Do you have a guidebook/ local map?	¿Tiene una guía/un plano de la ciudad?
What are the main attractions?	¿Cuáles son las atracciones principales?
What is that?	¿Qué es eso?
How old is it?	¿Es antiguo?; ¿De cuándo es?
Can I take photographs?	¿Puedo tomar fotos?
What time does it open/close?	¿A qué hora abren/cierran?
Is there an admission charge?	¿Hay que pagar?
Is there a discount for ...?	¿Hay descuentos para ...?
children	niños
students	estudiantes
pensioners	pensionados; jubilados (Arg)

GUIDED TOURS

Do you organise group tours?	¿Organizan excursiones en grupo?
What type of people participate?	¿Qué tipo de gente participa?
Will I have free time?	¿Voy a tener tiempo libre?
Is it necessary to join in all the group activities?	¿Es obligatorio hacer todas las actividades con el grupo?
How long will we stop for?	¿Cuánto tiempo vamos a parar?
What time do I have to be back?	¿A qué hora tengo que volver?
The guide has paid/will pay.	La/El guía ha pagado/va a pagar.
I'm with them.	Voy con ellos.
I've lost my group.	He perdido a mi grupo.
Have you seen a group of (Australians)?	¿Ha visto un grupo de (australianos)?

GOING OUT

There's a vast choice of entertainment in Latin America and it's an experience not to be missed. From the mariachi bands in Mexico City to the tango clubs in Buenos Aires you're sure to have a great time. There's casinos, cinemas, concerts, nightclubs, salsotecas – put your dancing shoes on and enjoy yourself.

Where to Go

What's there to do in the evenings?	¿Qué se puede hacer por las noches?
Where can I find out what's on?	¿Dónde puedo averiguar qué hay esta noche?
What's on tonight?	¿Qué hay esta noche?
Which paper are the concerts listed in?	¿En qué periódico se anuncian los conciertos?
In the entertainment guide.	En la guía de diversiones.

I feel like going to …   Tengo ganas de ir …
 a bar/café   a un bar/café
 the cinema   al cine
 a concert   a un concierto
 a disco   a una discoteca
 a disco (with salsoteca)   un boliche (Arg)
     una salsoteca (Ecu)
     un salseadero (Col)
     un rumbeadero (Col)

 the opera   a la ópera
 a restaurant   a un restaurante
 the theatre   al teatro

I feel like …   Tengo ganas de …
 a stroll   pasear
 dancing   bailar
 going for tapas   ir de tapas;
     tragos (CAm)
     botanas (Mex)

Invites

What are you doing this evening/this weekend?	¿Qué haces esta noche/este fin de semana?
Would you like to go out somewhere?	¿Quieres salir conmigo?
Do you know a good restaurant (that is cheap)?	¿Conoces algún restaurante (que no sea muy caro)?
Would you like to go for a drink/meal?	¿Quieres que vayamos a tomar algo/a cenar?
My shout (I'll buy).	Te invito.
Do you want to come to the (Barricada) concert with me?	¿Quieres venir conmigo al concierto de (Barricada)?
We're having a party.	Vamos a hacer una fiesta.
Come along.	¿Quieres venir?

Responding to Invites

Sure!	¡Por supuesto!
Yes, I'd love to.	Me encantaría.
That's very kind of you.	Es muy amable de tu parte.
Yes, let's. Where shall we go?	Sí, vamos. ¿Pero, dónde?
No, I'm afraid I can't. What about tomorrow?	Lo siento pero no puedo. ¿Qué tal mañana?

Nightclubs & Bars

Are there any discos?	¿Hay alguna discoteca?
How much is it to get in?	¿Cuánto cuesta la entrada?
How do you get to this disco?	¿Cómo se llega a esta discoteca?
Shall we dance?	¿Vamos a bailar?
I'm sorry, I'm a terrible dancer.	Lo siento, pero bailo fatal.
Come on!	¡Venga, vamos!
What type of music do you prefer?	¿Qué tipo de música prefieres?
I really like (reggae).	Me encanta (el reggae).

Where can we dance some (salsa)?	¿Dónde se puede bailar (salsa)?
Do you want to go to a karaoke bar?	¿Quieres ir a un karaoke?
How much is the cover charge?	¿Cuánto vale/cuesta entrar?
Do you have to pay to enter the dance?	¿Hay que pagar para entrar al baile?
No, it's free.	No, es gratis.
Yes, it's (700) pesetas.	Sí, vale (setecientos) pesos.
This place is great!	¡Este lugar me encanta!
I'm having a great time!	¡La estoy pasando muy bien!

I don't like the music here,
  La música no me gusta.
Shall we go somewhere else?
  ¿Vamos a otro sitio?

THEY MAY SAY ...

Spanish has many words related to going out. El ocio is a concept that can't easily be translated, but basically it means 'going out and enjoying oneself'. All of these verbs mean 'to go out and have a good time':

ir de copas
ir de farra
ir de rumba
ir de juerga
ir de fiesta
ir de pachanga

ARRANGING TO MEET

What time shall we meet?
  ¿A qué hora quedamos?
Where shall we meet?
  ¿Dónde nos encontramos?
Let's meet at (eight o'clock) in the (Plaza Mayor).
  Nos encontramos a las (ocho) en la (Plaza Mayor).
OK. I'll see you then.
  De acuerdo. Nos vemos.
Agreed/OK!
  ¡Hecho!
I'll come over at (six).
  Vendré a las (seis).
I'll pick you up at (nine).
  Te recogeré a las (nueve).

GOING OUT

CLASSIC PICK–UP LINES

Would you like a drink?	¿Quieres una copa?
Do you have a light?	¿Tienes fuego, por favor?
Do you mind if I sit here?	¿Te importa si me siento aquí?
Shall we get some fresh air?	¿Vamos a tomar el fresco?
Do you have a girlfriend/ boyfriend?	¿Tienes novia/o?
Can I take you home?	¿Puedo llevarte a casa?

CLASSIC REJECTIONS

No thank you.	No, gracias.
I'd rather not.	Mejor que no.
I'm here with my girlfriend/ boyfriend.	Estoy aquí con mi novia/ novio.
I'm sorry, I've got better things to do …	Lo siento, pero tengo otras cosas más importantes que hacer.
Stop hassling me.	Por favor, deje de molestarme.
Leave me alone!	¡Déjeme en paz!
Excuse me, I have to go now.	Lo siento, pero tengo que irme.
Get lost!	¡Hasta nunca!

I'll try to make it.	Intentaré venir.
If I'm not there by (nine), don't wait for me.	Si no estoy a las (nueve), no me esperen.
I'll be along later. Where will you be?	¡Llegaré más tarde. Dónde van a estar?
See you later/tomorrow.	Hasta luego/mañana.
Sorry I'm late.	Siento llegar tarde.
Never mind.	No importa/No pasa nada.

DATING & ROMANCE
The Date

Would you like to do something …?	¿Quieres hacer algo …?
tomorrow	mañana
tonight	esta noche
at the weekend	este fin de semana
Yes, I'd love to.	Me encantaría.

GOING OUT

THE PARTY

More than going out to bars and nightclubs, home parties or fiestas are the best alternative for meeting people, doing lots of dancing and getting to know Latin American life at heart. It is almost guaranteed that any friend you get to know in Latin America will invite you to one.

I brought some spirits.	Traje algo de trago.
I have we run out of spirits?	¿Se acabó el trago?
I want to dance.	Quiero bailar.
How do you dance this?	¿Como se baila esto?
What sort of music is this?	¿Que clase de música es esta?

bolero	unlike the fast bolero of Spain, the Latin American version is slow and romantic
cha cha cha	related to mambo, the Cuban 50s cha cha cha developed the off-beat step to include a quick change of step on the last two beats of the rhythm; said to have been designed specifically to appeal to white dancers
cueca	also known as the marinera and, in Mexico, the chilena, the cueca originated as a folk dance in Chile, north Argentina and Peru
cumbia	Afro-Caribbean rhythm
habanera	a dance which developed in Cuba in the late 19th century. It's slow and provocative, and accompanied by high-pitched singing reminiscent of flamenco

mambo	ballroom dance of Cuban origin, performed as an off-beat rumba
merengue	originating in the French-speaking Caribbean, it is always danced with the weight on one foot, thus creating a limp-like movement
pasodoble	a fast dance in duple time
ranchera	Mexican country music
rumba	a dance style of Afro-Cuban origin in which the rhythm is provided by maracas (drums) and a singer; known for its erotic side-to-side hip movements
salsa	developed in New York, and popular in the Caribbean in the '60s and '70s, the catchy salsa is a mix of son and other Latin American rhythms
samba	of Brazilian origin, with an African influence, the samba is a lively ballroom dance in double time
son	the Cuban equivalent of American country music
tango	originally a fast, sensual dance which developed in Argentina in the 1880s, it became a more slow, melancholy dance in the 1920s. The most well-known singer of tangos is Carlos Gardel, who died tragically in an air crash in Colombia, in 1935.
vallenato	based on the European piano accordian

GOING OUT

INTIMATE BODY

I really like your …	Me encanta(n) tu(s) …
body	cuerpo
breasts	pechos/tetas
bum; ass	culo;
	nalgas (Mex)
eyes	ojos
hair	pelo
hands	manos
lips	labios
mouth	boca
skin	piel

Thanks, but I'd rather not..	Gracias, pero no tengo ganas.
I'm afraid I'm busy.	Me parece que estoy ocupada/o.
Where would you like to go?	¿Dónde quieres ir?
Will you take me home?	¿Me acompañas a casa?
Do you want to come inside for a while?	¿Quieres subir a tomar algo?
Can I see you again?	¿Quieres que nos veamos de nuevo?
Can I call you?	¿Puedo llamarte?
I'll call you tomorrow.	Te llamaré mañana.
Goodnight.	Buenas noches.

INTIMATE SPANISH

cuddle	abrazo	lover	amante
erection	erección	to masturbate	masturbarse
to fuck	follar; joder; echar un polvo; tirar (Col); coger (Arg, Uru, Chi)		
orgasm	orgasmo	oral sex	sexo oral
safe sex	sexo seguro	kiss	beso

Useful Words

boyfriend	el novio
to chat up	ligar
girlfriend	la novia
date	una cita
to date	citarse
to go out with	salir con
to pick up	levantar
relationship	una relación
single	soltera/o
I (don't) like that.	Eso (no) me gusta.
Please stop!	¡Por favor, para!
	¡No sigas, por favor! (Mex)
Please don't stop!	¡Sigue!; ¡Por favor, no pare!
I think we should stop now.	Creo que deberíamos parar.
Kiss me!	¡Dame un beso!
Take this off.	Sácate/Quítate esto.
Touch me here.	Tócame aquí.
I want to make love to you.	Quiero hacerte el amor.
Let's go to bed!	¡Vámonos a la cama!
Do you have a condom?	¿Tienes un condón/ preservativo?
Let's use a condom.	Quiero que usemos un condón.

Afterwards

That was great.	Ha sido fantástico; Estuvo fantastico.
Would you like a cigarette?	¿Quieres un cigarro?
Can I stay over?	¿Puedo quedarme a pasar la noche?
You can't sleep here tonight.	No puedes quedarte aquí esta noche.
When can I see you again?	¿Podemos vernos alguna otra vez?
I'll call you.	Ya te llamaré.

GOING OUT

Love

I love you.	Te quiero; Te amo.
I'm in love with you.	Estoy enamorada/o de ti.
I'm really happy with you.	Soy muy feliz contigo.
Do you love me?	¿Me quieres?; ¿Me amas?
Do you want to go out with me?	¿Quieres salir conmigo?
I'd love to have a relationship with you.	Me gustaría que tuviéramos una relación.
Let's move in together.	¿Por qué no nos vamos a vivir juntos?
Will you marry me?	¿Quieres casarte conmigo?

Leaving & Breaking Up

I have to leave tomorrow.	Tengo que irme mañana.
I'll miss you.	Te voy a echar de menos.
I'll come and visit you.	Vendré a visitarte.
I really want us to keep in touch.	Me gustaría que nos mantuviéramos en contacto.
I don't think it's working out.	Creo que no está funcionando.
I want to end the relationship.	Quiero que terminemos.
I want to remain friends.	Me gustaría que quedáramos como amigos.

QUESTIONS

Are you married?	¿Estás casada/o?
Do you have a girlfriend/ boyfriend?	¿Tienes novia/o?
How many children do you have?	¿Cuántos hijos tienes?
How many brothers/sisters do you have?	¿Cuántas/os hermanas/os tienes?
How old are they?	¿Cuántos años tienen?
Do you live with your family?	¿Vives con tu familia?
Do you get along with your family?	¿Te llevas bien con tu familia?

REPLIES

I'm …

single	Soy soltera/o.
married	Estoy casada/o.
separated	Estoy separada/o.
divorced	Estoy divorciada/o.
a widow/widower	Soy viuda/o.

I have a partner.	Tengo pareja.
We live together but we're not married.	Vivimos juntos pero no estamos casados.
I don't have any children.	No tengo hijos.
I have a daughter/a son.	Tengo una hija/un hijo.
I live with my family.	Vivo con mi familia.

FAMILY MEMBERS

baby/children	el bebé/los hijos
boy	el chico; muchacho
christian name	el nombre de pila
daughter/son	la hija/el hijo
family	la familia

FAMILY

father	el padre; papá
girl	la chica; muchacha
grandmother/grandfather	la abuela/el abuelo
husband	el esposo; marido
mother	la madre; mamá
mother/father-in-law	la suegra/el suegro
mum/dad	la mamá/el papá
nickname	el apodo
sister/brother	la hermana/el hermano
wife	la esposa; mujer

TALKING WITH PARENTS

When is the baby due?	¿Para cuándo esperas el bebé?
What are you going to call the baby?	¿Cómo se va a llamar?
Is this your first child?	¿Es tu primer bebé?
How many children do you have?	¿Cuántos hijos tienes?
How old are your children?	¿Cuántos años tienen tus hijas/os?
I can't believe it! You look too young.	¡No lo puedo creer! Y pareces tan joven.
Does s/he attend school?	¿Va a la escuela?
Who looks after the children?	¿Quién cuida de las hijas (f)/ los hijos? (m)
Do you have grandchildren?	¿Tienes nietos?
What's the baby's name?	¿Cómo se llama el bebé?
Is it a boy or a girl?	¿Es niña o niño?
Is s/he well-behaved?	¿Se porta bien?
Does s/he let you sleep at night?	¿Te deja dormir por las noches?

DID YOU KNOW ... Todo el mundo means everyone. However, all the world is el mundo entero.

FAMILY

S/he's very big for her/his age!	¡Está muy grande para su edad!
What a beautiful child!	¡Es un/a niño/a precioso/a!
S/he looks like you.	Se parece a ti.
S/he has your eyes.	Tiene tus ojos.
Who does s/he look like, Mum or Dad?	¿A quién ha salido, al padre o a la madre?

TALKING WITH CHILDREN

What's your name?	¿Cómo te llamas?
How old are you?	¿Cuántos años tienes?
When's your birthday?	¿Cuándo es tu cumpleaños?
Have you got brothers and sisters?	¿Tienes hermanos y hermanas?
Do you have a pet at home?	¿Tienes alguna mascota?; ¿Tienes un animal domestico?
Do you go to school or kinder?	¿Vas a la escuela o a la guardería; kinder (Mex)?

Is your teacher nice?	¿Es simpática/o tu maestra/o?
Do you like school?	¿Te gusta ir a la escuela?
Do you play sport?	¿Practicas algún deporte?
What sport do you play?	¿Qué deporte practicas?
What do you do after school?	¿Qué haces después de la escuela?
Do you learn English?	¿Aprendes inglés?
We speak a different language in my country so I don't understand you very well.	En mi país hablamos otra lengua/idioma diferente y no te entiendo bien.
I come from very far away.	Vengo de muy lejos.
Do you want to play a game?	¿Quieres jugar conmigo?
What shall we play?	¿A qué jugamos?
Have you lost your parents?	¿Has perdido a tus padres?

PETS

Do you like animals?	¿Te gustan los animales?
What a cute (puppy)!	¡Qué (cachorrito) más lindo!
What's s/he called?	¿Cómo se llama?
Is it female or male?	¿Es hembra o macho?
How old is s/he?	¿Cuánto tiempo tiene?
Does s/he bite?	¿Muerde?

I have a …	Tengo …
bird	un pájaro
canary	un canario
cat/kitten	una gata/una gatita
dog/puppy	un perro/un cachorro
fish	un pez
guinea pig	un conejillo
hamster	un hámster
mouse	un ratón
rabbit	un conejo
tortoise	una tortuga

Common pet names include Puqui, Benyi and Capitán.

COMMON INTERESTS

What do you do in your spare time?	¿Qué te gusta hacer en tu tiempo libre?

Do you like …?   ¿Te gusta …?
I (don't) like …   (No) me gusta …

basketball	el baloncesto/basket
dancing	bailar
films	el cine
food	la comida
football	el fútbol
hiking	el excursionismo
music	la música
reading	leer
shopping	ir de compras
skiing	esquiar
swimming	nadar
talking	hablar
travelling	viajar

STAYING IN TOUCH

Tomorrow is my last day here.	Mañana es mi último día aquí.
Let's swap addresses.	¿Por qué no nos damos las direcciones?
Do you have a pen and paper?	¿Tienes papel y lápiz?
What's your address?	¿Cuál es tu dirección?
Here's my address.	Ésta es mi dirección.
If you ever visit (Scotland) you must come and visit us.	Si alguna vez vas a (Escocia) tienes que venir a vistarnos.
If you come to (Melbourne) you've got a place to stay.	Si vas a (Melbourne) tienes casa.
Do you have an email address?	¿Tienes correo electrónico?
Do you have access to a fax?	¿Tienes acceso a fax?

I'll send you copies of the photos.	Te enviaré copias de las fotos.
Don't forget to write!	¡No te olvides de escribirme!
It's been great meeting you.	Me ha encantado conocerte.
Keep in touch!	¡Nos mantendremos en contacto!

Writing

If you want to contact your new friends by writing to them in Spanish when you get back home, here are some useful words and phrases:

INTERESTS

Dear ...	Querida/o ...
I'm sorry it's taken me so long to write.	Siento haber tardado tanto en escribir.
It was great to meet you.	Me encantó conocerte (sg)/ conocerlos (pl).
Thank you so much for your hospitality.	Muchísimas gracias por tu (sg)/su (pl) hospitalidad.
I miss you (sg).	Te echo mucho de menos.
I miss you (pl).	Los echo mucho de menos.
I had a fantastic time in Chile.	Lo pasé muy bien en Chile.
My favourite place was ...	Mi lugar preferido fue ...
I hope to visit Guatemala again soon.	Espero visitar otra vez Guatemala pronto.
Say 'hi' to (Isabel) and (Miguel) for me!	Saluda a (Isabel) y a (Miguel) de mi parte.
I'd love to see you again.	Tengo ganas de verte/verlos otra vez.
Write soon!	¡Escríbeme pronto!
With love/regards,	Un beso/besos/un abrazo

South Americans tend to be quite informal when ending a letter. It is usual to finish with un abrazo (a hug) or un beso (a kiss), even when writing to casual friends.

ART
Seeing Art

When is the gallery open?	¿A qué hora abren el museo/la galería?
What kind of art are you interested in?	¿Qué tipo de arte te interesa?
What is in the collection?	¿Qué hay en la colección?

I'm interested in …	Me interesa(n) …
animation	los dibujos animados; los caricaturas
cyber art	el arte cibernético
design	el diseño
graphic art	el arte gráfico
painting	la pintura
performance art	la acción plastica
Renaissance art	el arte renacentista
Romanesque art	el arte románico
sculpture	la escultura

INTERESTS

Many other words associated with art styles are similar to English. For instance, baroque is barroco

altarpiece	el retablo
building	el edificio
church	la iglesia
cloakroom	el guardarropa; la ropería (Mex)
curator	una conservadora/un conservador
epoch	la época
etching	el aguafuerte/guaro
gardens	los jardines
permanent collection	una exposición permanente
photographer	la/el fotógrafa/o
a print	un grabado
salon	la sala
sculptor	una escultora/un escultor
souvenir shop	la tienda de recuerdos/souvenirs
statue	una estatua

Opinions

I like the works of ...	Me gustan las obras de ...
What do you think of ...?	¿Qué te parece ...?
It's not as good as ...	No es tan bueno como ...
It's reminiscent of ...	Me recuerda a ...

It's ...	Es ...
awful	horrible
beautiful	bonito
dramatic	dramático
interesting	interesante
marvellous	maravilloso
unusual	extraño
incomprehensible	incomprensible

Doing Art

artwork	una obra de arte	opening	una inauguración
bookshop	la librería	painter	una pintora/
canvas	el lienzo		un pintor
exhibit	exponer	studio	el estudio
exhibition	una exposición	style	el estilo
installation	una instalación	technique	la técnica

MUSIC
Regional Music

There are so many rhythms, dances, regional styles and songs that it would take a whole book to begin describing them. As anywhere modern popular music runs the gamut of tastes, while pre-Columbian, Latin, Caribbean, African, US (especially country & western), and Spanish influences have contributed to the proliferation of varieties. However, here are a few of the many you will come across.

Andean

Andean music employs a number of interesting instruments. The charango is similar to a ukulele, while the violín chapaco is a variationof the European violin. Instruments of pre-

INTERESTS

Columbian origins are typically woodwind instruments, such as the quena (reed flute) and the zampoña (pan flute). The breathy lead instrumentsof the rural altiplano are the tarka and the sikuri. Drums include the caja (tambourine-like) and the huankara.

The Colombian Andean music has been strongly influenced by Spanish music: typical forms are teh bambuco, pasillo and torbellino, all of which use stringed instruments.

Mariachi
Perhaps the most 'typical' Mexican music, with a heavy portion of brass

Music of Los Llanos
Music of Venezuela and Colombia, it is sung and accompanied by a cuatro (harp) and maracas. The most popular rhythm in venezuela is the joropo.

Música Criolla
With its roots in Spain and Africa, its main instruments are guitars and a cajón (wooden box used as a drum)

Reggae Influence
the reggae influence is felt throughout the Caribbean coast of Central America

Salsa
dance music which spread through the Caribbean in the 1960s

Tango
This famous music and dance is ever-popular

Vallenato
Emanating in Colombia, this is a more recent style of music, based on the European accordian

Do you like …?	Te gusta …?
listening to music	escuchar música
to dance	bailar
Do you …?	
play an instrument	¿Tocas algún instrumento?
sing	¿Cantas?

INTERESTS

What music do you like?	¿Qué tipo de música te gusta?
Which bands do you like?	¿Qué grupos te gustan?
I like (the) ...	Me gustan (los) ...
Have you heard the latest record by ...?	¿Has escuchado lo último de ...?
Which station plays salsa?	¿En qué emisora/estación de radio ponen salsa?
Which is a good station for (jazz)?	¿Qué emisora/estación de radio es buena para escuchar (jazz)?
What frequency is it on?	¿En qué frecuencia está?
Where can you hear traditional music around here?	¿Dónde se puede escuchar música folklórica en esta ciudad?
Shall we sit or stand?	¿Sentados o de pie?
Where shall we sit?	¿Dónde nos sentamos?

¡GUAY – COOL!

El concierto de la semana que viene será ...	The concert next week will be ...
Es una película ...	It's a ... film.
El tiempo ayer fue ...	The weather yesterday was ...
La excursión de ayer resultó ...	Yesterday's trip was ...
La fiesta mañana va a ser muy ...	The party tomorrow will be really ...
Es/Está ...	It's ...
extraordinaria/o; increíble	amazing
buenísíma/o; chiva/o (CAm);	great
la berraquera; brilante	brilliant
loca/o	crazy
guay (chévere, vacano?)	cool
heavy	full on
de pena (malisimo, fatal, terrible, horrible?)	terrible

Shall we go closer to the stage? ¿Vamos más cerca del escenario?

What a fantastic concert! ¡Qué concierto fantastico!
It's terrible! ¡Suena fatal/horrible!
This singer is brilliant. Esta/e cantante es genial.

See also On Tour, page 224.

Useful Words

ballroom	salón de baile
band	el grupo
concert	el concierto
drums	la batería
famous	conocida/o; famosa/o
gig	presentación
guitar	la guitarra
karaoke bar	karaoke
keyboard	los teclados
musician	una/un música/o
opera	la ópera
opera house	la ópera
orchestra	la orquesta
performance	la actuación
rock group	el grupo de rock
saxophone	el saxofón
song	la canción
show	el espectaculo
singer	la/el cantante
singer-songwriter	la cantautora/el cantautor
stage	el escenario
tickets	las entradas
ticket office	la taquilla/boletería
tune	la melodía
venue	el local
voice	la voz

INTERESTS

> **TRILLS**
>
> It's important to emphasise the rr in Spanish as it can mean the difference between one meaning and another.
>
> perro = dog
> pero = but

INTERESTS

CINEMA & THEATRE

I feel like going to a/an ...	Tengo ganas de ir ...
ballet	al ballet
comedy	a una comedia
film	al cine
play	al teatro

What's on at the cinema tonight?
¿Qué película dan en el cine esta noche?

Where can I find a cinema guide?
¿Dónde puedo encontrar la cartelera del cine?

Are there any tickets for ...?
¿Hay entradas para ...?

Sorry, we are sold out.
Lo siento pero se han agotado las localidades.

Is it in English?
¿Es en inglés?

Does it have English subtitles?
¿Tiene subtítulos en inglés?

Is there a short before the film?
¿Hay algún corto antes de la película?

Are those seats taken?
¿Están libres estos asientos?

Have you seen ...?
¿Has visto ...?

Have you seen the latest film by (Litín)?
¿Has visto la última película de (Litín)?

Who is in it?
¿Quién actúa?

It stars ...
Actúa ...

Who's it by?
¿Quién la dirige?

TICKETS PLEASE

You'll come across a couple of different words for tickets:

If you're buying tickets for a show, you'll need to ask for boletas.

Tickets for trains, buses, etc are called tiquetes/boletas.

It's directed by ...	La dirige ...
It's been really well reviewed.	La crítica la deja muy bien.

I (don't) like ...	(No) me gusta/n ...
action movies	las películas de acción
amateur film	el cine aficionado
animated films	las películas de dibujos animados
art films	el arte y ensayo
black comedy	la comedia negra
classical theatre	el teatro clásico
comedy	la comedia
documentary	los documentales
drama	el drama
film noir	el cine negro
horror movies	el cine de terror
period dramas	el cine de época
realism	el cine realista
sci-fi movies	el cine de ciencia ficción
short films	los cortos
thrillers	el cine de suspenso
war films	el cine bélico

INTERESTS

CINE

The countries with major developments in the film industry are Argentina, Cuba and Mexico. Known films include:

Alfonso Arau	*Como Agua para el Chocolate* *Like Water for Chocolate*
Fernando Solana	*Sur*
Tomás Gutierrez Alea	*Fresa y Chocolate* *Strawberry and Chocolate*
Arturo Ripstein	*El Callejon de los Milagros* *Miracle Alley*
Sergio Cabrera	*La Estrategia del Caracol*

INTERESTS

Opinions

Did you like the …?	¿Te ha gustado la/el …?
film	película
performance	actuación
play	obra

I liked it very much.	Me ha gustado mucho.
I didn't like it very much.	No me ha gustado mucho.

I thought it was …	Creo que ha sido …
excellent	fantástica/o
OK	regular

I had a few problems with the language.	He tenido dificultades para entender la lengua/el idioma.

LITERATURE

Who is your favourite author?	¿Quién es tu autora/autor favorita/o?
I read (Gabriel García Marquez).	Leo mucho a (Gabriel García Marquez)
I've read everything by (Isabel Allende).	Lo he leído todo de (Isabel Allende)
I prefer the works of (Jorg Luis Borges).	Prefiero las obras de (Jorg Luis Borges).
What kind of books do you read?	¿Qué tipo de libros lees?

I (don't) like …	(No) me gusta(n) …
comics	los cómics/las tiras cómicas
crime/detective novels	la novela negra
fantasy literature	la literatura fantástica
fiction	la ficción
non-fiction	el ensayo

AUTHORS

A postwar literary boom thrust many Latin American authors into the international sphere. Authors such as Isabelle Allende and Mario Vargas Llosa are widely translated. Nobel laureates and their most famous works include:

1945	Gabriela Mistral	(Chi)	*Desolación*
			Desolation
1967	Miguel Angel Asturias	(Gua)	*El Señor Presidente*
			The President
1971	Pablo Neruda	(Chi)	*Canto General*
			General Song
1982	Gabriel García Márquez	(Col)	*Cien Años de Soledad*
			A Hundred Years of Solitude
1990	Octavio Paz	(Méx)	*El Laberinto de la Soledad*
			The Labyrinth of Solitude

INTERESTS

novels	las novelas
poetry	la poesía
romance	la literatura romántica
science-fiction	la ciencia ficción
short stories	los cuentos
the classics	la literatura clásica
travel writing	los libros de viajes

Have you read *(One Hundred Years of Solitude)*?	¿Has leído *(Cien años de soledad)*?
What did you think of ...?	¿Qué te pareció ...?
Can you recommend a book for me?	¿Me puedes recomendar algún libro?

INTERESTS

Opinions

I thought it was …	Creo que es …
boring	aburrido
entertaining	entretenido

I thought it was …	Me pareció …
badly written	muy mal escrito
better/worse than the	mejor/peor que su
previous book	libro anterior
well-written	bien escrita/o

HOBBIES

Do you have any hobbies?	¿Tienes algún pasatiempo?

I like …	Me gusta …
gardening	la jardinería
travelling	viajar

I like to …	Me gusta …
cook	cocinar
draw	dibujar
paint	pintar
sew	coser
take photographs	sacar/tomar fotos

I make …	Hago …
pottery	cerámica
jewellery	joyería

I collect …	Colecciono …
books	libros
coins	monedas
comics	cómics/caricaturas
dolls	muñecas
miniature cars	coches miniatura
stamps	estampillas

TALKING ABOUT TRAVELLING

Have you travelled much?	¿Has viajado mucho?
How long have you been travelling?	¿Cuánto tiempo llevas viajando?
I've been travelling for (two) months.	Llevo (dos) meses viajando.
Where have you been?	¿Dónde has estado?
I've been to …	He estado en …
What did you think of (Quito)?	¿Qué te pareció (Quito)?

I thought it was …   Me pareció …
- boring   aburrida/o
- great   fantástica/o
- OK   normal
- too expensive   demasiado cara/o
- horrible   horrible

There are too many tourists there.	Hay demasiados turistas.
Not many people speak (English).	Poca gente habla (inglés).
I was ripped off in (Sucre).	Me estafaron en (Sucre).

People are really friendly there.
    Allí la gente es muy amable.
What is there to do in (Bogota)?
    ¿Qué se puede hacer en (Bogota)?
There's a really good restaurant/hotel there.
    Allí hay un restaurante/ hotel muy bueno.
I'll write down the details for you.
    Ya te escribiré los detalles.

INTERESTS

> ### THEY MAY SAY …
>
> Es importante.
>   It's important.
> No es importante.
>   It's not important.
> (No) es posible.
>   It's (not) possible.
> No es nada.
>   It's nothing.
> No importa.
>   It doesn't matter.

The best time to go is in (December).	La mejor época para ir es (diciembre).
Is it expensive?	¿Es caro?
Did you go alone?	¿Fuiste sola/o?
Is it safe for women travellers on their own?	¿Es seguro para mujeres que viajan solas?
Is it safe to hitch?	¿Es seguro hacer auto-stop?

STARS
Astrology

When's your birthday?	¿Cuándo es tu cumpleaños?
What star sign are you?	¿De qué signo eres?
I don't believe in astrology.	No creo en los signos del zodíaco.

I'm …	Soy …
Aries	aries
Taurus	tauro
Gemini	géminis
Cancer	cáncer
Leo	leo
Virgo	virgo
Libra	libra
Scorpio	escorpión
Sagittarius	sagitario
Capricorn	capricornio
Aquarius	acuario
Pisces	piscis

Ah, That explains it!	¡Ah, eso lo explica todo!

(Leo's) are very …	(Los leo) son muy …
aggressive	agresivos
caring	bondadosos
charming	encantadores
crafty	habilidosos/ingeniosos
creative	creativos

BAD SPANISH – CURSES

¡Maladita sea!	Fucking hell!
¡Condenado!	Damn!
¡No joda!	Damn it!
¡Coño! (Ven)	Fuck!
¡Mierda!	Shit!
¡Me cago en dios!	Christ!
¡Que cagada!; ¡Carajo!	Gosh!
¡Hijo de puta!	Son of a bitch!

INTERESTS

emotional	emocionales
indecisive	indecisos
intense	intensos
interesting	interesantes
jealous	celosos
loyal	leales
outgoing	abiertos
passive	pasivos
proud	orgullosos
self-centred	egoístas
sensual	sensuales
stingy	tacaños

I get on well with (Virgos).   Me llevo bien con los (virgo).

ascendent	el ascendente
chart	la carta astral
descendent	el descendiente
horoscope	el horóscopo
personality	la personalidad
zodiac	el zodíaco

Astronomy

Are you interested in astronomy?	¿Te interesa la astronomía?
I'm interested in astronomy.	Me interesa la astronomía.

INTERESTS

Do you have a telescope?	¿Tienes un telescopio?
Is there a planetarium/ observatory nearby?	¿Hay algún observatorio por aquí cerca?
Where is the best place near here to see the night sky?	¿Cuál es el mejor lugar para observar el cielo de noche?
Will it be cloudy tonight?	¿Va a estar nublado esta noche?

When can I see …?	¿Cuándo puedo ver …?
Mercury	Mercurio
Mars	Marte
Uranus	Urano
Pluto	Plutón

What time does it rise?	¿A qué hora sale?
What time will it set?	¿A qué hora se pone?
Can I see it at this time of year from here?	¿Se puede ver en esta época del año desde aquí?
Which way is north?	¿Dónde está el norte?
Is that Orion?	¿Aquello es Orión?
It's the other way up in the southern/northern hemisphere.	Se ve al revés en el hemisferio sur/norte.

Earth	La Tierra
Milky Way	La Vía láctea
Ursa Major/The Great Bear/ The Big Dipper	La osa mayor
The Little Bear	La osa menor
The Plough	El carro

DID YOU KNOW …   el cometa is a 'comet'
la cometa means 'kite'

WHAT ARE YA?

cursi	dag; jerk
pendejo (Mex)	
grosero (Arg)	
nuevo rico	flash; nouveau riche type
heavy (jevi); pesado	heavy
intelectual	intellectual type
mamerta/o	left-wing type
izquierdista; zurdo (Arg)	trendy
moderna/o	
yupi	yuppie

INTERESTS

astronaut	una/un astronauta
astronomer	una/un astrónoma/o
atmosphere	la atmósfera
comet	el cometa
full moon	la luna llena
galaxy	la galaxia
meteor	el meteorito
moon	la luna
NASA	NASA
nebula	la nebulosa
planet	un planeta
shuttle	la lanzadera/trasbordador espacial
sky	el cielo
space	el espacio
space exploration	la exploración espacial
stars	las estrellas
sun	el sol
telescope	el telescopio
universe	el universo

INTERESTS

The Unexplained

Do you believe there's life out there?

¿Crees que hay vida fuera de la tierra?

Do you believe in ...?
  (black) magic
  extraterrestrials
  ghosts
  life after death

  mediums
  miracles
  Satan
  telepathy
  UFOs
  witchcraft

¿Crees en ...?
  la magia negra
  los extraterrestres
  fantasmas
  la vida después de la muerte
  las/los médiums
  los milagros
  Satanás
  la telepatía
  los OVNIs
  la brujería

Have you ever seen one?
Are there haunted places in (Colombia)?

¿Alguna vez has visto alguna/o?
¿Hay lugares embrujados en (Colombia)?

People here/in my country tend (not) to be ...
  imaginative
  realistic
  scientific
  superstitious

La gente aquí/en mi país tiende a (no)ser ...
  imaginativa
  realista
  científica
  supersticiosa

SOCIAL ISSUES

POLITICS

Politics play a large part in daily Latin American life and are the topic of much conversation.

Did you hear about ...?	¿Has oído que ...?
	¿Te has enterado de que ...?
I read in (*El Tiempo*) today that ...	Hoy he leído en (*El Tiempo*) que ...
What do you think of the current/new government?	¿Qué te parece el nuevo gobierno/el gobierno actual?
I (don't) agree with their policy on ...	(No) Estoy de acuerdo con su política sobre ...
drugs	drogas
education	educación
the environment	el medio ambiente
military service	el servicio militar
privatisation	la privatización
social welfare	el estado del bienestar; asistencia/bienestar social
the economy	la economía
I am ...	Estoy ...
against ...	en contra de ...
in favour of ...	a favor de ...

DID YOU KNOW ...

Propaganda in Spanish doesn't have the negative connotations that it does in English – it simply means 'publicity' or 'advertising'.

SOCIAL ISSUES

I support the ... party.	Apoyo al partido ...
I'm a member of the ... party.	Soy miembro del partido ...
communist	comunista
conservative	conservador
green	verde
social democratic	socialdemócrata/
	Social Demócrata
socialist	socialista
Who do you vote for?	¿Por quién votas?
I'm an anarchist.	Soy anarquista.
I'm an abstainer.	Yo me abstengo; Yo dejo en blanco.
In my country we have a (socialist) government.	En mi país tenemos un gobierno (socialista).
Politicians are all the same.	Todos los políticos son iguales.
Politicians can never be trusted.	No se puede confiar en los políticos.

candidate's speech
  mitin/discurso
corrupt
  corrupta/o
counting of votes
  escrutinio
democracy
  democracia
demonstration
  manifestación
dole
  subsidio de desemple
electorate
  electorado
exploitation
  explotación
legislation
  legislación
legalisation
  legalización
parliament
  parlamento

policy	política
polls	sondeos de opinión/encuestas
president	presidenta (f)/presidente (m)
prime minister	primera ministra (f)/primer ministro (m)
racism	racismo
rally	concentración
rip-off	estafa
sexism	sexismo
strike	huelga
term of office	mandato
trade union	sindicatos
unemployment	desempleo
vote	votar

WHICH PAST?

If you want to say something without a specific time reference, you can use the verb haber with the past participle, just as we do in English with the verb 'to have'. So 'We have bought the tickets' will be Hemos comprado los boletos.

Once you put a specific day or time to an event or action you use the simple past: 'We bought the tickets yesterday' – Compramos boletos ayer.

SOCIAL ISSUES

... elections	elecciones ...
local council	municipales
regional	estatales; regionales; provinciales
general/national	generales

ENVIRONMENT

Does (Chile) have a pollution problem?	¿Hay un problema de contaminación en (Chile)?
Does (Buenos Aires) have a recycling program?	¿Hay algún programa de reciclaje en (Buenos Aires)?
Is this recyclable?	¿Esto es reciclable?

Are there any protected ... here?	¿Hay ... protegidas/os aquí?
Is this a protected ...?	¿Este ... está protegida/o?
park(s)	parque(s)
forest(s)	bosque(s)
species	especie(s)

Where do you stand on ...?	¿Qué piensas de ...?
pollution	la contaminación
deforestation	la deforestación
nuclear testing	las pruebas nucleares

antinuclear group	el grupo antinuclear
biodegradable	biodegradable
conservation	la conservación
disposable	desechable
drought	la sequía
ecosystem	el ecosistema
endangered species	las especies en peligro de extinción
hunting	la caza
hydroelectricity	la energía hidroeléctrica
industrial pollution	la contaminación industrial
irrigation	la irrigación
nuclear energy	la energía nuclear
ozone layer	la capa de ozono

SOCIAL ISSUES

pesticides	los pesticidas
recyclable	reciclable
recycling	reciclar
reservoir	el embalse
	la represa (CAm)
	el depósito (Mex)
toxic waste	los residuos tóxicos
water supply	el suministro de agua

SOCIAL ISSUES

| How do people feel about ...? | ¿Qué piensa la gente de ...? |
| What do you think about ...? | ¿Qué piensas de ...? |

I'm in favour of ...	Estoy a favor de ...
I'm against ...	Estoy en contra de ...
abortion	el aborto
animal rights	los derechos de los animales
equal opportunity	la igualdad de oportunidades
euthanasia	la eutanasia
immigration	la inmigración

THEY MAY SAY ...

¡Estoy de acuerdo!	I agree!
¡Por supuesto!	Absolutely!
¡Exactamente!	Exactly!
¡Desde luego!	Of course!
¡Ni hablar!	No way!
¡Para nada!	
¡No estoy de acuerdo!	I disagree!
¡Eso no es verdad!	That's not true!
¡Sí hombre!	Yeah, sure!
Sí pero ...	Yes, but ...
¡Anda ya!	In your dreams!
¡No me jodas!	Come off it!
Lo que sea.	Whatever.

SOCIAL ISSUES

party politics	los partidos políticos
racism	el racismo
tax	los impuestos
unions	los sindicatos

What is the current policy on (immigration)?	¿Cuál es la política actual sobre (inmigración)?
Is there an (unemployment) problem here?	¿Existe un problema de (desempleo) aquí?
Is there an adequate social welfare program?	¿Hay un buen programa de servicios/asistencia sociales?

What assistance is there for ...?	¿Qué tipo de asistencia reciben ...?
the aged	los ancianos
homeless	los sin hogar
street kids	los jóvenes callejeros

activist	una/un activista
citizenship	la ciudadanía
class system	el sistema de clases
demonstration	una manifestación
dole	el subsidio de desempleo
equality	la igualdad
human rights	los derechos humanos
inequality	la desigualdad
petition	la petición
protest	una protesta
race	la raza
social security	la seguridad social
strike	la huelga
unemployment	el desempleo
welfare	el bienestar social
political speech	un discurso político

SOCIAL ISSUES

DRUGS

All drugs are illegal in Latin American countries. However, you may find yourself in a position where the issue is being discussed, and the following phrases may help you understand the conversation but, if referring to your own interests, use discretion.

I don't take drugs.	No consumo ningún tipo de drogas.
I'm not interested in drugs.	Las drogas no me interesan.
I take (cocaine) occasionally.	Tomo (cocaína) de vez en cuando.
I smoke regularly.	Fumo regularmente.
Do you want to have a smoke?	¿Nos fumamos un porro/puro/cigarro?

DOPE – COLLOQUIAL TERMS

One problem with being in another country is that it is often difficult to assess situations and people as easily as you can back home, especially when you are unfamiliar with the language. Here are some colloquial terms common amongst drug-users – if you hear them in use around you, you're probably in the wrong bar.

tripi; acid	acid
coca; perico; línea	cocaine
mono	cold turkey
camello; dealer	drug dealer
chocolate	hash
jaco; caballo	heroin
yonki	heroin addict
chutarse	to inject
maría; mota; monte; mecha	marijuana
liar un porro	to roll a joint
chuta	syringe

I'm a heroin addict.	Soy (heroinómana).
Where can I find clean syringes?	¿Dónde puedo conseguir jeringas sin usar?
Do you sell syringes?	¿Vende jeringas?
I'm stoned.	Estoy pijeada/moteada.
I'm out of it.	Estoy colocada/o.
My friend has taken an overdose.	Mi amigo/a ha sufrido una sobredosis.
This drug is for personal use.	Esta droga es para consumo propio.
I'm trying to get off it.	Estoy intentando desintoxicarme.
Where can I get help with a drug problem?	Necesito ayuda, tengo un problema de drogadicción. ¿A dónde puedo acudir?
Do you have a methodone program in this country?	¿Hay algún programa de metadona en este país?
Can I register?	¿Me puedo inscribir?
I'm on a methadone program.	Estoy en un programa de metadona.

acid	LSD; ácidos
addiction	la adicción
cocaine	la cocaína
cocaine addict	una/un cocainómana/o
cold turkey	el síndrome de abstinencia
drug addiction	la toxicomanía
drug dealer	un traficante de drogas
heroin addict	una/un heroinómana/o
to inject	inyectarse
overdose	una sobredosis
syringe	una jeringa
syringe disposal	la recogida de jeringas usadas

LOOKING FOR ...

Where can I buy ...?	¿Dónde puedo comprar ... ?
Where is the nearest ...?	¿Dónde está la/el ... más cercana/o?
camera shop	la tienda de fotografía
clothing store	la tienda de ropa
craft shop	la tienda de artesanía
delicatessen	la fiambrería
department store	los grandes almacenes
fish shop	la pescadería
general store; shop	la tienda; el almacén
	la pulpería (Cos, Chi)
	la tienda de abarrotes (Bol,CAm, Ecu, Mex, Per, Col)
	el abasto (Ven)
	la bodega (CAm)
greengrocer	la verdulería; frutería
launderette	la lavandería;
	el lavadero;
market	el mercado
newsagency	el quiosco;
	puesto de periodícos (Mex)
optician	la óptica
pharmacy	la farmacia
	la droguería (Col)
record shop	la tienda de discos/disquería
shoe shop	la zapatería
souvenir shop	la tienda de recuerdos/souvenirs
stationers	la papelería
supermarket	el supermercado
tailor	la sastrería
travel agency	la agencia de viajes

MAKING A PURCHASE

I'm just looking.	Sólo estoy mirando.
How much is this?	¿Cuánto cuesta esto?;
	¿Cuánto vale esto?
Can you write down the price?	¿Puede escribir el precio?
I'd like to buy ...	Quisiera comprar ...
Do you have others?	¿Tiene otros?
Can I look at it?	¿Puedo verla/o?
I don't like it.	No me gusta.
I'll buy it.	Me la/lo llevo.
Do you accept credit cards?	¿Aceptan tarjetas de crédito?
Can I have a receipt?	¿Podría darme un recibo?
Does it have a guarantee?	¿Tiene garantía?
Can I have it sent overseas?	¿Pueden enviarlo por correo a otro país?
I'd like to return this please.	Me gustaría devolver esto, por favor.
It's faulty.	Es defectuosa/o.
It's broken.	Está estropeada/o.
I'd like my money back.	Quiero que me devuelvan el dinero.

THEY MAY SAY ...

¿En qué puedo servirle?; ¿Qué desea?	Can I help you?
¿Algo más?	Will that be all?
¿Se lo envuelvo?	Would you like it wrapped?
Lo siento, es el único que tenemos.	Sorry, this is the only one.
¿Cuánto/s quiere?	How much/many would you like?

BARGAINING

Really?	¡En serio!; ¡De veras!
That's very expensive!	¡Es carísimo!
The price is very high.	Cuesta demasiado.
Do you have something cheaper?	¿Tiene algo más barata/o?
I don't have much money.	No tengo mucha plata/ dinero.
Could you lower the price?	¿Podría bajar un poco el precio?
I'll give you (80) pesos.	Le doy (ochenta) pesos.
No more than (50).	No más de (cincuenta).

AMOUNTS

Give me a ...	Deme ...
gram	un gramo
kilogram	un quilo
millimetre	un milímetro
centimetre	un centímetro
metre	un metro
kilometre	un kilómetro
half	un medio
half a litre	medio litro
quarter	un cuarto

ESSENTIAL GROCERIES

Where can I find the ...?	¿Dónde puedo encontrar ...?
I'd like ...	Quisiera ...
batteries	pilas
bread	pan
butter	mantequilla
	manteca (Arg)
cheese	queso
chocolate	chocolate
eggs	huevos

flour	harina
gas cylinder	cilindro de gas
ham	jamón
honey	miel
margarine	margarina
marmalade	mermelada
matches	fósforos; cerillos
milk	leche
... olives	aceitunas ...
black	negras
green	verdes
stuffed	rellenas
olive oil	aceite de oliva
pepper	pimienta
salt	sal
shampoo	champú
soap	jabón
sugar	azúcar
sunflower oil	aceite de girasol
toilet paper	papel higiénico
toothpaste	pasta dentífrica/de dientes
washing powder	jabón de lavar
yoghurt	yogur

SOUVENIRS

embroidery	bordado
earrings	pendientes/aretes
	aritos (Arg, CAm)
	caravanas (Uru)
	chapas (Nic)
handicrafts	la artesanía
jewellery	la joyería
leathergoods	los artículos de cuero
necklace	el collar
panama hat	un panamá
pottery	la alfarería; cerámica
ring	el anillo

run	la alfombra; el tapete
silverware	la plata
T-shirt	una camiseta

CLOTHING

clothing	la ropa
boots	las botas
coat	un abrigo
dress	un vestido
hat	un sombrero
jacket	una chaqueta; chupa
jeans	los tejanos; vaqueros
jumper (sweater)	un chompa; buzo; saco; suéter
raincoat	el impermeable
sandals	las sandalias
	las ojotas (Bol, Ecu, Per)
shirt	una camisa
shoes	los zapatos
skirt	una falda; la enagua
	una pollera (Arg, Uru)
socks	los calcetines; las medias
trousers	el pantalon (Col)

It's ...	Es ...
too big	demasiado grande
too small	demasiado pequeño
too short	muy corto
too long	muy largo
too tight	muy apretado
too loose	demasiado suelto

DID YOU KNOW ... Contestar means to answer.
Asistir means to attend.

SHOPPING

swimsuit	un bañador; traje de baño
T-shirt	una camiseta
umbrella	el paraguas
underwear	la ropa interior
Can I try it on?	¿Me la/lo puedo probar?
My size is ...	Uso la talla ...
It doesn't fit.	No me queda bien.

MATERIALS

bronze	el bronce
cashmere	el casimir; la cachemira
copper	el cobre
cotton	el algodón
handmade	hecho a mano
glass	el vidrio
leather	el cuero
of brass	de latón
of gold	de oro
of silver	de plata
plastic	el plástico
silk	la seda
stainless steel	el acero inoxidable
synthetic	la fibra sintetica
wood	la madera
wool	la lana

COLOURS

dark ...	... oscuro
light ...	... claro
black	negra/o
blue	azul
brown	marrón; café
green	verde

NO NOT NEVER

The easiest way to make a negative statement is to put no in front of the verb.

No va.
    It doesn't go.

To say 'never', say no + verb + nunca or ¡jamás!

Jamás also means 'ever':

¿Has estado en Nueva York alguna vez?
    Have you ever been to New York?

No he estado en Nueva York nunca.
    No, I've never been to New York.

SHOPPING

grey	gris
orange	naranja; anaranjada/o
pink	rosa
purple	lila; púrpura; morada/o
red	roja/o
white	blanca/o
yellow	amarilla/o

TOILETRIES
See also page 215.

aftershave	la loción para después del afeitado/afeitarse
bath/shower gel	el gel de baño
comb	el peine
condoms	los preservativos; condones
dental floss	el hilo dental; la seda dental
deodorant	el desodorante
hairbrush	el cepillo (para el cabello)
moisturising cream	la crema hidratante
panty liner	una salva slip
	los panti protectores (Mex)
pregnancy test kit	la prueba de embarazo
razor	la afeitadora
razor blades	las cuchillas/hojas de afeitar
sanitary napkins	las compresas;
	toallas femeninas
shampoo	el champú
shaving foam	la crema de afeitar
soap	el jabón
scissors	las tijeras
sunblock cream	la crema solar/bronceador
tampons	los tampones
tissues	los pañuelos de papel
toilet paper	el papel higiénico

SHOPPING

toothbrush	el cepillo de dientes
toothpaste	la pasta dentífrica/de dientes; la crema dental
water purification tablets	las pastillas para purificar el agua

FOR THE BABY

baby food	la comida de bebé; potitos
baby powder	el talco
bib	el babero

INDIGENOUS PRODUCTS

Some original Latin American products you must enjoy ... if you haven't already.

	L.Am.Spanish	Amerindian
avocado	aguacate/palta	ahuacatl (Nahuatl)
cashew	marañon/anacardo	acajú (Tupi)
coca leaf	coca	kúka (Quechua)
custard apple	chirimoya	
chewing gum	chicle	chictli (Nahuatl)
chilli	chile/ají	chilli (Nahuatl)
chocolate	chocolate	xocolatl (Aztec)
guava	guayaba	
hammock	hamaca	hamaca (Taino)
maize	maiz/milpa/choclo	mahiz (Taino)
marijuana	marihuana	
paw paw	papaya	ababai (Carib)
peanut	cacahuate/maní	cacahuatl (Nahuatl)
pineapple	ananás/piña	ananas (Quechua)
potato	patata/papa	Batata (Taino)
quinine	quina	kina (Quechua)
rubber	caucho	
tobacco	tabaco	tabaco (Taino)
tomato	jitomate/tomate	xitomatl (Nahuatl)

disposable nappies	los pañales
dummy; pacifier	el chupete; chapín
feeding bottle	el biberón
	la mamadera (Arg)
nappy	el pañal
nappy rash cream	la crema para la irritación de los pañales
powdered milk	la leche en polvo
teat	la tetina

STATIONERY & PUBLICATIONS

Is there an English-language bookshop nearby?	¿Hay alguna librería que venda libros en inglés por aquí cerca?
Where is the English-language section?	¿Dónde está la sección de libros en inglés?
Do you have the latest novel by ...?	¿Tienen el último libro de ...?
Do you have a copy of ...?	¿Tienen el libro ...?
Can you recommend a good Latin American book available in English?	¿Me puede recomendar un buen libro latinoamericano traducido al inglés?
Do you know if this author is translated into English?	¿Sabe si esta/e escritora/escritor está traducida/o al inglés?
Do you sell magazines/ newspapers?	¿Venden revistas/periódicos?
Is there a local entertainment guide?	¿Tienen alguna guía de actividades?
dictionary	un diccionario
envelope	un sobre
newspaper in English	un periódico en inglés
... map	un mapa de ...
city	la ciudad
regional	la zona
road	carreteras

paper	el papel
pen (ballpoint)	el bolígrafo
	la birome (Arg)
	el esfero (Col)
popular magazines	las revistas del corazón

MUSIC

I'm looking for a salsa CD.	Quisiera un compact de salsa.
Do you have any mambo records?	¿Tienen discos de mambo?
What is her/his best recording?	¿Cuál es su mejor disco?
Who is the best (ballad) singer?	¿Cuál es el mejor cantante de (baladas)?
What's the latest record by ...?	¿Cuál es el último disco de ...?
What music can you recommend to take back to (Australia)?	¿Qué música me recomienda para llevar de recuerdo a (Australia)?
Can I listen to this CD here?	¿Puedo escuchar este compact aquí?

Do you have this on ...?	¿Tienen este en ...?
CD	compact;
	disco compacto
record/cassette	disco/casete

I need (a) ...	Necesito ...
blank tape	una cinta virgen
headphones	unos auriculares/audífonos
batteries	unas pilas

PHOTOGRAPHY

How much is it to process this film?	¿Cuánto cuesta revelar este rollo?
When will it be ready?	¿Cuándo estará listo?
I'd like a film for this camera.	Quiero un rollo para esta cámara.

Can you put the film in for me please?	¿Puede colocarme usted el rollo?
Do you have one-hour processing?	¿Tienen servicio de revelado en una hora?
I'd like to have some passport photos taken.	Me gustaría hacerme fotos de pasaporte.
The film is jammed.	El rollo está trabado.
This camera doesn't work.	Esta cámara no funciona.
Can you repair it?	¿Pueden arreglarla?

battery	la pila
B&W (film)	película en blanco y negro
camera	la cámara (fotográfica)
colour (film)	(película) en color
film	el rollo
film speed	la sensibilidad
flash	la bombilla/flash
lens	el objetivo/lente
light meter	el fotómetro
slides	las diapositivas
video tape	la cinta de vídeo

SMOKING

A packet of cigarettes, please.	Un paquete de cigarrillos, por favor.
Are these cigarettes strong/mild?	¿Son fuertes o suaves estos cigarrillos?
Do you have a light?	¿Tiene fuego?
Do you mind if I smoke?	¿Le importa si fumo?
Please don't smoke here.	Por favor, no fume aquí.
Would you like one?	¿Quieres uno?
Could I have one?	¿Me das uno?
I'm trying to give up.	Estoy intentando dejar de fumar.

| carton | cartón |

SHOPPING

cigarette machine	máquina de tabaco
cigarette papers	papel de fumar
cigarettes	los cigarrillos
	los cigarros (CAm, Mex, Ven)
cigars	los tabacos/habanos/puros
filtered	con filtro
lighter	el encendedor
matches	los fósforos;
	los cerillos (Mex)
menthol	mentolado
pipe	la pipa
tobacco (pipe)	el tabaco de pipa
... tobacco	el tabaco ...
dark	negro
light	rubio
rolling	de enrollar; para armar
without filter	sin filtro

SIZES & COMPARISONS

small	pequeña/o; chica/o
big	grande
as big as	tan grande como
heavy	pesada/o
light	leve; ligera/o; livana/o
more	más
less	menos
too much/many	demasiado/s
many	muchos
some	algunas/os
few	pocas/os
also	también
neither	tampoco
enough	bastante; suficiente
a little bit	un poco; un poquito; un pedazo
a lot	mucho

One of the great pleasures of travelling in Latin America is sampling the huge variety of fruit, vegetables and local dishes, not to mention the alcoholic beverages.

Markets are the best places to buy food if you want to cook. Towns and cities have numerous restaurants which vary widely in both cuisines and price. You will also find the inevitable fast-food outlets. Many restaurants provide a set menu for lunch which usually consists of soup, a main course and a drink. This is also the main meal of the day.

breakfast	desayuno
lunch	almuerzo; comida
tea	merienda
dinner	cena

I'm ...

I'm hungry is
   Tengo hambre.

I'm thirsty is
   Tengo sed.

Variations

lunch	comida (Mex)
	colación (Chi)
set lunch	almuerzo completo (Arg, CAm, Chi)
	almuerzo corriente (Col)
	casado (Cos)
	comida corrida (Chi)
	cubierto (Mex)
	el menú (Per)
	merienda (Ecu)
set dinner	comida

VEGETARIAN & SPECIAL MEALS

Vegetarians should have little trouble finding a dish without meat on the menu, although in Argentina this can be more difficult.

I'm a vegetarian.	Soy vegetariana/o.
I don't eat meat.	No como carne.

FOOD

I don't eat chicken, fish or ham.	No como pollo, ni pescado, ni jamón.
Do you have any vegetarian dishes?	¿Tienen algún plato vegetariano?
Does this dish have meat?	¿Lleva carne este plato?
Can I get this without the meat?	¿Me puede preparar este plato sin carne?
Does it contain eggs/dairy products?	¿Lleva huevos/productos lácteos?

I'm allergic to (peanuts).	Soy alérgica/o a (los cacahuetes).
Is this kosher?	¿Es apto/bueno para los judíos?
Is this organic?	¿Es orgánico?

EATING OUT

restaurant	restaurante; restorán
Chinese restaurant	restaurante chino
	restaurante chifa (Bol, CAm, Per)
cheap restaurant	restaurante barato; comedor soda;
	fuente de soda (Cos)
	bar (Per)
	lonchería (Gua)
steakhouse	parrillada (Arg, Chi, Col)
	churrasquería (Ecu)

Table for ..., please.	Una mesa para ..., por favor.
Can I see the menu please?	¿Puedo ver la carta/el menú, por favor?
Do you have a menu in English?	¿Tiene una carta en inglés?
What is that?	¿Qué es esto?
I'd like ...	Quisiera ...
I'd like the set lunch, please.	Quisiera el almuerzo completo; almuerzo corriente, por favor.
What does it include?	¿Qué está incluido?; ¿Qué incluye?

FOOD

Is service included in the bill?	¿El servicio está incluido en la cuenta?
Does it come with salad?	¿Viene con ensalada?
What's the soup of the day?	¿Cuál es la sopa del día?
What's the speciality here?	¿Cuál es la especialidad de este restaurante?
What do you recommend?	¿Qué me recomienda?
What are they eating?	¿Qué están comiendo ellas/os?
I'll try what she's having.	Probaré lo que ella está comiendo.
What's in this dish?	¿Qué ingredientes tiene este plato?
Do you have sauce?	¿Tiene salsa?
Not too spicy please.	Sin tanto picante, por favor.
It's not hot.	No está caliente.
I didn't order this.	No pedí esto.
I'd like something to drink.	Quiero algo para beber.
Do you have a highchair for the baby?	¿Tienen una sillita para el bebé?
Can you please bring me …?	¿Me puede traer … por favor?
some salt	la sal
more water	más agua
more wine	más vino
some pepper	la pimienta
more bread	más pan
The bill, please.	La cuenta, por favor.
Anything else?	¿Algo más?
Thank you, that was delicious.	Muchas gracias, estaba buenísimo.

ashtray	cenicero
the bill	cuenta
cup	taza
dessert	postre
a drink	una bebida

FOOD

first course/entrée	primer plato; de entrado
fork	(un) tenedor
fresh	fresca/o
a glass	un vaso
	una copa (for wine or spirits)
house wine	vino de la casa
knife	(un) cuchillo
plate	(un) plato
second/main course	segundo plato; plato fuerte
set menu	menú del día
spicy	picante
spoon	cuchara
stale	pasado/rancio
stale (bread)	(pan) duro/añejo
sweet	dulce
teaspoon	cucharita
toothpick	palillo/escarbadientes

Condiments

chilli	ají (SAm)
	chile (CAm)
	locoto (Bol, Per)
chilli sauce	salsa picante; ají
garlic	ajo
mustard	mostaza
pepper	pimienta
salt	sal
sugar	azúcar
vinegar	vinagre

EAT & DRINK

to eat is
  comer
to drink is
  beber or tomar

FOOD

Desserts & Snacks

appetiser in sauce	coctel
crème caramel; egg custard	flan
ice cream	helado
rice pudding	arroz con leche
sandwich	sandwich; emparedado; sánduche
soup	sopa; consomé; locro

Methods of Cooking

baked	al horno; horneado
boiled	hervido; cocido
chargrilled	al carbón
fried	frito
grilled	asado/a la parilla
medium	a punto; termino medio
rare	jugoso; poco cocido
roasted	asado
smoked	ahumado
stewed	guisado
well-done	bien hecho; bien asado; bien cocido

FOOD

MENU DECODER

a la plancha	grilled	asado	roasted
aceite	oil	bien asado	well done
aceituna	olive	atún	tuna
aceitunas rellenas	stuffed olives	auyama; calabaza	pumpkin
adobo	battered	bacalao	salted cod
agua	water	batata	sweet potato
agua del grifo; tubo; la llave	tap water	una bebida	a drink
agua mineral	mineral water	beicon/tocino	cold bacon
sin gas	plain	con queso	with cheese
con gas	fizzy	berberechos	cockles
aguacate	avocado	berenjena	aubergine; eggplant
ahumado/a	smoked		
ají	red chilli	besugo	bream
ajo	garlic	betabel	beetroot
ajoporro; puerros	leek	bife (Arg)	steak
		bistec	
al ajillo	in garlic	bistec con patatas	steak & chips
alcaucil	artichoke		
al horno	baked	blanco	white (wine)
albaricoque	apricot	bocadillo	tapa in a sandwich
albóndigas	meatballs		
alcachofa	artichoke	bollos	bread rolls
allioli	garlic sauce	boniato (Arg)	sweet potato
almejas	clams	boquerones;	anchovies
almendra	almond	boquerones en vinagre	anchovies in vinaigrette
alubias	kidney beans	boquerones fritos	fried anchovies
ananá	pineapple		
anchoas	anchovies	borrar (Mex)	glass
anguila	eel	una botella	bottle
un anís	anise	breva; higo	fig
apio	celery	buey	ox
arroz	rice	cabra	goat
arroz con leche	rice pudding	cacahuete; maní	peanut
arvejas	peas		

MENU DECODER

FOOD

café	coffee	cereales	cereal
con leche	with milk	cereza	cherry
cortado	with a little milk	una cerveza	a beer
		ciruela	plum
descafeinado	decaffeinated	cochinillo	suckling pig
helado	iced	cocina	kitchen
solo; negro	black	coco	coconut
calabacín	zucchini; courgette	col	cabbage
		colabaza (Mex)	pumpkin
calabaza	pumpkin	coles de	Brussels
calamares	calamari; squid	bruselas	sprouts
		coliflor	cauliflower
calamares a la romana	squid rings fried in butter	un combinado	cocktail
		un coñac	brandy
caldereta	stew	conejo	rabbit
caldo	broth; stock; consommé	una copa (de ...)	a glass (of ...)
		cordero	lamb
callampas	mushrooms	costillas	ribs
callos; tripa	tripe	crudo	raw
cambur	banana	cuajada	milk junket with honey
camarón	small prawn; shrimp		
		una cuchara	a spoon
camote (Cos)	sweet potato	cucharita	teaspoon
canelones	cannelloni	un cuchillo	a knife
cangrejo	crab	la cuenta	the bill
cangrejo de río	crayfish	chabacano	apricot
carabinero	large prawn	un champán;	champagne
caracol	snail	un cava	
carajillo	with liqueur	champiñones	mushrooms
carne	meat	champiñones	garlic
caza	game (meat)	al ajillo	mushrooms
cazuela	casserole; fish stew (Arg)	chauchas (Arg)	beans
		chipirón	small squid
cebolla	onion	chirimoya	custard apple
cenicero	ashtray	chivo	kid; baby goat
cerdo	pig; pork	choclo	corn on the cob

FOOD

MENU DECODER

choco	cuttlefish	frutila	strawberry
chorizo	spicy red/ white sausage	fuerte	strong
		galleta	biscuit/cookie
chorizo al horno	spicy baked sausages	gamba	prawn/shrimp
		gambas a la plancha	grilled prawns
chuleta	chop/cutlet	garbanzo	chickpea
damasco	apricot	gazpacho	cold tomato and vegetable soup
dátil	date		
doble	long black		
dorada	sea bass		
dulce	sweet	girasol	sunflower
ejotes	green beans	granada	pomegranate
elote (Cos)	corn	grasa	fat
empanada	pie	gratinada	au gratin
ensalada	salad	guindilla	hot chilli
ensalada rusa	vegetable salad with mayonnaise	guisado (Mex)	stew
		guisantes	peas
		guiso (Cos)	stew
entremeses	hors-d'oeuvres	un güisqui	whisky
espárragos	asparagus	hígado	liver
espagueti	spaghetti	haba	broad bean
espinacas	spinach	hamburguesa	hamburger
espumoso	sparkling	harina	flour
estofada/o	braised	helado	ice cream
estofado	stew	hervida/o	boiled
faba	type of dried bean	hierbabuena	mint
		higo	fig
filete	fillet	hongos	mushrooms
filete	pork, cheese	bien hecho	well done
flan	crème caramel	hongos (Cos)	mushrooms
frambuesa	raspberry	horneado	baked
fresa	strawberry	horno	oven
fresca/o	fresh	hortalizas	vegetables
frijoles	beans	huevos	eggs
frita/o	fried	cocidos; duros	boiled
fruta	fruit		

MENU DECODER

estrellados; fritos	fried	mango	mango
pasados	boiled	maní	peanut
pericos; revueltos	scrambled	manzana	apple
		marinado	marinated
infusión	herbal tea	marisco	shellfish
jabalí	wild boar	un martini	martini
jamón	ham	mayonesa	mayonnaise
jamón dulce	boiled ham	mazorca	corn on the cob
jamón serrano	cured ham	una mediana	bottle ($^1/_3$ litre)
una jarra	jug	mejillones	mussels
jengibre	ginger	mejillones al vapor	steamed mussels
judías (verdes)	(green) beans	melocotón	peach
judías blancas	butter beans	melón	melon
jitomate	tomato	membrillo	quince
jugo	juice	menta	mint
jugoso	rare	menú del día	set menu
langosta	spiny lobster	merluza	hake
langostino	large prawn	merluza a la plancha	fried hake
lechuga	lettuce		
legumbre	pulse	miel	honey
lengua	tongue	migas	fried breadcrumb dish
lenguado	sole		
lentejas	lentils	mojama	cured tuna
lima	lime	montado	tiny tapas sandwich
limón	lemon		
una litrona	a litre bottle	morcilla	blood sausage,
lomo	pork loin; sausage	muy hecho	well done
		naranja	orange
lomo con pimientos	pork sausage with peppers	nata	cream
		natilla (Cos)	sour cream
longaniza	dark pork sausage	natillas	creamy milk dessert
macarrones	macaroni	nuez/nueces	nut; walnut;
maíz	sweet corn	olla	pot
mandarina	tangerine	orejón	dried apricot

FOOD

MENU DECODER

ostras	oysters	piña	pineapple
pajarito	small bird	piñón	pine nut
palillo	toothpick	pistacho/e	pistachio
paloma	pigeon	plancha	grill; grilled;
palta (Chi)	avocado		on a hot plate
pan	bread	plátano	plantain
parrilla	grilled	platija	flounder
papa	potato	un plato	a plate
pasa	raisin	poco hecho;	rare
pasado/rancio	stale	se hace poco (Mex)	
pastel	pastry/cake	pollo	chicken
pata	pigs' trotters	porotos	beans
patata/papa	potato	postre	dessert
patatas fritas	chips;	potaje	stew
	French fries	potta	avocado
patisería	cake shop	primer plato	first course;
pato	duck		entrée
pavía	battered	puerros	leeks
pavo	turkey	pulpo (a la	octopus (in
pechuga	chicken breast	gallega)	sauce)
pepino	cucumber	a punto	medium (steak)
pera	pear	queque (Cos)	cake
perdiz	partridge	queso	cheese
peregrina	scallop	un quinto	very small
pescadilla	whiting		bottle
pescado	fish	rábano	radish
pescaíto/	tiny fried fish	rabo	tail
pescado frito		ración	small tapas
pez espada	swordfish		plate or dish
picadillo	minced meat	rape	monkfish
picada (Arg)	snack	rebozado/a	battered &
picante	spicy		fried
pil pil	garlic sauce	refrescos	soft drinks
	often spicy	rellena/o	stuffed
pimentón	capsicum/	remolacha	beetroot
	paprika	repollo/col	cabbage

MENU DECODER

FOOD

riñón	kidney	tinto	red
un ron	rum	tocino	bacon
rosada	ocean catfish/ wolf-fish	tomate	tomato
		tortilla	omelette
rosado	rosé	tortilla de patata;	egg and potato
sal	salt	española (Mex)	omelette
salado	salted/salty	tostada	toast
salmón	salmon	trigo	wheat
salsa de ajo (Mex)	garlic sauce	trucha	trout
		trufa	truffle
sandía	watermelon	un tubo	tall glass
una sangría	sangría (red wine punch)		(¼ litre)
		turrón	almond nougat
sardina	sardine	uva	grape
seco	dry/dried	(carne de) vaca	beef
segundo plato	second/main course	un vaso; una copa	glass
sepia	cuttlefish	vegetal	vegetable
serrano	mountain- cured ham	vegetariano/a	vegetarian
		venera	scallop
sesos	brains	verdura	green vegetable
seta	wild mushroom	vieira	scallop
		vino	wine
una sidra	cider	vino de la casa	house wine
sobrasada	soft pork sausage		
		xes (Mex)	beef
soja	soy	zanahoria	carrot
solomillo	sirloin	zapallo	pumpkin
sopa	soup	zarzuela	fish stew
tapa	bite-sized snack	zarzuela de marisco	shellfish stew
tarta	cake	zumo/jugo	fruit juice
una taza	a cup		
té	tea		
un tenedor	a fork		
ternera	beef/veal		

FOOD

TYPICAL DISHES

Within Latin America there is an incredible variety of cuisines and specialities. Just some of the dishes and snacks that you will find are described here.

ceviche; cebiche
  An essential experience for anyone travelling in Latin America. It is usually raw seafood that has been marinated in lemon, chilli, onions, garlic, tomatoes, sometimes coriander. It's served cold as an appetiser.

empanadas
  A meat or cheese pasty sometimes with rice, egg and olives. They can be either fried, empanada frita, or baked, empanada al horno. In Chile the meat empanadas are called empanada de pino.

parrillada; parrilla; asado
  Mixed grill of steak and other cuts, such as small intestines (chinchulines), large intestine (tripa gorda), udder (ubre), kidneys (riñones), blood sausage (morcilla; xellena Mex)

pollo asado
  Roast chicken

tacos
  Found mainly in Mexico, these are soft corn tortillas filled with beef, chicken or cheese with a variety of accompaniments

tamales
  Corn dough stuffed with meat, beans, chillis or nothing at all, usually wrapped in banana leaves, sometimes in corn husks and then steamed in onion and chicken sauce

FOOD

Argentina, Paraguay & Uruguay

Argentina is known for its beef dishes, generally eaten in grill houses (parrilladas).

bife de chorizo
A thick, tender, juicy steak

carbonada
Beef stew with rice, potatoes, sweet potatoes, maize, squash, chopped apples and peaches

dulce de leche
Caramelised milk

húngaros
Spicy sausages on a hot dog roll

locro
Maize stew

matambre arrollado
Rolled beef stuffed with spinach, onion, carrots and eggs

puchero
Slow-cooking casserole with beef, chicken, bacon, sausage, blood sausage, maize, peppers, tomatoes, onions, cabbage, sweet potatoes and squash. Sometimes beans are added. It's accompanied by rice cooked in the broth.

Bolivia

anticuchos
A speciality of La Paz, these are beef-heart shishkebabs

charque kan
Dried jerked beef served with mashed maize

chuños/tunta
Freeze-dried potatoes, eaten as snacks or with meals

fricasés
Pork soup, a speciality in La Paz

humitas
Corn-meal tamales filled with spiced beef, vegetables and potatoes. They are wrapped in a maize husk and fried, grilled or baked.

papa rellena
Potatoes mashed with vegetables and deep fried. Street vendors sell them.

pique a lo macho
Diced, grilled beef and sausage served with potatoes, lettuce, tomatoes, onions and locoto

pollo a la canasta
Chicken in a basket served with chips, mustard and a spicy sauce

rostro asado
Sheep's head, this dish is popular in Oruro

salteña
The Bolivian version of the empanada, they are smaller, spicier and have more juice than the typical empanada

thimpu
Spicy lamb and vegetable stew

Central America

arreglados
little puff pastries stuffed with beef, chicken or cheese

baleadas
white flour tortillas folded over a filling of refried beans, cream and crumbled cheese, typical of Honduras

bocas/boquitas
side dishes such as black beans, ceviche, chicken stew

casado
a set, filling meal that contains rice, black beans, fried plaintain, beef, chopped cabbage and maybe an egg or an avocado

cazuela de mariscos
Chile is well known for its marvellous seafood and this is a seafood stew

cazuela de pollo
boiled chicken, served in broth, with potato and vegetables

completo
a hot dog with salad, sauce or mustard

curanto
A very rich combination of seafood, chicken, pork, lamb, beef and potato. It's a speciality of Chiloé Island.

elote
corn served boiled or roasted on the cob

frijoles con arroz
this is a typical dish in all Central American countries and is simply white rice with black beans, maybe served with plaintain

guacamole
a salad of mashed avocados mixed with onion, chilli, lemon and tomatoes

gallo pinto
literally 'spotted rooster', the refried version of beans and rice

olla de carne
a beef and vegetable soup containing potatoes, plaintains, corn, squash and a local tuber called yuca

onces
the habit of eating bread, jam and cheese and having tea at about 5.30 to 6 pm

paila
pan-fried or poached eggs served with bread

FOOD

FOOD

patacones
a coastal speciality, especially on the Caribbean side, consisting of slices of deep fried plaintain

pupusas
El Salvadoran-style small, thick, corn tortilla with a filling of sausage, cheese or beans

sancocho
spicy meat and vegetable stew, Panama's national dish

tajaditas
crispy fried banana chips

tortillas
the bread substitute; a corn or wheat flat pancake

tres leches
a moist cake prepared with cream, condensed and evaporated milk

nocatamal
Nicaragua's less spicy version of the tamale

Chile

curanto
a hearty stew of fish, shellfish, chicken, pork, lamb, beef and potato

chupe de congrio
conger eel stew

lomo a lo pobre
this is the biggest standard meal in Chile and consists of an enormous slab of beef topped with two fried eggs

pastel de choclo
a maize casserole filled with vegetables, chicken and beef

Colombia

ajiaco
A speciality of Bogotá, this is a soup made of chicken and several different kinds of potato. It is served with corn on the cob, capers and avocado.

arepa
a toasted or fried maize pancake, which is eaten in place of bread

bandeja paisa; plato montañero
dish consisting of ground beef, a sausage, chorizo, red beans, rice, plantain, fried egg, a piece of pork crackling and avocado

cazuela de mariscos
a stew of shellfish, fish, squid and vegetables

hormiga culona
large fried ants; probably the most exotic Colombian speciality, unique to Santander and available only in season (March to May)

mazamorra
boiled maize in milk, typical to Antioquia

rondón
the most typical dish of San Andrés is made with coconut milk, yuca, plaintain, fish and sea snails

sancocho
soup – basically vegetable with fish, meat or chicken. It varies from region to region.

Ecuador

cuy
whole roasted guinea pig. It tastes rather like a cross between rabbit and chicken.

churrasco
a hearty plate with a slice of fried beef, one or two fried eggs, vegetables, fried potatoes, a slice of avocado and tomato and rice

FOOD

FOOD

hunitas
    sweet corn tamales often served for breakfast with coffee

llapinglchos
    mashed potato and cheese pancakes that are fried, often they
    are served with fritada (scraps of fried or roast pork)

seco
    stew, usually meat, served with rice

yaguarlocro
    potato soup with chunks of barely congealed blood sausage
    floating in it

Mexico

antojitos
    traditional snacks or light dishes

burrito
    any combination of beans, cheese, meat, chicken or seafood
    seasoned with salsa or chilli and wrapped in a flour tortilla

chiles rellenos
    chillis stuffed with cheese, meat or other foods, deep fried
    and baked in sauce

enchiladas
    ingredients similar to those used in tacos and burritos rolled
    up in a tortilla, dipped in sauce and then baked or semi-fried

frijoles
    beans, boiled, fried and refried in soups or tortillas (or with
    just about anything)

gazpacho
    chilled vegetable soup spiced with hot chillis

huevos rancheros
    fried eggs on tortillas, covered in salsa

FOOD

machaca
cured, dried and shredded beef or pork mixed with eggs, onions, cilantro and chillis

menudo
tripe soup made with the spiced entrails of various four-legged beasts

papadzules
tortillas sprinkled with chopped boiled eggs, rolled up and topped with a sauce made with squash or pumpkin seeds; typical of Yucatán

pollo pibil
chicken marinated in achiote sauce, sour Seville orange juice, garlic, black pepper, cumin and salt, then wrapped in banana leaves and baked; typical of Yucatán

pozole
rich, spicy stew of hominy (large maize kernels) with meat and vegetables

quesadilla
flour tortilla topped or filled with cheese and occasionally other ingredients and then heated

sopa de lima
a chicken stock containing shredded chicken, bits of tortilla and lime juice; an authentic Yucatecan lunch or supper

tacos
soft or crisp corn tortillas filled with beef, chicken or cheese with a variety of accompaniments; salbutes are the Yucatecan version filled with turkey meat

tortillas
thin, round patties of pressed corn or wheat flour dough cooked on griddles; in Costa Rica omelettes are sometimes called tortillas

tostada
a flat, crisp tortilla topped with meat or cheese, tomatoes, beans and lettuce

FOOD

Peru

ceviche/cebiche
An essential experience for any person travelling in Peru. It is usually fish that has been marinated in lemon, chilli and onions, sometimes coriander. It is served cold as an appetiser, with sweet potato. Its spiciness varies but it's quite delicious. Ceviche can be made with other seafood. Dried potatoes (cuños) sometimes accompany the ceviche

lomo saltado
similar to stir-fried beef, cooked with onions, tomatoes and sometimes potatoes; served with rice. (Pique macho is the Bolivian version.)

sopa a la criolla
a lightly spiced noodle soup with beef, egg, milk and vegetables

palta a la jardinera
an appetiser of avocado stuffed with cold vegetable salad

Venezuela

arepa
this plain maize pancake is often served as a snack stuffed with a variety of fillings

cachapa
a round pancake made of fresh corn, served with cheese or jam

chachito
a sort of croissant filled with chopped ham and served hot

casabe
a very large, dry bread made from yuca amarga; common in the Gran Sabana

hallaca
chopped pork, beef and/or chicken with vegetables and olives, all folded in a maize dough, wrapped in banana leaves and steamed; particular popular during Christmas

hervide
    a hearty soup made of beef or chicken with potatoes, carrots
    and a variety of local root vegetables

muchacho
    roast loin of beef served in sauce

FOOD

pabellon criollo
    a main course consisting of shredded beef, rice, black beans,
    cheese and fried ripe plaintain; Venezuela's national dish

sancocho
    a vegetable stew with fish, beef or chicken

tequeño
    white cheese strips wrapped in pastry and deep-fried

SELF-CATERING
Shops

baker	una panadería
butcher	una carnicería
delicatessen	una fiambrería
fish shop	una pescadería
greengrocer's	una verdulería, una frutería
patisserie/cake shop	una pastelería

In the Delicatessen

How much is (a kilo of cheese)?	¿Cuánto vale/cuesta (un quilo de queso)?
Do you have anything cheaper?	¿Tiene algo más barato?
What is the local speciality?	¿Cuál es la especialidad de la zona?
Give me (half) a kilo, please.	Deme (medio) quilo, por favor.
I'd like (six slices of ham).	Deme (seis lonchas/rebanadas de jamón).
Can I taste it?	¿Puedo probarla/lo?

FOOD

Making Your Own Meals

Where can I find the (sugar)?	¿Dónde puedo encontrar (el azúcar)?
I'd like some …	Quisiera un poco de …
bread	pan
butter	mantequilla; manteca (Arg)
cheese	queso
chocolate	chocolate
eggs	huevos
flour	harina
ham	jamón
honey	miel
jam	jalea
margarine	margarina
marmalade	mermelada
milk	leche
… olives	aceitunas …
black	negras
green	verdes
stuffed	rellenas
olive/sunflower oil	aceite de oliva/girasol
pepper	pimienta
salt	sal
sugar	azúcar
yoghurt	yogurt

AT THE MARKET
Meat & Poultry

bacon	tocino
beef	carne de vaca; carne de res lomo (Per)
chicken	pollo
duck	pato
goat	cabra; cabrito; chivo
ham	jamón

FOOD

hamburger	hamburguesa
hot dog	perro caliente
lamb	cordero
liver	hígado
(mince) meat	carne (molida)
mutton	carne de cordero; cordero
pork	cerdo; chancho
	puerco (Mex)
pork crackling	chicharrón
rabbit	conejo
ribs	costillas
roast meat	carne asada; churrasco
sausage	salchicha
	chorizo (Chi, Mex)
tripe	tripa
	panza (Bol)
	guatitas (Chi)
	mondongo (Arg, Per, Uru)
steak	bistec
turkey	pavo
	guajolote (Mex)
veal	ternera

Cuts & Cooking

beefsteak	bistec/borrar biftec/bife
breast (poultry)	pechuga
chop	chuleta;
	bife de costilla (Arg)
fat	grasa
grilled	asado; a la parrilla
medium	a punto
rare	jugoso
ribs	costillas
tongue	lengua
trotters (pig's feet)	pata
	patitas de cerdo (Arg)
well-done	bien hecho/asado

FOOD

Fish & Seafood

abalone	abulón
	oreja marina (Arg)
bass	corvina
catfish	bagre
clams	almejas
crab	cangrejo
fish (once caught)	pescado
flounder (or sole)	lenguado
king crab	centolla
lobster	langosta
mackerel	sierra
	macarela (Cos)
mussels	mejillones
	cholgas (Chi)
octopus	pulpo
oyster	ostra
perch	mojarra
prawns	camarones
	lengostine (Arg)
salmon	salmón
scallops	callos
	vieiras (Ven)
	ostiones (Chi)
seafood	mariscos
shark	tiburón
shellfish	concha
shrimps	camarones
snails	caracoles
squid	calamares
swordfish	pez espada
trout	trucha
tuna	atún
turtle	tortuga/caguama

Vegetables

asparagus	espárragos
aubergine (eggplant)	berenjena
avocado	aguacate
	palta (Arg, Chi, Peru, Uru)
beans	(borrar) frijoles
	frijoles porotos (Arg, Chi, Uru)
beetroot	remolacha
	betabel (Mex)
broccoli	brócoli
cabbage	repollo
	col (Mex)
capsicum	pimentón/pimiento
carrot	zanahoria
cauliflower	coliflor
celery	apio
	céleri (Ven)
corn	maíz
corn on the cob	choclo
	clote (CAm)
	mazorca (Col)
cucumber	pepino
garlic	ajo
green beans	ejotes
	chauchas (Arg)
leek	puerro
lentils	lentejas
lettuce	lechuga
mushroom	hongos; champiñones
	callampas (Chi)
olive	oliva
	aceituna (Arg, Bol, Chi, Col)
onion	cebolla
peas	guisantes
	arvejas (Arg, Bol, Chi, Col)
	chícharos (Mex)

FOOD

FOOD

plantain (a green banana requiring cooking)	plátano
potato	papa(Mex); patata
pumpkin	calabaza
	auyama (Col, Ven)
	zapallo (Arg, Bol, Chi)
radish	rábano/rabanito
red beans	frijoles; porotos colorados
red chilli pepper	aji
spinach	espinaca
squash	calabaza/zapallito/ayote
sweet potato	camote/batata
tomato	tomate
	jitomate (Mex)
vegetable	verdura
zucchini	calabacín

Fruit & Nuts

fruit	fruta
apple	manzana
apricot	damasco; albaricoque
	chabacano (Mex)
avocado	palta (SAm)
	aguacate (CAm, Col, Mex)
banana	banana; plátano dulce; cambur (Ven)
blackberry	mora
cherry	cereza
coconut	coco
custard apple	chirimoya; anona (Cos)
date	dátil
fig	higo
	breva (Col)

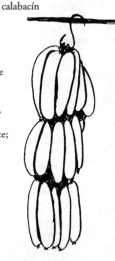

FOOD

grape	uva
grapefruit	toronja
	pomelo (Arg)
guava	guayaba
lemon	limón
mandarin	mandarina
mango	mango
melon	melón
orange	naranja
papaya	papaya
	lechosa (Ven)
passionfruit	maracuyá; parchita
peach	durazno; melocotón
pear	pera
pineapple	piña
	ananás (Arg)
plum	ciruela
pomegranate	granada
raisin	pasa
raspberry	frambuesa
strawberry	fresa; frutilla
watermelon	sandía
	patilla (Col)

almond	almendra	peanut	maní; cacahuate
nut	nuez	pinenut	piñón
hazelnut	avellana	pistachio	pistacho/e

Dairy Products

butter	mantequilla
	manteca (Arg, Uru)
cheese	queso
cream	crema; nata
icecream	helado
margarine	margarina
milk	leche

FOOD

sour cream	crema agria
	natilla (Cos)
yoghurt	yogurt

Eggs

egg	huevo
boiled eggs	huevos cocidos; pasados; duros; tibios
fried eggs	huevos fritos; estrellados
omelette	tortilla (de huevos)
	torta de huevos (CAm)
scrambled eggs	huevos revueltos
	huevos pericos (Col)

Breads & Cereals

bread	pan
cake	torta; pastel; queque (Cos)
	ponqué (Col, Ven)
biscuits; cookies	galletas; bizcochos
savoury biscuits	saltinas; galletas saladas
corn	maíz
croissant	medialuna (Arg)
flour	harina
oats	avena
pancake	panqueque; panqué
pastry	factura (Arg)
	repostería (Cos)
rice	arroz
sweet	dulce
sweet bread	pan dulce
toast	pan tostado
	tostadas calao (Col)
wheat	trigo

DRINKS
Nonalcoholic Drinks
Fruit juices can be bought in most countries. All well-known soft drinks are available in South America, along with some lesser known varieties such as inca cola (Peru), a bubblegum-flavoured, bright yellow drink.

FOOD

water	agua	orange juice	jugo de naranja
soft drink	gaseosa	pure juice	jugo puro
	bebida (Chi)		batido (Ven)
	refrescos (Mex, Pan)	watered juice	refresco
	sodas (Pan)		licuado (Mex)
	colas (Ecu)		fresco (Sal)
juice	jugo		chicha (Pan, Per)

FOOD

ice	hielo
without ice	sin hielo
a cold fizzy drink	una gaseosa, bien helada
mineral water	agua mineral

jugo con leche; batido en leche (Cos)
  juice with milk (this is similar to a fruit milkshake, such as
  blackberry juice with milk, (jugo de mora con leche)
pipas
  green coconuts which have a hole in the top so you can drink
  the milk with a straw – slightly bitter but refreshing and filling

Alcoholic

Wine is popular in Chile and Argentina, where some marvellous and very cheap wines can be bought. Beer is consumed in
great quantities, especially in the Central American countries.
The alternatives to these drinks are rum or home-brewed spirits
which are cheap, get you very drunk very quickly and leave you
with a rotten hangover!

beer	cerveza
white wine	vino blanco
red wine	vino tinto
rum	ron
spirit	aguardiente; pisco; chichamezcal
	pulque (Mex)
	caña (Rpl)
	guaro (Cos)

chicha
  A fruity, corn-based drink found in Peru and Bolivia. It can
  be alcoholic or nonalcoholic.
pisco
  The Peruvian clear spirit which is made into a pisco sour in
  Chile, Peru and Bolivia. Like a tangy Margarita – fantastic.
guinda
  the Bolivian speciality

FOOD

Hot Drinks

coffee	café
black coffee	café negro
	café tinto (Col)
	café americano (Mex)
milk coffee	café con leche
	perico (Col)
instant coffee	nescafé
	café instantáneo (Mex)
small cup of coffee	un cafecito
	un café chico (Arg)
with milk	con leche
	un cortado (Arg)
without milk	sin leche
with/without sugar	con/sin azúcar
tea	té
herb tea	té aromático
	agua aromática (Col)
coca leaf tea (found in Bolivia and supposed to help with altitude sickness)	mate de coca
with lemon	con limón
hot chocolate	chocolate

Your Shout, My Shout

I'll buy you a drink.	Te invito (a) una copa.
What would you like?	¿Qué quieres tomar?
What will you have?	¿Qué vas a tomar?
I'll have …	Me apetece …
	Para mí, …
	Yo tomaré …
	Apetezco ... (Mex)
	Quiero ... (Arg)
It's on me.	Pago yo.
	Yo pago. (Mex)

FOOD

It's my round.	Es mi ronda.
You can get the next one.	La próxima la pagas tú.
	Tu pagas la otra. (Mex)
Same again, please.	Otra de lo mismo.

One Too Many?

Thanks, but I don't feel like it.	Lo siento, pero no me apetece.
I don't drink (alcohol).	No bebo/tomo.
This is hitting the spot.	Me la estoy pasando muy bien.
I'm a bit tired, I'd better get home.	Estoy cansada/o, quiero irme a la casa.
Where is the toilet?	¿Dónde está el lavabo/baño?
Is food available here?	¿Sirven comida aquí?
I'm feeling drunk.	Esto se me está subiendo mucho.
I think I've had one too many.	Creo que he tomado demasiadas copas.
I'm pissed.	Estoy borracha/o; bolinga; pedo.
I feel ill.	Me siento mal.
I want to throw up.	Tengo ganas de vomitar.
S/he's passed out.	Está durmiendo la mona.
I'm hung over.	Tengo resaca.
	Estoy cruda/o. (Mex)
	Estoy de goma. (Cos)

IN THE COUNTRY

The countryside in Latin America is a very different experience to the city. The pace of life is generally much slower. You will find that as you travel through the Americas you will start to identify strong regional differences even within the same country.

CAMPING

campsite	camping; campamento (Mex)
site/space	parcelas; espacios (Arg) lugares (Mex) campos (Cos)

Is there a campsite nearby?	¿Hay algún camping cerca?
Where's the nearest campsite?	¿Dónde está el camping más cercano?
Do you have any sites available?	¿Tiene parcelas libres?

SIGNS	
CAMPING PROHIBIDO ACAMPAR	CAMPING GROUND NO CAMPING

How much is it ...?	¿Cuánto vale/cuesta ...?
per person	por persona
per tent	por tienda; carpa
per vehicle	por vehículo
Where are the ...?	¿Dónde están las ...?
showers	duchas regaderas (Mex)
washing facilities	instalaciones
Can I camp here?	¿Se puede acampar aquí?

IN THE COUNTRY

Who owns this land?	¿Quién es el propietario de este terreno?
Can I talk to her/him?	¿Puedo hablar con ella/él?
backpack	la mochila
	el morral
	el salveque (Cos)
can opener	el abrelatas
canvas	el sobretoldo
	la lona (Mex)
compass	la brújula
crampons	los crampones
firewood	la leña

WEATHER

What's the weather like?	¿Qué tiempo hace?
The weather is fine/bad today.	Hace buen/mal tiempo hoy.
It's raining.	Llueve.
It's hot (today).	Hace calor (hoy).
It'll be hot (tomorrow).	Hará calor (mañana).

	Today	Tomorrow
cloudy	Está nublado.	Estará nublado.
cold	Hace frío.	Hará frío.
foggy	Hay niebla.	Habrá niebla.
frosty	Está helando.	Helará.
hot	Hace calor.	Hará calor.
raining	Llueve.	Lloverá.
snowing	Nieva.	Nevará.
sunny	Hace sol.	Hará sol.
windy	Hace viento.	Hará viento.

gas cartridge	el cartucho de gas
	la garaffa de gas (Arg)
hammer	el martillo
hammock	la hamaca
ice axe	el pico; la pica; el piolet
mat	la esterilla
mattress	el colchón
penknife	la navaja
rope	la cuerda
sleeping bag	el saco de dormir
stove	la estufa; cocina
tent	la carpa; tienda (de campaña)
tent pegs	las estacas
torch (flashlight)	la linterna
water bottle	la cantimplora

HIKING & MOUNTAINEERING
Getting Information

Where can I find out about hiking routes in the region?	¿Dónde hay información sobre caminos rurales de la zona?
Are there guided treks/climbs?	¿Se organizan excursiones/ escaladas guiadas?
Do I need a guide?	¿Necesito un guía?
I'd like to hire a guide.	Me gustaría contratar un guía.
I'd like to talk to someone who knows this area.	Quisiera hablar con alguien que conozca este sector.
How long is the trail?	¿Cuántos kilómetros tiene el camino?
Is the track (well-)marked?	¿Está (bien) marcado el sendero?
How high is the climb?	¿A qué altura se escala?
Which is the shortest/easiest route?	¿Cuál es el camino más corto/ fácil?

IN THE COUNTRY

Is the path open all year?	¿Está la ruta abierta todo el año?
When does it get dark?	¿A qué hora oscurece?
Is it very scenic?	¿Tiene bonita vista?
Where can I rent mountain gear?	¿Dónde se alquila el material de montaña?
Where can we buy supplies?	¿Dónde podemos comprar comida?
How many hours per day will we walk?	¿Cuántas horas por día vamos a caminar?
Does the price include food?	¿El precio incluye comida?
Where do we meet?	¿Dónde vamos a encontrarnos?
How far is it from ... to ...?	¿Cuánto hay de ... a ...?
Is it a difficult walk?	¿Es una caminata difícil?
Is it a safe walk?	¿Es una caminata segura?
Do I need to bring ...?	¿Tengo que llevar ...?

On the Path

Where have you come from?	¿De dónde vienes?
How long did it take you?	¿Cuánto has tardado?
Does this path go to ...?	¿Este camino va a ...?
I'm lost.	Estoy perdida/o.
Where are we on this map?	¿Dónde estamos aquí en el mapa?
Can we stay in this village?	¿Podríamos quedarnos en este pueblo?
Where can I spend the night?	¿Dónde puedo pasar la noche?
Can I leave some things here for a while?	¿Puedo dejar algunas cosas aquí durante un rato?
May I cross your property?	¿Puedo cruzar su propiedad?
Is the water OK to drink?	¿Se puede beber el agua?
Can we swim here?	¿Se puede nadar aquí?
Can I/we sleep here?	¿Podría/Podríamos dormir aquí?

altitude	la altura
backpack	la mochila; el morral; el salveque
binoculars	los prismáticos
	las larga vistas (Arg)
cable car	el teleférico
candles	las velas
cave	una cueva; caverna
cliff	un acantilado; barranco
to climb	subir
compass	la brújula
cross-country trail	el camino
downhill	cuesta abajo
first-aid kit	el maletín de primeros auxilios
forest	el bosque
gap; narrow pass	un portillo; una pasada
	una brecha (Mex)
glacier	el glaciar

IN THE COUNTRY

IN THE COUNTRY

gloves	los guantes
guide	la/el guía
guided trek	la excursión guiada
harness	el arnés
to hike	ir de excursión
hiking boots	las botas de montaña

SEASONS	
summer	el verano
autumn	el otoño
winter	el invierno
spring	la primavera

itinerary	el itinerario
ledge	el saliente
lookout	el mirador
map	el mapa
mountain	la montaña
mountaineering	alpinismo
mountain hut	el refugio de montaña
mountain path	el sendero
pass	el paso
peak	la cumbre
pick	la piqueta; el pico
provisions	los víveres; las provisiones
rock climbing	escalar
rope	la cuerda
to scale	trepar
signpost	un cartel indicator la señal (Mex)
steep	escarpada/o
trek	la excursión
uphill	cuesta arriba
view	la vista
to walk	caminar

AT THE BEACH

Can we swim here?	¿Podemos nadar aquí?
Is it safe to swim?	¿Es seguro nadar aquí?
What time is high/low tide?	¿A qué hora es la marea alta/baja?

coast	la costa
rock	el peñón
sand	la arena
sea	el mar
sunblock	la crema solar; el bronceador
sunglasses	las gafas de sol
	los lentes ascuros (Arg, Mex)
towel	la toalla
wave	la ola

See also Aquatic Sports, page 190.

GEOGRAPHICAL TERMS

agriculture	la agricultura
bay	la bahía
beach	la playa
bridge	el puente
cape	el cabo
cave	la cueva
cliff	el acantilado
coral island	la isla de coral
the country	el campo
desert	el desierto
earth	la tierra
earthquake	el terremoto
farm	la hacienda; el rancho; la finca
	la estancia (Arg, Uru)
	el fundo (Chi)
field	el campo
footpath	el camino
forest	el bosque
glacier	el glaciar; el ventisquero
harbour	el puerto
high plateau	el altiplano
hill	la colina; el cerro
hot spring	la fuente termal; las aguas termales

IN THE COUNTRY

island	la isla
jungle	la selva
lake	el lago
landslide	el derrumbe/terr
marsh	el estero; el pantano; la ciénaga
mountain range	la cordillera; sierra; serranía
mud brick	el adobe
national park	el parque nacional
pass	el paso
peak	la cumbre; la cima
plain	la llanura
	el llano (Ven, Cos)
plateau	la meseta
rapids	los raudales
	los rápidos (Arg, Mex)
river	el río
road	la carretera
	la ruta (Arg)
rock	la roca
salt lake	el lago salado
sea	el mar
sound; fjord	el fiordo
spring	la fuente
stone	la piedra
stream	el arroyo
swamp	la ciénaga; el pantano
tide	la marea
trail	el sendero
trail (mountain)	el sendero; el camino
valley	el valle
vegetation	la vegetación
village	el pueblo
vineyard	el viñedo
volcano	el volcán
waterfall	la cascada; la catarata
	el salto (Mex)
wave	la ola

FAUNA
Domestic Animals

bull	el toro
calf	el ternero
cat	el gato
chicken	el pollo
cockerel	el gallito
cow	la vaca
dog	el perro
donkey	el burro
duck	el pato
goat	la cabra
goose	el ganso
hen	la gallina
lamb	el cordero
horse	el caballo
mule	la mula
ox	el buey
pig	el cerdo;
	el cohino; el chancho; el marrano
sheep	la oveja

> ### STRESS
>
> If a word ends in a vowel, -n or--s, the stress is on the second-last syllable.
>
> sombrero, tienen muchos
>
> If a word ends in a consonant (except -n and -s) the stress falls on the last syllable.
>
> hablar, ciudad

See also Pets, page 98.

Wildlife

What's that animal/bird/ insect called?	¿Cómo se llama este animal/ pájaro/insecto?
wild animal	animal salvaje

armadillo	el armadillo; el cachicamo
deer	el ciervo/venado
dolphin	el delfín
goat	la cabra
guinea pig	el cuy
	el cobayo (Arg)
	el conejillo de india (Mex)
jaguar	el jaguar

IN THE COUNTRY

monkey	el mono; el mico
mouse	el ratón
panther	la pantera; el leopardo
	el jaguar (Arg, Mex)
tapir	la danta
	el tapir (Arg, Mex)
tiger	el tigre
wolf	el lobo

Reptiles

lizard	el lagarto
rattlesnake	la víbora de cascabel
snake	la serpiente; la culebra; la víbora

Aquatic Wildlife

crocodile	el cocodrilo; el caimán
dolphin	el delfín
fish	el pez (for live fish)
	el pescado (in LAm 'pescado' is often used instead of 'pez')
frog	la rana
seal	la foca
shark	el tiburón
shellfish	los mariscos/moluscos
toad	el sapo
turtle	la tortuga
whale	la ballena

Birds

bird	el pájaro
buzzard	el ratonero;
	el zopilote (CAm)
	el carancho (Arg, Uru)
	el gallinazo (Bol, Ecu, Per)
	el chulo (Col)

crane	la grulla
eagle	el águila
flamingo	el flamenco
	el flamingo (Mex)
hummingbird	el colibrí
macaw	el papagayo
	la lalapa (Cos)
	el guacamayo (Ven)
owl	el búho; la lechuza
parrot	el loro
pelican	el pelícano
seagull	la gaviota
vulture	el cuervo; el buitre
	el chulo (Col)
	el zamuro (Ven)

IN THE COUNTRY

Insects & Others

ant	la hormiga
bee	la abeja
butterfly	la mariposa
cockroach	la cucaracha
fly	la mosca
leech	la sanguijuela/babosa
mosquito	el mosquito; el zancudo
scorpion	el alacrán; el escorpión
snail	el caracol
spider	la araña
wasp	la avispa

FLORA

bamboo	el bambú
cactus	el cacto
	cactus (Arg, Mex)
coconut palm	la palma de coco
	la palmera cocotera (Arg)

IN THE COUNTRY

crops	el cultivo
flower	la flor
grapevine	la vid; la parra
harvest	la cosecha
leaf	la hoja
lemon tree	el limonero
market garden/ orchard	la huerta
olive tree	el olivo
orange tree	el naranjo
orchid	la orquídea
palm tree	la palma; la palmera
sugar cane	la caña de azúcar
vine	la vid
vineyard	la viña
wheat	el trigo
wood	la madera

TYPES OF SPORT

What sport do you play?	¿Qué deporte practicas/juegas?
I play/practise …	Practico …
American football	el fútbol americano
athletics	el atletismo
Australian Rules Football	el fútbol australiano
baseball	el béisbol
basketball	el baloncesto
	el basquetbol (Mex)
boxing	el boxeo
cricket	el críquet
cycling	el ciclismo
diving	el submarinismo/buceo
fencing	la esgrima
football	el fútbol
handball	el balonmano
hockey	el hockey
indoor soccer	el fútbol sala
judo	el judo
pelota	la pelota vasca
rowing	el remo
rugby	el rugby
skiing	el esquí
soccer	el fútbol
surfing	el surf
swimming	la natación
tennis	el tenis
gymnastics	la gimnasia rítmica
weightlifting	el levantamiento de pesas

ACTIVITIES

TALKING ABOUT SPORT

Do you like sport?	¿Te gustan los deportes?
Yes, very much.	Me encantan.
No, not at all.	No me gustan nada.
I like watching rather than participating.	Me gusta verlos pero no practicarlos.
What sport do you follow?	¿A qué deporte eres aficionada/o?
I follow …	Soy aficionada/o a …
Who's your favourite …?	¿Quién es tu … favorita/o.
player	jugadora/jugador
sportsperson	deportista
What's your favourite team?	¿Cuál es tu equipo favorito?
How do you play (basketball)?	¿Cómo se juega al (baloncesto)?
Can you play (rugby)?	¿Sabes jugar al (rugby)?
Yes, I know how to play.	Sí, sé jugar.
No, I don't know how to play.	No, no sé jugar.
Do you feel like (going for a swim)?	¿Te gustaría (nadar); tiene ganas/desea (de nadar)?
Yes, that'd be great.	Me gustaría muchísimo.
Not at the moment, thanks.	No gracias, ahora no.
Do you want to go (skiing) this weekend?	¿Quieres ir a (esquiar) este fin de semana?
Yes, why not?	¡Por supuesto!
I'm sorry, I can't.	Lo siento, pero no puedo.

GOING TO THE MATCH

Would you like to go to a (basketball) game?	¿Te gustaría ir a un partido de (baloncesto)?
Where is it being held?	¿Dónde se juega?
How much are the tickets?	¿Cuánto valen/cuestan las entradas?
What time does it start?	¿A qué hora empieza?
Who's playing?	¿Quién juega?

Who do you think will win?	¿Quién crees que va a ganar?
Who are you supporting?	¿Para qué equipo vas?
I'm supporting …	Voy por …
Who's winning?	¿Quién gana?
Which team is winning/ losing?	¿Qué equipo/quién va ganando/va perdiendo?
What's the score?	¿Cómo van?

What a …!	¡Qué; Vaya …!
goal	gol
hit	tiro
kick	chute
	puntapié (Arg)
pass	pase

What a great performance!	¡Qué bien esta jugada!
The referee has disallowed it.	El árbitro lo ha anulado.
How much time is left?	¿Cuánto tiempo queda de partido?
That was a really good game!	¡Qué partidazo!
What a boring game!	¡Qué partido á aburrido!
What was the final score?	¿Cómo han quedado?
It was a draw.	Empate.

international championships	los campeonatos internacionales
medal	la medalla
national championships	los campeonatos nacionales
Olympic Games	los juegos olímpicos
referee	el árbitro
seat (actual seat)	el asiento
seat (place)	la localidad
ticket	la entrada
ticket office	la taquilla
	la boletería (Arg)

ACTIVITIES

THEY WILL SAY ...

¡Venga!/¡Aupa!/¡Vamos!	Come on!
¡Goooooooool!	Goal!
¡Penalty/Penal clarísimo!	That was clearly a penalty!
¡Árbitro casero/vendido!	The ref's an amateur!
¡Ha sido falta!	That was a foul!
¡Eso es fuera de juego; lugar (Mex)!	Offside!

¡Campeones, campeones, eo eo eo eo!
(Common football chant)

SOCCER

In Latin America, sport means soccer. Argentina and Uruguay have both won the World Cup twice, though many of the best athletes have abandoned their own countries to play for higher salaries in Europe.

Do you follow soccer?	¿Eres aficionada/o al fútbol?
Who do you support?	¿De qué equipo eres?
I support (Boca Juniors).	Soy del (Boca Juniors).
What a terrible team!	¡Vaya equipo más malo!; ¡Qué equipo más malo! (Arg)
(Guadalajara) are much better.	(Guadalaraja) es mucho mejor.
Who's the best team?	¿Cuál es el mejor equipo?
Who's at the top of the league?	¿Quién va primero en la liga?
Who plays for ...?	¿Quién juega en el ...?
My favourite player is ...	Mi jugador favorito es ...
He's a great player.	Es un gran jugador.
He played brilliantly in the match against (Italy).	Jugó un partidazo contra (Italia).

Common Soccer Teams

América (Mex, Col)	Colo Colo (Chi)
Alianza Lima (Perú)	River Plate (Arg)

coach	entrenadora (f)/entrenador (m)
corner	corner
	tiro de esquina (Col)
cup	la copa
fans	la afición; los aficionados
	las hinchas; la hinchada (Arg)
free kick	el tiro libre
foul	la falta
goal	el gol
goalkeeper	portera/o
	arquero (Arg)
kick off	el saque
league	la liga
manager	el mánager
offside	fuera de juego
	fuera de lugar (Mex)
penalty	el penalty
	el penal (Arg, CAm)
player	la jugadora/el jugador
to score/shoot	marcar/chutar

Important Tournaments

Copa Libertadores de América	Copa de la Concacaf
Copa América	Supercopa

FOOTBALL & RUGBY

I play ...	Juego al ...
Have you ever seen ...?	¿Has visto alguna vez ...?
Are you familiar with ... ?	¿Sabes lo que es el ...?
American football	fútbol americano
Aussie Rules	fútbol australiano
rugby	rugby
It's a contact sport.	Es un deporte de contacto.
Do you want me to teach you to play?	¿Quieres que te enseñe a jugar?
field goal	el gol de campo
forward	el delantero
fullback	el defensa
to kick for touch	intentar mandar el balón fuera del campo de juego; patear afuera (Arg)
kick-off	el saque (inicial)
pass	el pase
scrum	melée
tackle	el placaje
to touch down	poner el balón en el suelo
try	un ensayo
winger	el lateral

(English words are commonly used in Argentina for rugby.)

DID YOU KNOW ...   A letter you write to someone is *una carta*; a letter of the alphabet is *una letra*.

KEEPING FIT

Where's the best place to jog/ run around here?	¿Cuál es el mejor sitio para trotar/correr por aquí cerca?
Where's the nearest …?	¿Dónde está … más cercana/o?
gym	el gimnasio
swimming pool	la piscina
	la alberca (Mex)
tennis court	la cancha de tenis
What is the charge per …?	¿Cúanto cobran por …?
day/hour	día/hora
game	juego; partida
Can I hire …?	¿Es posible alquilar …?
a bicycle	una bicicleta
a racquet	una raqueta
shoes	zapatillas/zapatos
Do I have to be a member to attend?	¿Hay que ser socia/o para entrar?
Is there a women-only session/pool?	¿Hay alguna clase de gimnasia/ piscina sólo para mujeres?
Where are the change rooms?	¿Dónde están los vestuarios/ vestidores?
May I see the gym?	¿Puedo ver el gimnasio?
Is there a crèche?	¿Tienen servicio de guardería?

exercise bicycle	la bicicleta aeroestática fija (Mex)
jogging	footing; correr
massage	el masaje
rowing machine	la máquina de remar
sauna	el sauna
shower	la ducha regadera (Mex)
towel	la toalla
weights	las pesas
workout	entreno

WALKING & MOUNTAINEERING

See In the Country, pages 171 to 174 for trekking terms.

TENNIS

Do you like tennis/ table tennis?	¿Te gusta jugar tenis/ ping pong?
Do you play tennis?	¿Sabes jugar tenis?
I play tennis.	Juego tenis.
Would you like to play tennis?	¿Quieres jugar al tenis?
Is there a tennis court near here?	¿Hay alguna cancha de tenis aquí cerca?
How much is it to hire the court?	¿Cuánto vale alquilar la cancha de tenis?
Can you play at night?	¿Se puede jugar de noche?
Is there racquet and ball hire?	¿Se alquilan raquetas y pelotas?
Are there instructors?	¿Tienen instructoras/es?
What type of surface does the court have?	¿Qué tipo de superficie tiene la pista de tenis?

tennis court	la cancha de tenis
tournament	el torneo
ace	ace
advantage	ventaja
deuce	iguales
fault	falta
game	el juego
game ball	la pelota de juego
grass court	la cancha de hierba el césped (Arg, Mex)
hard court	la cancha dura
hire	alquilar rentar (Mex)
line	la línea

ACTIVITIES

love	cero a cero
	cero (Arg)
match	el partido
match ball	la pelota de partido
net	la red
ping pong ball	la pelota de ping pong
play doubles (v)	jugar dobles
point	el punto
racquet	la raqueta
serve	el servicio
	el saque (Arg)
set	el set
set ball	la pelota de set
table tennis	el ping pong
table tennis table	la mesa de ping pong
table tennis bat	la pala
	la raqueta (Mex)

CYCLING

Where does the race pass through?	¿Por dónde pasa la carrera?
Who's winning?	¿Quién va ganando?
Is today's leg very hard?	¿Es muy dura la etapa de hoy?
How many kilometres is today's race?	¿Cuántos kilómetros tiene la etapa de hoy?
Where does it finish?	¿Dónde termina?
My favourite cyclist is ...	Mi ciclista favorito es ...

cyclist	ciclista
leg (in race)	etapa
winner of a leg	vencedora/vencedor de etapa
(yellow) jersey	camiseta (amarilla)
hilly stage of the race	etapa de montaña
race against the clock	contra reloj

SKIING

How much is a pass for these slopes?	¿Cuánto vale/cuesta el forfait para estas pistas?
What are the skiing conditions like at …?	¿Cuáles son las condiciones de las pistas de esquí en …?
Is it possible to go cross-country skiing at …?	¿Es posible hacer esquí de fondo en …?
At what levels are the different slopes?	¿De qué nivel son las pistas?
Where are the (black) level slopes?	¿Dónde están las pistas (negras)?

cross-country	la carrera de fondo
downhill	el descenso
instructor	la profesora/ el profesor; la instructora/ el instructor (Arg)
safety binding	la fijación de seguridad
skis	los esquíes
ski-boots	las botas
ski-lift	el tele-arrastre
ski-pass	forfait boleto (Mex)
ski slope	la pista
ski-suit	el traje de esquí
stock	el bastón de esquí
sunblock	la crema solar

AQUATIC SPORTS

diving	el buceo
diving equipment	el equipo de inmersión el buceo (Mex)
motorboat	la lancha a motor
surfboard	la tabla de surf
surfing	el surf

ACTIVITIES

swimming	la natación
water-skiing	el esquí acuático
water-skis	los esquís para el agua
wave	la ola
windsurfing	el windsurf

See also At the Beach, page 174.

BULLFIGHTING

The corrida (bullfight) is a spectacle with a long history and many rules. It is not, as many would suggest, simply a ghoulish alternative to the slaughterhouse (itself no pretty sight). Aficionados will say that the bull is better off dying at the hands of a matador than in the matadero (abattoir). The corrida is about many things – death, bravery, performance. No doubt, the fight is bloody and cruel, and about that hackles will always rise. To witness the fight is not necessarily to understand it, but it might clue you in to some of the thought and tradition behind it. Although many locals themselves consider it a cruel and 'uncivilised' activity (no-one would call it a sport), there is no doubting its popularity.

In many countries such as Costa Rica, killing the bull at the end is illegal. The torero should only show his skills and then get out of the ring.

Do you like bullfighting?	¿Te gustan los toros?
Is bullfighting popular in this area?	¿Son los toros populares en esta región?
Would you like to go to a bullfight?	¿Quieres ir a una corrida?
I'd like to go to a bullfight.	Me gustaría ir a una corrida de toros.
Do you agree with bullfighting?	¿Estás de acuerdo con los toros?
I don't agree with bullfighting.	No estoy de acuerdo con los toros.
Is there a bullfight today/ soon?	¿Hay alguna corrida de toros hoy/pronto?

ACTIVITIES

Where is the bullring?	¿Dónde está la plaza de toros?
Who's appearing tonight?	¿Quién torea esta tarde?
Where can I get tickets for the bullfight?	¿Dónde se compran las entradas para los toros?
What's the bullfighter called?	¿Cómo se llama el torero?
What's that music?	¿Qué es esa música?
What's happening now?	¿Qué pasa ahora?
What does this mean?	¿Qué significa esto?
Why are people shouting?	¿Por qué grita la gente?

Bullfighting Terms

las almohadillas	cushions, thrown at a poorly performing bullfighter
las banderillas	short prods with decorated harpoon-style ends
los banderilleros	those who place the coloured banderillas into the bull's neck
la capa	cape
el capote	cloak
la corrida	bullfight

THEY MAY SAY ...

¡Olé!
¡Torero, torero!

Es tan bueno que le han concedido ...

He's so good they've given him ...

una oreja	an ear
las dos orejas	both ears
el rabo	the tail

ACTIVITIES

la cuadrilla	the torero's team
los cuernos	horns
la espada	sword
la estocada	the final (and fatal) plunge of the sword into the bull's neck
las faenas	moves of the matador in the ring
la lidia	the art of bullfighting
el matador	the bullfighter who kills the bull
la montera	the bullfighter's hat
las orejas	ears
los peones	junior bullfighters under the orders of the matador
los picadores	those on horseback who try to weaken the bull with their lances
las plaza de toros	bullring
el rabo	tail

ACTIVITIES

el ruedo	arena
el sol/la sombra	sun/shade
el tendido	section of the stand in which you are seated
el torero	name given to different types of bullfighters
el toro	bull
el toro bravo	fighting bull
el traje de luces	'suit of lights' – the specially decorated suit made for bullfighters
la vuelta al ruedo	lap of honour

COCK FIGHTING

Cock fighting is very popular in Costa Rica, Cuba and Mexico and less so in other parts of South and Central America.

	las peleas de gallos
fighting cock	gallo de pelea
fighting ring	redondel
cages	rejones
spurs	espuelas

HORSE RACING

Where are horse races held?	¿Dónde hay carreras de caballos?
Where is the [horse] racetrack?	¿Dónde está el hipódromo?
Shall we have a bet?	¿Apostamos algo?
How much do you want to put on?	¿Cuánto quieres apostar?
Which horse is favourite?	¿Qué caballo es el favorito?
Which horse should I back?	¿A qué caballo apuesto?
At what odds is this horse?	¿Cuánto dan los corredores por este caballo?
This horse is five to one.	Este caballo está cinco a uno.
What weight is the horse carrying?	¿Qué peso lleva el caballo?

ACTIVITIES

THE HORSES MAY HEAR ...

| ¡Arreeee! | Gee up! |
| ¡Sooooo! | Whoah! |

bet	la apuesta
bookmaker	el corredor de apuestas
horse	el caballo
jockey	la/el jockey
photo finish	el foto finish
race	la carrera
ride (v)	montar a caballo

HORSE RIDING

Is there a horse-riding school around here?	¿Hay alguna escuela de equitación?
Are there rides available?	¿Es posible dar un paseo a caballo?
How long is the ride?	¿Cuánto dura el paseo?
How much does it cost?	¿Cuánto vale/cuesta?
Do you offer rides for beginners?	¿Ofrecen paseos para principiantes?
I'm an experienced rider.	Soy una/un jinete experimentada.
Can I rent a hat and boots?	¿Se pueden alquilar el casco y las botas de montar?

canter	el medio galope
crop	la fusta
horse	el caballo
mare	la yegua
gallop	el galope
stables	la cuadra
stallion	el semental
trot	el trote

ACTIVITIES

ACTIVITIES

CAR RACING

a crash	un accidente
to crash; collide	chocar
driver	la corredora/el corredor; la/el piloto
to fall behind	quedarse atrás; rezagarse
Formula One	Fórmula Uno
helmet	el casco
... kilometers an hour	... kilómetros por hora
lap	una vuelta
to overtake; pass	pasar; adelantar
racetrack	el autódromo; la pista de carreras
racing car	el coche de carreras
to skid	patinar
to take the lead	llevar la delantera

GOLF

bunker	el búnker
flagstick	la banderola
follow-through	el impulso
golf course	el campo de golf
golf trolley	el carrito de golf
golfball	la pelota de golf
hole	el hoyo
iron	el bastón de hierro; el iron
teeing ground	la salida; el 'tee'
wood	el bastón de madera; un driver

GAMES

Do you play ...	¿Te gusta jugar ...?
billiards	al billar
bingo	al bingo
	la lotería (Mex)
cards	a las cartas

chess	al ajedrez
computer games	con juegos de computador
dominoes	al dominó
draughts	a las damas
ludo	al parchís
	al parkase (Mex)
	a ludo (Arg)
noughts and crosses	tres en raya
	triqui (Col);
	ta-te-tí (Arg)
pinball	al millón
pool	el billar pool
roulette	a la ruleta
table football	al futbolín

Shall we play (dominoes)?	¿Jugamos al (dominó)?
I'm sorry, I don't know how to play (chess).	Lo siento, pero no sé jugar al (ajedrez).
How do you play (dominoes)?	¿Cómo se juega al (dominó)?
What are the rules?	¿Cuáles son las reglas?
Whose turn is it?	¿A quién le toca tirar ahora?
It's my turn.	Es mi turno.
	Me toca. (Mex)
I'm winning/losing.	Estoy ganando/perdiendo.
Stop cheating!	¡Deja de hacer trampas!

Cards

Do you want to play …?	¿Quieres jugar …
cards	a las cartas
bridge	al bridge
poker	al póquer
I don't know how to play.	No sé jugar.
I'll teach you.	Yo te enseño.

THEY MAY SAY …

¡Afortunada/o!	Lucky!
¡Bingo/Lotería (Mex)!	Bingo!
¡Línea!	Line! (in bingo)
¡Qué mala suerte!	Hard luck!
¡Qué suerte tengo!	I'm on a roll!
¡Tramposa/o!	Cheat!
Tengo gafe.	I'm jinxed.

pick up (a card)	coger
	levantar (Arg)
	robar (Mex)
to deal	repartir
hand	la mano
deck	la baraja
to shuffle	barajar

It's your turn to pick up a card.	Te toca coger una carta.
I can't go.	No voy.
I'll bet (110) pesos.	Apuesto (ciento diez) pesos.
I'll see you.	Te igualo.
I'll raise you (50) pesos.	Y (cincuenta) más.

Spanish Deck (naipe)

ace	el as
king	el rey
queen	el caballo – in a Spanish deck the Queen is replaced by a knight
jack	la sota
spades	las espadas – appear as swords
clubs	los bastones;
	bastos (Arg, Mex) – appear as a club or baton
diamonds	los oros – appear as a gold coin
hearts	las copas – appear as a goblet

ACTIVITIES

French Deck (poker)

ace	el as
king	el rey
queen	la reina, la dama
jack	el valet
	el jack/jota (Arg)
joker	el comodín
spades	las picas
	espadas (Arg)
clubs	los tréboles
diamonds	los diamantes
hearts	los corazones

Poker

four of a kind	póquer
full hand	ful
pair	pareja
	par (Arg)
poker	póquer
royal flush	escalera de color
straight	escalera
three of a kind	trío
	tercia (Mex)
two pairs	doble pareja
	par doble (Arg)

Chess

Do you like chess?	¿Te gusta jugar al ajedrez?
Shall we play chess?	¿Jugamos al ajedrez?
White starts.	Las blancas empiezan.
It's my move.	Ahora muevo yo.
Hurry up and make a move!	¡Mueve de una vez!
Check!	¡Jaque!
Check to the king!	¡Jaque al rey!
Checkmate!	¡Jaque mate!
Cheat!	¡Tramposa/o!

ACTIVITIES

bishop; rook
    el alfil
black pieces
    las negras
castle
    la torre
chess board
    el tablero de ajedrez
chess tournament
    el campeonato de ajedrez
    el torneo de ajedrez (Arg)
king
    el rey
knight
    el caballo
pawn(s)
    el peón(es)
pieces
    las fichas
    las piezas (Arg)

queen   la reina
white pieces   las blancas
stalemate   tablas
                                   ahogado (Mex)

> ### HARD G
>
> When u is added to g
> it makes the g hard.
> When gu is followed
> by e or i, the u is not
> pronounced:
>
> > guerra (war) is
> > said as gerra not
> > gwerra.
>
> However when the gu
> is followed by a or o it
> is pronounced as gw:
>
> > guapa (attractive)
> > is said as gwapa.

THE LOTTERY
lottery ticket   décimo
                                   cachito (Mex)

I'd like a lottery ticket please. ¿Me da un décimo de lotería
                                   por favor?
Which number do you want?   ¿Qué número desea?

TV & VIDEO
Do you mind if I put the   ¿Te importa si enciendo/
    TV on?   prendo (Mex) la tele?
Turn the TV off!   ¡Apaga la tele!

Do you mind if I turn the volume up/down?	¿Te importaría subir/bajar el volumen?
Can I change the channel?	¿Puedes cambiar de canal?
Which channel do you want to watch?	¿Qué canal quieres ver?

I feel like watching …	Me gustaría ver …
cartoons	los dibujos animados
	las caricaturas (Mex)
current affairs	un noticiero
a documentary	un documental
a film	una película
a game show	un concurso
kids' programs	la programación infantil
news	las noticias
a series	una serie de televisión
a soap opera	una telenovelón
sport	la programación deportiva
	los deportes (Mex)
a variety program	un programa de variedades
the weather	el tiempo

Can we watch the English-language TV?	¿Podemos poner la tele en inglés?
I prefer to watch in Spanish.	Yo prefiero el castellano.
Where's the remote control?	¿Dónde está el mando a distancia?
It's over there/here.	Está allí/aquí.
The TV isn't working.	La televisión no funciona.

antenna	la antena
buttons	los botones
cable TV	el cable
channel	el canal
remote control	el mando a distancia
	el control remoto (Mex)
satellite dish	la antena parabólica

television	la televisión
TV	tele
TV set	el televisor
volume	el volúmen

Video

| to hire (a video) | alquilar |
| | rentar (Mex) |

Where can I hire videos?	¿Dónde alquilan películas de vídeo?
Do you loan videos here?	¿Alquilan películas aquí?
Yes, we loan them.	Sí, alquilamos películas.
No, I'm sorry, we only sell them.	No, lo siento, sólo las vendemos.
Do I have to be a member to borrow videos?	Para alquilar una película, hay que ser socio de este video club?
How much is it to hire this video?	¿Cuánto vale alquilar esta película?
Is this film for daily or weekly hire?	¿Esta película es de alquiler diario o semanal?
How long can I borrow this for?	¿Por cuántos días se alquila esta película?
Do you have ...?	¿Tienen ...?

FESTIVALS & HOLIDAYS

champagne   la cava; el champán
to celebrate (an event)   celebrar
to celebrate (in general)   festejar
church   la iglesia
to exchange gifts   regalar
gift   el regalo
holiday   el día festivo/feriado
party   la fiesta

BIRTHDAYS & SAINTS' DAYS

When is your …?   ¿Cuándo es tu …?
    birthday   cumpleaños
    saint's day   santo

My … is on (24 January).   Mi … es el día (veinticuatro de enero).

Congratulations!   ¡(Muchas) felicidades!
Happy birthday!   ¡Feliz cumpleaños!
Happy saint's day!   ¡Feliz santo!
Many happy returns!   ¡Que cumplas muchos más!
Blow out the candles!   ¡Sopla las velas!

birthday cake   pastel/queque de cumpleaños
candles   velas

HAPPY BIRTHDAY TO YOU …

¡Cumpleaños feliz!
¡Cumpleaños feliz!
¡Todas/os te deseamos!
¡Cumpleaños feliz!

CHRISTMAS & NEW YEAR

Christmas begins on 24 December but gifts aren't usually exchanged until 6 January (Epiphany).

In Colombia gifts are exchanged at midnight on 24 December. On 6 January kids find a small present in ther shoe when they get up (a gift from the wise kings).

Christmas Day	la Navidad	25 December
Christmas Eve	la Nochebuena	24 December
New Year's Eve	el fin de año; la nochvieja (Arg)	31 December
New Year's Day	el año nuevo	1 January
Epiphany	día de los reyes magos	6 January

| Happy Christmas! | ¡Feliz navidad! |
| Happy New Year! | ¡Feliz año nuevo!
¡Próspero año nuevo! |

Christmas Delicacies

mazapán	marzipan
polvorones	soft Christmas biscuits
roscón de reyes;	special ring-shaped cake eaten
rosea de reyes (Arg);	at Epiphany
rosca de reyes (Mex)	
turrón	Christmas candy

Every region and country has its delicacies.

In Colombia:

natilla	a jelly-like dessert made from corn
buñuelos	balls made from cheese and flour
pavo relleno	stuffed turkey

SOME FESTIVALS & TRADITIONS

There are numerous local festivals, however the following are among the most celebrated.

Semana Santa

(Holy Week) The week before Easter, celebrated with religious processions.

Todos Santos

(All Saint's Day) Held on November 1, this is public holiday

Día de los Muertos

(All Soul's Day) Held on November 2, this is celebrated with gifts of food, drink and flowers taken to family graves.

Armar el pesebre (Col);

Poner el nacimiento (Mex)

Literally meaning 'to place the nativity scene', this tradition involves placing figures of the three Kings at a distance from a set of nativity figures on 24 December and moving them a little closer each day, culminating on 6 January, 'el día de los reyes magos', 'the day of the Three Wise Men'.

Cotillón (not in Col or Arg)

> On New Year's Eve you can go from party to party, collecting a cotillón at each one, which is a kind of party bag containing sweets, party whistles and other goodies.

Día de los Reyes Magos

> Epiphany: this involves a procession featuring the Three Wise Men and other Christmas and popular characters, either on the night of January 5, or on January 6.

Los Quince Años (especially in Cos)

> When a young girl turns 15 there is a special celebration to welcome her into womanhood.

EASTER

Happy Easter!
  ¡Felices pascuas!
chocolate eggs
  los huevos de chocolate
chocolate figures
  la mona de pascua
easter cake
  el roscón de Pascua
  la rosea de Pascua (Arg)
  la rosca de Pascua (Mex)
Holy Week
  la Semana santa
religious procession
  la procesión religiosa

> **YOU MAY SAY ...**
> Good health!; Cheers!
>
> ¡Salud!
> ¡A tu/su salud!
> ¡Chin chin!
> ¡Toda la suerte!
> ¡Por ti/ustedes/
>   nosotros!

CHRISTENINGS & WEDDINGS

Congratulations!	¡Felicidades!
To the bride & groom!	¡Vivan los novios!
baptism	el bautizo
	el bautismo (Arg)

engagement	el compromiso
honeymoon	la luna de miel
wedding	la boda
wedding anniversary	el aniversario de bodas
wedding cake	la ponqué de novia (Col)
	la torta de bodas (Arg)
	el pastel de bodas (Mex)
wedding present	el regalo de bodas

TOASTS & CONDOLENCES

And the most popular of all, accompanied by arm movements
forming the shape of the cross:

> ¡Arriba, abajo, al centro y … pa'dentro!
> (lit: 'up, down, in the centre and inside')

Bon appétit!	¡Buen provecho!
	¡Que aproveche!
Bon voyage!	¡Buen viaje!

Sickness

Get well soon!	¡Que te mejores!
Bless you! (after sneezing)	¡Jesús!; ¡Salud!

Death

I'm very sorry.	Lo siento muchísimo.
My deepest sympathy.	Mi más sentido pésame.
My thoughts are with you.	Te acompaño en el sentimiento.

Luck

Good luck!	¡Buena suerte!
Hope it goes well!	¡Qué te vaya bien!
What bad luck!	¡Qué mala suerte!
Never mind!	¡No te preocupes!

HEALTH

You will find that in most big cities there are well-equipped medical services where you can go in the case of an emergency. In the country the regional clinics are usually the best place to seek medical advice. Ask a local where the closest one is if you need to there quickly.

AT THE DOCTOR

I am sick.	Estoy enferma/o.
My friend is sick.	Mi amiga/o está enferma/o.
I need a doctor (who speaks English).	Necesito una doctora/un doctor (que hable inglés).
Could you please call a doctor?	¿Podría llamar a un doctor, por favor?
Could the doctor come here?	¿Puede visitarme la doctora/ el doctor?

THEY MAY SAY ...

¿Qué le pasa?	What's the matter?
¿Le duele?	Do you feel any pain?
¿Dónde le duele?	Where does it hurt?
¿Tiene la regla?	Are you menstruating?
¿Tiene fiebre?	Do you have a temperature?
¿Desde cuándo se siente así?	How long have you been like this?
¿Ha tenido esto antes?	Have you had this before?
¿Se encuentra bajo medicación?	Are you on medication?
¿Fuma?	Do you smoke?
¿Bebe?	Do you drink?
¿Toma drogas?	Do you take drugs?
¿Es alérgica/o a alguna medicina?	Are you allergic to anything?
¿Está embarazada?	Are you pregnant?

HEALTH

Where's the nearest ...?	¿Dónde está ... más cercano?
clinic	la clínica
doctor	el doctor/el médico
hospital	el hospital
chemist	la farmacia
	la droguería (Col)
dentist	el dentista

AILMENTS

I'm ill.	Estoy enferma/o.
I've been vomiting.	He estado vomitando.
I feel under the weather.	Tengo malestar general.
I feel ...	Me siento ...
dizzy	mareada/o
shivery	destemplada/o
	escalofrios (Mex)
weak	débil
I feel nauseous.	Tengo náuseas.
I can't sleep.	No puedo dormir.
I have ...	Tengo ...
an allergy	una alergia
altitude sickness	soroche
	mal de montaña (Mex)
	el apunamiento (Chi)
anaemia	anemia
a blister	una ampolla
a bruise	un cardenal
	un morado (Col)
	un moretón (Arg)
a burn	una quemadura
cancer	cáncer
cholera	cólera
a cold	un resfriado; un catarro
	un resfrío (Arg)

HEALTH

cystitis	cistitis
constipation	estreñimiento
a cough	tos
diarrhoea	diarrea
dysentry	disentería
earache	dolor de oído
fever	fiebre
frostbite	congelación
glandular fever	mononucleosis
a headache	dolor de cabeza
hayfever	alergia al polen
	fiebre de heno (Arg)
hepatitis	hepatitis
indigestion	indigestión
an infection	una infección
an inflammation	una inflamación
influenza	gripe
itch	comezón; escozor; rasquiña
lice	piojos
a lump	un bulto
	una bolita (Mex)
a migraine	migraña; jaqueca
a pain	dolor
a rash	una irritación/erupción/sarpullido
sore throat	dolor de garganta
sprain	una torcedura/tronchadura/esquince
an STD	una enfermedad de transmisión sexual
a stomachache	dolor de estómago
sunburn	una quemadura de sol
sunstroke	una insolación
swelling	una hinchazón
thrush	afta
travel sickness	mareo
worms	lombrices; gusanos; parasitos
yellow fever	fiebre amarilla

HEALTH

USEFUL PHRASES

I feel better/worse.	Me siento mejor/peor.
This is my usual medicine.	Éste es mi medicamento habitual.
I have been vaccinated.	Estoy vacunada/o.
Do you have a student/ pensioner discount?	¿Hay algún descuento para estudiantes/pensionados?
Can I have a receipt for my health insurance?	¿Puede darme un recibo para mi seguro médico?

WOMEN'S HEALTH

Could I see a female doctor?	¿Puede examinarme; revisarme (Mex) una doctora?
I'm on the Pill.	Tomo la píldora.
I think I'm pregnant.	Creo que estoy embarazada; encinta.
I haven't had my period for ... weeks.	Hace ... semanas que no me viene la regla.
I'd like to get the morning-after pill.	Quisiera tomar la píldora del día siguiente.
I'd like to have a pregnancy test.	¿Puede hacerme la prueba del embarazo?
I'm pregnant.	Estoy embarazada/encinta.
I'd like to terminate my pregnancy.	Quisiera interrumpir mi embarazo.
I'd like to use contraception.	Quisiera usar algún método anticonceptivo.

abortion	el aborto
cystitis	la cistitis
diaphragm	el diafragma
IUD	el DIU
mamogram	la mamografía
menstruation	la regla
	la menstruación (Arg)

miscarriage	el aborto natural
pap smear	la citología
	la papanicolau (Arg)
period pain	el dolor menstrual
the Pill	la píldora
pregnant	embarazada; encinta
premenstrual tension	la tensión pre-menstrual
thrush	el afta
ultrasound	el ultrasonido

HEALTH

SPECIAL HEALTH NEEDS

I'm ...	Soy ...
asthmatic	asmática/o
diabetic	diabética/o
epilectic	epiléptica/o

HEALTH

I'm allergic to ...	Soy alérgica/o ...
antibiotics	a los antibióticos
aspirin	a la aspirina
bees	a las abejas
codeine	a la codeína
dairy products	a los productos lácteos
penicillin	a la penicilina
pollen	al polen

I have high/low blood pressure.	Tengo la presión baja/alta.
I have a weak heart.	Tengo el corazón débil.
I'm on regular medication for ...	Estoy bajo medicación para ...
I'm on a special diet.	Sigo una dieta especial.
I have a skin allergy.	Tengo un alergia en la piel.
I have my own syringe.	Tengo mi propia jeringa.
I don't want a blood transfusion.	No quiero que me hagan una transfusión de sangre.

inhaler	el inhalador
pacemaker	el marcapasos

ALTERNATIVE TREATMENTS

aromatherapy
  la aromaterapia
herbalist
  el herborista;
  el homeopata
  la herbolaria (Mex)
homeopathy
  la homeopatía
massage
  el masaje

HEALTH

massage therapist	la masajista
meditation	la meditación
naturopath	el naturópata
	la naturista (Mex)
reflexology	la reflexología
yoga	el yoga

PARTS OF THE BODY

My ... hurts.	Me duele ...
I have a pain in my ...	Siento dolor en ...
I can't move my ...	No puedo mover ...

ankle	el tobillo	knee	la rodilla
appendix	el apéndice	leg	la pierna
arm	el brazo	liver	el hígado
back	la espalda	mouth	la boca
bladder	la vejiga	muscle	el músculo
blood	la sangre	nose	la nariz
bone	el hueso	penis	el pene
breast	el pecho	ribs	las costillas
chest	el pecho	shoulders	los hombros
ear	la oreja	skin	la piel
eye	el ojo	spine	la columna (vertebral)
finger	el dedo	stomach	el estómago
foot	el pie	teeth	los dientes
hand	la mano	throat	la garganta
head	la cabeza	tongue	la lengua
heart	el corazón	vagina	la vagina
jaw	la mandíbula	vein	la vena

AT THE CHEMIST

In Latin America many drugs are sold over the counter without a prescription. It's important to know exactly what you need and to check the use-by dates on any drugs you buy.

HEALTH

Where is the nearest all-night chemist?	¿Dónde está la farmacia de guardia más cercana?
I need something for ...	Necesito algo para ...
I have a prescription.	Tengo receta médica.
How many times a day?	¿Cuántas veces al día?
Take (two) tablets (four) times a day.	Tome (dos) píldoras (cuatro) veces al día.
before/after meals	antes/después de la comidas

Could I please have ...?	¿Me dá ... por favor?
antibiotics	antibióticos
aspirin	las aspirinas
contraceptives	los anticonceptivos
cough medicine	algo para el catarro
laxatives	los laxantes
painkillers	los analgésicos
sleeping pills	las pastillas para dormir
a vaccine	una vacuna

AT THE DENTIST

I have a toothache.	Me duele una muela.
I have a cavity.	Tengo una caries.
I've lost a filling.	Se me ha caído un empaste.
I've broken a tooth.	Se me ha roto un diente.
My gums hurt.	Me duelen las encías.
I don't want it extracted.	No quiero que me lo arranque.
Please give me an anaesthetic.	Por favor, póngame anestesia.
Ouch!	¡Ay!

SPECIFIC NEEDS

DISABLED TRAVELLERS

Is there a special service for disabled people?
¿Tienen servicios para minusválidos?

What services are available for disabled people?
¿Qué servicios tienen para minusvalidos?

I need assistance,
I'm …
Necesito asistencia, porque soy …

- disabled — minusválida/o
- blind — ciega/o
- deaf — sorda/o
- mute — muda/o

Is there wheelchair access?
¿Hay acceso para la silla de ruedas?

I might be in a wheelchair, but I'm not stupid/ hard of hearing.
Puede que vaya en silla de ruedas, pero tonta/o; sorda/o no soy.

Are guide dogs allowed?
¿Se permite la entrada a los perros guía?

Is there a guide service for blind people?
¿Hay algún servicio de guía para personas ciegas?

Will there be a guide to describe things?
¿Es una excursión guiada?

Could you please speak more slowly/clearly?
Por favor hable más despacio/claro.

I'm deaf but I can lip-read.
Soy sorda/o pero puedo leer los labios.

Is there anyone here who speaks sign language?
¿Hay alguien aquí que pueda hablar el lenguaje de las manos/de señas (Mex)?

I'm hard of hearing.
Tengo problemas de oído.

| Speak into my other ear please. | Hábleme por el otro oído, por favor. |
| I wear a hearing aid. | Llevo audífono. |

guide dog	perro lazarillo
disabled	minusválida/o
hearing aid	audífono
paraplegic	parapléjica/o
wheelchair	silla de ruedas

SPECIFIC NEEDS

GAY TRAVELLERS

The words for 'gay, lesbian, heterosexual', etc are more or less the same in Spanish as they are in English – though with Spanish pronunciation of course!

Are there any gay bars around here?	¿Hay algún bar gay/de ambiente por aquí?
Is there a gay telephone hotline?	¿Hay alguna línea telefónica de información gay?
Is there a local gay publication?	¿Conoces alguna revista de tema homosexual?
Is there a gay bookshop?	¿Hay alguna librería homosexual?
Am I likely to be harassed for being gay?	¿Me van a molestar por ser homosexual?

TRAVELLING WITH A FAMILY

I'm travelling with my family.	Viajo con toda mi familia.
Are there facilities for babies?	¿Hay facilidades para bebés?
Is there a childminding service	¿Tienen guardería en el hotel?

Are there other families in the …?	¿Hay otras familias en …?
hotel	el hotel
tour group	la excursión

Is there a childminding service in the hotel?	¿Tienen guardería en el hotel?
Can you provide an English-speaking babysitter?	¿Disponen de un servicio de niñeras que hablen inglés?

(In LAm the English word 'babysitter' is also commonly used.)

Can you add an extra bed to the room?	¿Pueden añadir una cama en la habitación?
Do you hire out family cars?	¿Alquilan coches familiares?
Does this car have a child seat?	¿Este coche tiene sillita para niños?
Is there family entertainment?	¿Hay alguna diversión para toda la familia?
Is there children's entertainment here?	¿Hay algún espectáculo para niños aquí?
Is it for all ages?	¿Es para todos los públicos?
Is it suitable for all the family?	¿Es adecuado para toda la familia?; ¿Es adecuado para todo spublico (Mex)?
Is there a family price?	¿Hay un precio especial para familias?
Are children allowed?	¿Se admiten niños?
Is there a children's menu?	¿Tienen menú infantil?
Could you make it a child's portion?	¿Puede prepararme una ración para niños?
What time is the children's program on?	¿A qué hora dan el programa infantil; familiar (Mex)?
Is there a playground around here?	¿Hay algún parque infantil por aquí cerca?

LOOKING FOR A JOB

Where is the best place to look for a job?	¿Cuál es el mejor sitio; lugar (Mex) para buscar trabajo?

I'm looking for work.	Estoy buscando trabajo.
I'd like to find work.	Me gustaría encontrar trabajo.
Do you have any vacancies for a …?	¿Hay algún puesto de trabajo para una/un …?
I have a qualification in …	Estoy cualificada para …

I have experience in …	Tengo experiencia …
acting	como actriz/actor
cleaning	en trabajos de limpieza
construction work	en la construcción
design	en el diseño
fruit picking	en la recolección de fruta
looking after children	como niñera/cuidadora; en cuidar niños
photography	en la fotografía
office work	en trabajo de oficina
sales	como vendedora/vendedor
secretarial work	como secretaria/o
teaching	en la enseñanza
using computers	en computadoras
waiting	como camarera/o
writing	como escritora/escritor

I can …	Puedo …
cook	cocinar
draw	pintar
drive	conducir
	manejar (Arg, Mex)
type	escribir a máquina

I'm looking for …	Estoy buscando trabajo …
part-time	de tiempo parcial
	de medio tiempo (Mex)
full-time	de tiempo completo
casual work	esporádico
	eventual (Mex)

What's the salary?	¿Cuál es el salario?
How is the salary paid?	¿Cómo me van a pagar?
How often would I get paid?	¿Cada cuánto me van a pagar?
Do I have to pay tax?	¿Tengo que pagar impuestos?
What are the working hours?	¿Cuál es el horario?
Is this a live-in job?	¿Es un trabajo que requiere vivir en la casa?
I'd like to apply for the position.	Me gustaría presentar una solicitud.
Here is my resumé.	Aquí está mi currículum.
I can provide references.	Puedo presentarle mis referencias.
I have a valid work permit.	Tengo permiso de trabajo.
I would be pleased to attend an interview.	Me gustaría tener una entrevista.
I'll be able to work for three months/until (May).	Puedo trabajar aquí durante tres meses/hasta (mayo).

SPECIFIC NEEDS

amateur	amateur; aficionada/o
application	solicitud
certificate	certificado
college	residencia de estudiantes
company	compañía
contract	contrato
degree	título
dismissal	despido
dole	paro
employer	jefa/e
exploitation	explotación
harrassment	acoso
high school	instituto; colegio secundario liceo (Arg)
income tax	impuesto sobre la renta
interview	entrevista
job	trabajo

job advertisement	anuncio de trabajo
job description	descripción del trabajo
qualification	calificaciones
	cualidades (Mex)
rate of pay	salario
reference	referencias
resignation	dimisión; renuncia
resumé	curriculum; currículo
salary	salario
	sueldo (Arg)
school	escuela
specialist	especialista
strike	huelga
university	universidad
work permit	
	permiso de trabajo

LATE AFTERNOON

Don't confuse tarde – late, with la tarde – the afternoon or evening.

ON BUSINESS

Here are some key words and phrases for that quick visit or conference. For more, try one of the many phrasebooks available which specialise in business language.

I'm here on business.	Estoy de viaje de negocios.
We're attending a conference/ trade fair.	Estamos asistiendo a una conferencia/feria de muestras.
Does the hotel have office facilities?	¿Dispone el hotel de servicios de oficinas?
I need an interpreter.	Necesito una/un intérprete.
I have an appointment with …	Tengo una cita con …
I need to …	Tengo que …
send a fax/email	enviar un fax/email
make photocopies	hacer fotocopias
	sacar copias (Mex)
use a computer	usar un computador

Thank you for seeing me.	Gracias por atenderme.
Let me introduce my colleague.	¿Puedo presentarle a mi colega?
It was a pleasure meeting you.	Encantada/o de conocerla/lo.
We'll be in touch.	Nos mantendremos en contacto.
Here's my business card.	Aquí tiene mi tarjeta de visita.

SPECIFIC NEEDS

ballpark figure	cifra aproximada
branch office	sucursal
business card	tarjeta de visita
	tarjeta de presentación (Mex)
client	clienta/e
colleague	colega
contract	contrato
director	director
distributor	distribuidora; distribuidor
figures	cifras
head office	oficina central
loss	pérdida
manager	encargada/o
	gerente (Arg)
mobile phone	teléfono móbil
modem	módem
overhead projector	proyector de transparencias; retro proyector
operations	operaciones
presentation	presentación
profit	ganancia
profitability	rentabilidad
projector	proyector
proposal	propuesta
sales	ventas
sales department	departamento de ventas
secretary	la/el secretaria/o
turnover	facturación

ON TOUR

We're travelling in a group.	Somos parte de un grupo.
I'm with a band/team.	Vengo con un grupo de música/equipo deportivo.
We're here for (three nights).	Nos quedaremos (tres noches).
We've lost our equipment.	Hemos perdido nuestras cosas.

Please talk to the ...	Por favor, hable con la/el ...
group leader	responsable del grupo
guide	guía
manager	mánager

We sent our gear in this ...	Hemos enviado nuestras cosas en este ...
plane	vuelo
train	tren
bus	bus

We're playing on (Saturday night).	Tocamos el (sábado por la noche).
Would you like some tickets?	¿Quieres entradas para nuestro concierto?
I'm still a groupie after all these years.	Todavía soy una/un fan después de tantos años.

band	grupo
coach	entrenadora/entrenador
equipment	equipo
manager	empresario
	jete (Mex)
	gerente (Arg)
member	miembro
player	música/o
roadie	transportista
team	equipo
van	furgoneta
	vagoneta (Mex)

FILM & TV

We're on location.	Estamos rodando los exteriores.
We're filming here for (six) days.	Vamos a rodar aquí durante (seis) días.
Who should we ask for permission to film here?	¿A quién tenemos que pedirle permiso para rodar aquí?
May we film here?	¿Podemos rodar aquí?

We're making a …	Estamos haciendo …
documentary	un documental
film	una película
series	una serie de televisión

actor	la actriz/el actor
camera operator	la operadora/el operador
continuity	la secretaria/el secretario
director	la directora/el director
editor	la editora/el editor
presenter	la presentadora/el presentador
producer	la productora/el productor
scriptwriter	la/el guionista

camera	la cámara
editing suite	control de edición
lights	las luces
make-up	el maquillaje
prop	el decorado
rushes	las primeras pruebas
script	el guión
sound	el sonido
stunt	la escena peligrosa
van	la caravana
wardrobe	el vestuario

SPECIFIC NEEDS

THEY MAY SAY …

¡Acción!
  Action!

¡Estamos rodando!
  We're filming!

¡Rodando!
  Rolling!

¡Toma uno!
  Take One!

¡Corten!
  Cut!

PILGRIMAGE & RELIGION

For a list of religions, see page 51

SPECIFIC NEEDS

Is there a church nearby?	¿Hay alguna iglesia aquí cerca?
Where can I pray/worship?	¿Dónde puedo rezar/hacer oración?
Can I receive communion here?	¿Puedo recibir la comunión aquí?
When are services held?	¿Cuándo se celebran los oficios?
When is the church/cathedral open?	¿A qué hora abre la iglesia/catedral?
Can I attend this service?	¿Puedo asistir a este oficio?

baptism	bautizo	mosque	mezquita
bible	la Biblia	nun	monja
candle	vela	Pope	Papa
chapel	la capilla	prayer	oración
church	iglesia	prayer book	devocionario;
communion	comunión		libro de rezos/
confession	confesión		de oraciónes
convent	convento	priest	sacerdote
funeral	funeral	service	oficio
God	Dios	shrine	capilla; altar
grave	tumba	synagogue	sinagoga
mass	misa	temple	templo
monastery	monasterio	wedding	boda
monk	monje	worship	adoración

Tracing Roots & History

My family/ancestors came from this area.	Mi familia/mis antepasados viene/n de esta zona.
Is there anyone here by the name of ...?	¿Hay alguien aquí que se llama ...?
Where is the cemetery?	¿Dónde está el cementerio?

TIME & DATES

TELLING THE TIME

What time is it?	¿Qué hora es?
It's one o'clock.	Es la una.
It's (two o'clock).	Son las (dos).
It's five past six.	Son las seis y cinco.
It's half past eight.	Son las ocho y media.
It's quarter to four.	Son las cuatro menos cuarto.
	Son cuarto para las cuatro. (Mex)
It's about eleven.	Son las once.

in the early morning (1–6am)	de la madrugada
in the morning (6am–1pm)	de la mañana
at midday (12–3pm)	del mediodía
in the afternoon (3–8pm)	de la tarde
in the evening (9pm–1am)	de la noche

DAYS

Monday	lunes
Tuesday	martes
Wednesday	miércoles
Thursday	jueves
Friday	viernes
Saturday	sábado
Sunday	domingo

MONTHS

January	enero
February	febrero
March	marzo
April	abril
May	mayo
June	junio
July	julio

August	agosto
September	setiembre;
	septiembre
October	octubre
November	noviembre
December	diciembre

DATES

Dates are expressed by cardinal numbers (two of May', '23 July', etc), except for the first day of the month which uses the ordinal number: '1st of April'.

What's the date today?	¿Qué día es hoy?
It's 26 April.	Es el veintiséis de abril.
It's 3 August.	Es el tres de agosto.
It's the 1st of October.	Es el primero de octubre.

PRESENT

today	hoy
this morning	esta mañana;
	madrugada
this afternoon	esta tarde
tonight	esta noche
this week	esta semana
this month	este mes
this year	este año
now	ahora
right now	en este momento

ADVERBS

The equivalent of –ly (to create an adverb) is – mente:

alegre (happy)

becomes

alegremente (happily)

PAST

yesterday	ayer
day before yesterday	anteayer; antier
yesterday morning	ayer por la mañana/madrugada

TIME& DATES

yesterday afternoon/night	ayer por la tarde/noche
last night	anoche
last week	la semana pasada
last month	el mes pasado
last year	el año pasado
(half an hour) ago	hace media hora
(three) days ago	hace (tres) días
(five) years ago	hace (cinco) años
a while ago	hace un rato
since (May)	desde (mayo)

FUTURE

tomorrow
    mañana
day after tomorrow
    pasado mañana
tomorrow morning
    mañana por la mañana
tomorrow afternoon
    mañana por la tarde
tomorrow evening
    mañana por la noche

next week
    la semana que viene/entra
next month
    el mes que viene/entra

next year	el año que viene/entra
in (five) minutes	dentro de (cinco) minutos
in (six) days	dentro de (seis) días
within an hour/month	dentro de una hora/un mes
until (June)	hasta (junio)

monday

Unlike English, Spanish does not use capital letters for languages, months or days of the week.

lunes 5 de abril
Monday the 5th of April

So Italian, the language, is italiano but note, an Italian is una/un Italiana/o

TIME & DATES

DURING THE DAY

It's early.	Es temprano.
It's late.	Es tarde.
afternoon (3–8 pm)	la tarde
evening (9 pm–1 am)	la noche
lunchtime	hora de comer
midnight	medianoche
morning (6 am–1 pm)	de la mañana
noon	mediodía
sunset	puesta del sol; atardecer
sunrise	amanecer

NUMBERS & AMOUNTS

CARDINAL NUMBERS

0	cero	30	treinta
1	uno	31	treinta y uno
2	dos	32	treinta y dos
3	tres	40	cuarenta
4	cuatro	41	cuarenta y uno
5	cinco	50	cincuenta
6	seis	51	cincuenta y uno
7	siete	60	sesenta
8	ocho	70	setenta
9	nueve	80	ochenta
10	diez	90	noventa
11	once	100	cien
12	doce	110	ciento diez
13	trece	200	doscientos
14	catorce	300	trescientos
15	quince	400	cuatrocientos
16	dieciséis	500	quinientos
17	diecisiete	600	seiscientos
18	dieciocho	700	setecientos
19	diecinueve	800	ochocientos
20	veinte	900	novecientos
21	veintiuno	1000	mil
22	veintidós	2000	dos mil
23	veintitrés	5000	cinco mil
24	veinticuatro	2200	dos mil doscientos

one million	un millón
48	cuarenta y ocho
157	ciento cincuenta y siete
1240	mil doscientos cuarenta
1999	mil novecientos noventa y nueve
14800	catorce mil ochocientos

ORDINAL NUMBERS

1st	primera/o (1r)
2nd	segunda/o
3rd	tercera/o
4th	cuarta/o
5th	quinta/o
6th	sexta/o
7th	séptima/o
8th	octava/o
9th	novena/o
10th	décima/o

¡PERMISO!

¡Permiso! is useful for getting past people.

To catch someone's attention, use ¡Disculpe! or ¡Perdón!

FRACTIONS

a quarter	un cuarto	three-quarters	tres cuartos
a third	un tercio	all	todo
half	medio/a	none	nada

USEFUL WORDS

a little (amount)	un poquito
double	(el) doble
a dozen	una docena
Enough!	¡Basta!
few	(unas) pocas/(unos) pocos
less	menos
many	muchas/os
more	más
once	una vez
a pair	un par
percent	por ciento
some	algunas/os
too much	demasiado
twice	dos veces

EMERGENCIES

Help!	¡Socorro!; ¡Auxilio!
Help me!	¡Ayúden me!
Call the police!	¡Llame a la policía!
Where is the police station?	¿Dónde está la comisaría?
It's an emergency!	¡Es una emergencia!
I need assistance!	¡Necesito ayuda!
Could you help me please?	¿Puede ayudarme, por favor?
Could I please use the telephone?	¿Puedo usar el teléfono, por favor?
I want to report an offence.	Deseo presentar una denuncia.

Look out!	¡Ojo! ¡Cuidado (Arg)! ¡Aquas (Mex)!
Fire!	¡Fuego!

There's been an accident!	¡Ha habido un accidente!
Call a doctor!	¡Llame a un médico!
Call an ambulance!	¡Llame a una ambulancia!
I am ill.	Estoy enferma/o.
My friend is ill.	Mi amiga/o está enferma/o.
I have medical insurance.	Tengo seguro médico.
I've been raped.	He sido violada/o.
I want to see a female police officer.	Deseo hablar con una mujer policía.
Could you please organise an official medical examination?	¿Pueden hacerme un examen médico oficial?

Go away!	¡Váyase!
I'll call the police!	¡Voy a llamar a la policía!
Thief!	¡Ladrón!

EMERGENCIES

I've been robbed!	¡Me han robado!
This woman/man has been robbed.	¡Han robado a esta/e señora/señor.
My ... was stolen.	Me robaron mi(s)...
bags	maletas
backpack	mochila
handbag	bolso
	cartera (Arg)
money	dinero
wallet	cartera; billetera
papers	todos mis papeles
travellers' cheques	cheques de viajero
passport	pasaporte
My possessions are insured.	Tengo seguro contra robo
I am lost.	Estoy perdida/o
I have lost my friend.	He perdido a mi amiga/o
I've lost…	He perdido …/Perdí …

SIGNS

POLICÍA	POLICE
COMISARÍA DE POLICÍA	POLICE STATION

DEALING WITH THE POLICE

I'm sorry (I apologise).	Lo siento/Discúlpeme.
I didn't realise I was doing anything wrong.	No sabía que no estaba permitido.
I'm innocent.	Soy inocente.
I didn't do it.	No lo he hecho yo.
I'm a foreigner.	Soy extranjera/o.
I'm a tourist.	Soy turista.

EMERGENCIES

THEY MAY SAY ...

¡Enséñeme su ...!
    pasaporte
    DNI; documentos
    carné de conducir;
    licencia de maneja (Mex)

Show me your ...
    passport
    identity papers
    drivers' licence

¡Identifíquese!

Show me your
    identification!

¡Muéstreme su permiso
    de trabajo!

Show me your work
    permit!

Está usted detenida/o;
¡Queda arrestada!

You've been arrested.

Vamos a ponerle una
    multa.

We're giving you a traffic
    fine.

Acompáñenos a
    la comisaría;
    delegación (Mex).

You must come with us to
    the police station.

Puede no hacer ninguna
    declaración hasta que
    esté en presencia
    de su abogada/o.

You don't have to say
    anything until you are
    in the presence of a
    lawyer.

¿Cuáles son sus datos
    personales?

What is your name and
    address?

Ahora va a pasar usted
    al juzgado de guardia.

Now you will be
    taken to the police court.

Le hemos asignado una/
    un abogada/o de oficio.

We have assigned
    you a duty solicitor.

What am I accused of?

¿De qué se me acusa?

Do I have the right to make
    a call?

¿Tengo derecho a hacer
    alguna llamada?

Can I call someone?

¿Puedo llamar a alguien?

EMERGENCIES

I wish to contact my embassy/ consulate.	Deseo comunicarme con mi embajada/consulado.
Can I call a lawyer?	¿Puedo llamar a una abogada/o?
I'd like to see a duty solicitor.	Quiero ver a una/un abogada/o de oficio.
I'll only make a statement in the presence of my lawyer.	Sólo declararé en presencia de mi abogada/o.
I understand.	Entiendo.
I don't understand.	No entiendo.
Is there someone here who speaks English?	¿Hay alguien aquí que hable inglés?
I'm sorry, I don't speak Spanish.	Lo siento, pero no hablo castellano.

police officer	policía
arrested	detenida/o
police station	comisaría
	estación de policia (Mex)
police car	furgón policial
	carro de la policia (Mex)
prison	cárcel
cell	celda
lawyer	abogada/o
police court	juzgado de guardia
judge	la/el juez

In this dictionary we have included the definite (la or el, corresponding to 'the' in English) or indefinite article (una or un, corresponding to 'a' or 'one' in English) with each noun. We have chosen either the definite or indefinite article according to the way the word is most likely to be used.

However, note that generally the articles are interchangeable. Thus un abanico, 'a fan' may also be el abanico, 'the fan'. La abuela, 'the grandmother', may also be una abuela, 'a grandmother'. Just remember, el becomes un, while la becomes una.

A

able (to be);		poder;
can		ser capaz de
Can (may) I take your photo?		
¿Puedo sacar una foto?		
Can you show me on the map?		
¿Me puede mostrar en el mapa?		
aboard		a bordo
abortion	el	aborto
above		arriba;
		sobre;
		encima de
abroad		en el
		extranjero;
		en el exterior
to accept		aceptar
accident	un	accidente
accommodation	el	alojamiento
acid (drug)		LSD; ácidos;
		tripi (slang)
across		a través de
action movies	las	películas de
		acción
activist	una/un	activista
actor	una/un	actriz/actor
addict	un	adicto
addiction	la	drogadicción;
	la	dependencia

address	la	dirección
to admire		admirar
admission	la	entrada
to admit		admitir
adult	una/un	adulta/o
advantage	una	ventaja
advice	el	consejo
aerogram	un	aerograma
aeroplane	el	avión
to be afraid of		tener miedo de
after		después de
[in the] afternoon		[de/en (Mex)]
(3–5pm)		la tarde
this afternoon		esta tarde
again		otra vez
against		contra
age	la	edad
aggressive		agresiva/o
[a while] ago		hace [un rato]
[half an hour] ago		hace [media
		hora]
[three days] ago		hace [tres días]
to agree		estar de
		acuerdo

I don't agree.
No estoy de acuerdo.
Agreed!
¡Hecho!

agriculture	la	agricultura
ahead		delante; adelante
aid (help)	la	ayuda
AIDS	el	SIDA
air	el	aire
air-conditioned		con aire condicionado
air mail		por vía aérea; correo aéreo (Mex)
airport	el	aeropuerto
airport tax	la	tasa/impuesto del aeropuerto
alarm clock	un	despertador
all		todo
an allergy	na	alergia
to allow		permitir
almost		casi
alone		sola/o
already		ya
also		también
altarpiece	el	retablo
altitude	la	altura
always		siempre
amateur	una/un	amateur; aficionada/o
amateur film	el	cine amateur
ambassador	la	embajadora
	el	embajador
among		entre
anaemia	la	anemia
anarchist	una/un	anarquista
ancient		antigua/o
and		y
angry		enojada/o
animals	los	animales
ankle	el	tobillo
annual		anual
answer	una	respuesta
answering machine	el	contestador automático

ant	la	hormiga
antenna	la	antena
anthologies	las	antologías
antibiotics	los	antibióticos
antinuclear group	un	grupo antinuclear
antiques	las	antigüedades
antiseptic		antiséptico
any		alguna/o
appendix	el	apéndice
appointment	una	cita
April		abril
arcades	los	portales
archaeological		arqueológica/o
architect		arquitecta/o
architecture	la	arquitectura
to argue		discutir
arm	el	brazo
aromatherapy	la	aromaterapia
to arrive		llegar
arrivals		llegadas
art	el	arte
art films	el	cine arte
art gallery	el	museo de arte
artist	una/un	artista
artwork	una	obra de arte
as big as		tan grande como
ASA; film speed	la	ASA; sensibilidad
ashtray	el	cenicero
to ask (for something)		pedir
to ask (a question)		preguntar
aspirin	la	aspirina
asthmatic		asmática/o
astronaut	una/un	astronauta
astronomer	una/un	astrónoma/o
athletics	el	atletismo
atmosphere	la	atmósfera
August		agosto
aunt	la	tía
automatic teller	el	cajero automático

autumn	el	otoño
avenue	la	avenida
awful		horrible

B

baby	un	bebé
baby food	la	comida de bebé;
	el	potito
baby powder	el	talco
babysitter	el	servicio de niñeras
back (body)	la	espalda
at the back (behind)		detrás de
backpack	la	mochila
bad		mala/o
badger	el	tejón
bag	el	bolso
baggage	el	equipaje
baggage claim	la	recogida de equipajes
bakery	la	panadería
balcony	un	balcón
ball	la	pelota; el balón
ballet	el	ballet
ballpark figure	una	cifra aproximada
ballroom	la	sala de fiestas
band (music)	el	grupo
bandage	el	vendaje
bank	el	banco
banknotes	los	billetes (de banco)
baptism	el	bautizo
a bar; café	un	bar; café
bar with music	un	bar musical; pub
baseball	el	béisbol
basket	la	canasta; cesta
basketball	el	baloncesto
bastard	un/una	cabrona/o; bastarda/o

bat	el	bate/bat (Mex)
bath; shower gel	el	gel de baño
bathing suit	el	bañador; vestito/traje de baño
bathroom	el	baño
battery	la	batería;
	el	acumulador
battery (small)	la	pila
to be		ser; estar
		see page 34.
beach	la	playa
beak	el	pico
bear	el	oso
beautiful		bonita/o; hermosa/o
because		porque
bed	lu	cama
bedroom	una	habitación;
	un	dormitorio (Arg)
bees	las	abejas
before		antes
beggar	una/un	mendiga/o
begin		comenzar
behind		detrás de
below		abajo
beside		al lado de
best	la/el	mejor
a bet	una	apuesta
between		entre
bib	el	babero
the Bible	la	Biblia
bicycle	la	bicicleta
big		grande
bike	una	bici
bill	la	cuenta
billiards	el	billar
binoculars	los	prismáticos; binoculares
biodegradable		biodegradable
biography	la	biografía
bird	el	pájaro

birth certificate	la	acta/partida de nacimiento
birthday	el	cumpleaños
birthday cake	el	pastel de cumpleaños
bite (dog)	una	mordedura; mordida (Mex)
bite (insect)	una	picadura;
	un	piquete (Mex)
black		negra/o
B&W (film)		blanco y negro
blanket	la	manta
to bleed		sangrar
to bless		bendecir
Bless you! (when someone sneezes)		¡Salud!; ¡Jesús! (not in Arg)
blind		ciega/o
a blister	una	ampolla
blood	la	sangre
blood group	el	grupo sanguíneo
blood pressure	la	presión arterial
blood test	un	análisis de sangre
blue		azul
to board (ship, etc)		embarcarse
boarding pass	la	tarjeta de embarque;
	el	pase de abordar (Mex)
boat	el	barco
body	el	cuerpo
Bon appétit!		¡Buen provecho!; ¡Bien apetito! (Mex)
Bon voyage!		¡Buen viaje!
bone	el	hueso
book	un	libro
to book		reservar
bookshop	la	librería
boots	las	botas
border	la	frontera
boring; bored		aburrida/o
to borrow		pedir
both		las/los dos; ambas/os
bottle	la	botella
bottle opener	el	abrebotellas; destapador
[at the] bottom		[en el] fondo
box	la	caja
boxing	el	boxeo
boy	el	chico; niño
boyfriend	el	novio
bra	el	sujetador; sostén; corpiño (Arg)
brakes	los	frenos
branch	la	rama
branch office	la	sucursal
of brass		de latón/bronce
brave		brava/o
bread	el	pan
to break		romper
broken (out of order)		rota/o; descompuesta/o
breakfast	el	desayuno
breast	el	pecho
breasts	los	senos
to breathe		respirar
a bribe	un	soborno;
	una	coima (Arg)
to bribe		sobornar coimear (Arg)
bridge	el	puente
brilliant		cojonuda/o; brillante
to bring		traer
broken		estropeada/o

bronchitis	la	bronquitis
brother	el	hermano
brown		marrón
a bruise	un	cardenal;
		moretón (Arg)
bucket	un	cubo; balde
Buddhist	una/un	budista
bug	un	bicho
to build		construir
building	el	edificio
bull	el	toro
a bullfight	una	corrida
bullfighting	los	toros
bullring	la	plaza de toros
bum; ass	el	culo
bus (city)	el	autobús
bus (intercity)	el	autocar;
		camión (Mex)
business	la	economía;
	los	negocios;
	el	comercio
business person	una/un	comerciante
busker	una/un	artista;
		callejera/o
bus station	la	estación de
		autobús/
		autocares
bus stop	la	parada de
		autobús
busy		ocupada/o
but		pero
butterfly	la	mariposa
to buy		comprar

I'd like to buy ...
Quisiera comprar ...
Where can I buy a ticket?
¿Dónde puedo comprar un billete/boleto (Mex)?

C

cable car	el	teleférico;
		cablecarril (Arg)
cable TV	el	cable
cake shop	la	pastelería
calendar	el	calendario
calf	el	ternero
camera	la	cámara
		(fotográfica)
camera operator	el	operador;
		camerógrafo
camera shop	la	tienda de
		fotografía
to camp		acampar

Can we camp here?
¿Está permitido acampar aquí?

campsite	el	camping
can (to be able)		poder; ser capaz de

We can do it.
Podemos hacerlo.
I can't do it.
No puedo hacerlo.

can (aluminium)	la	lata
can opener	el	abrelatas
canary	un	canario
to cancel		cancelar
candle	la	vela
canter	un	medio galope
canvas	el	lienzo
cape	la	capa
car	el	coche
car owner's title	los	papeles del coche
car registration	la	matrícula; patente
to care (about something)		preocuparse por
to care (for someone)		cuidar de

Careful!		¡Cuidado!; ¡Ojo!
cards	las	cartas
caring		bondadosa/o
carrier bag	la	bolsa;
	el	carro de la compra
to carry		llevar
carton	el	cartón
cartoons	los	dibujos animados
cash register	la	caja registradora
cashier	la	caja
cassette	el	casete
castle	el	castillo; la torre
cat	la/el	gata/o
cathedral	la	catedral
Catholic	la/el	católica/o
caves	las	cuevas
CD	el	compact
to celebrate		
(an event)		celebrar
(in general)		festejar
cemetary	el	cementerio
centimetre	el	centímetro
ceramic	la	cerámica
certificate	el	certificado
chair	la	silla
champagne	el	cava;
	el	champán
championships	los	campeonatos
chance	la	oportunidad
to change		cambiar
change (coins)	el	cambio
changing rooms	los	vestuarios
channel	el	canal
charming		encantadora; encantador
to chat up		ligar

cheap hotel	un	hotel barato
a cheat	una/un	tramposa/o
Cheat!		¡Tramposa/o!
to check		revisar
check-in (desk)	la	facturación de equipajes;
	la	recepción
checkmate		jaque mate
checkpoint (police)	el	control
cheese	el	queso
chemist	la	farmacia
chess	el	ajedrez
chess board	el	tablero de ajedrez
chest	el	pecho
chewing gum	el	chicle
chicken	el	pollo
child	una/un	niña/o
childminding service	la	guardería
children	los	hijos; niños
chocolate	el	chocolate
to choose		escoger
Christian	una/un	cristiana/o
christian name	el	nombre de pila
Christmas Day	la	Navidad
Christmas Eve	la	Nochebuena
church	una	iglesia
a cigarette	un	cigarro
cigarette machine	la	máquina de tabaco
cigarette papers	el	papel de fumar
cigarettes	los	cigarrillos
cinema	el	cine
circus	el	circo
citizenship	la	ciudadanía
city	la	ciudad

city centre	el	centro de la ciudad
city walls	las	murallas
class	la	clase
class system	el	sistema de clases
classical art	el	arte clásico
classical theatre	el	teatro clásico
clean		limpia/o
clean hotel	un	hotel limpio
cleaning		el trabajo de limpieza
client	la/el	clienta/e
cliff	el	acantilado
to climb		subir
cloak	el	capote
cloakroom	el	guardarropas
clock	el	reloj
to close		cerrar
closed		cerrada/o
clothing	la	ropa
clothing store	la	tienda de ropa
cloud	la	nube
cloudy		nublado
clown	la/el	payasa/o
clutch (car)	el	embrague; clutch (Mex)
coach (trainer)	la	entrenadora
	el	entrenador
coast	la	costa
coat	el	abrigo
cocaine	la	cocaína (coca)
cocaine addict	una/un	cocainómana/o
cockerel	el	gallito
cockroach	una	cucaracha
codeine	la	codeína
coins	las	monedas
a cold	un	resfriado;
	un	catarro
cold (adj)		fría/o

It's cold.		
Hace frío; Hará frío.		
to have a cold		
estar constipada/o		
cold turkey	el	síndrome de abstinencia;
	el	mono (slang)
cold water	el	agua fría
colleague	una/un	colega
college	la	residencia de estudiantes
colour	el	color
colour (film)	la	película en color
comb	un	peine
to come		venir
to come; arrive		llegar
comedy	la	comedia
comet	el	cometa
comfortable		cómoda/o
comics	los	comics
communion	la	comunión
communist	el	comunista
companion	una/un	compañera/o
company	la	compañía
compass	la	brújula
computer games	los	juegos de computador
a concert	un	concierto
concert hall	el	teatro
condoms	los	preservativos; condones
conductor	una	cobradora;
	un	cobrador
confession	una	confesión
to confirm		confirmar
Congratulations!		
¡Felicidades!;		
¡Felicitaciones! (Arg)		
conservative		conservadora; conservador

to be constipated		estar estreñida/o
constipation	el	estreñimiento
construction work	la	construcción
consulate	el	consulado
contact lenses	los	lentes de contacto
contraception	el	anticonceptivo
contraceptives	los	anticonceptivos
contract	el	contrato
convent	el	convento
to cook		cocinar
cool [colloquial]		chévere; ¡padre! (Mex)
cork oak	un	alcornoque
corner		
(interior)	el	rincón
(exterior)	la	esquina
corrupt		corrupta/o
to cost		costar; valer

How much does it cost to go to …?
¿Cuánto cuesta/vale ir a …?
It costs a lot.
Cuesta bastante.

cotton	el	algodón
country	un	país
countryside	el	campo
a cough	la	tos
to count		contar
coupon	un	cupón
court (legal)	el	tribunal; el juzgado
court (tennis)	la	cancha
cow	la	vaca
crafts	la	artesanía
crafty		habilidosa/o; ingeniosa/o
crag; wall of rock	un	peñón
crane (bird)	la	grulla
crazy		loca/o
credit card	una	tarjeta de crédito

creep (slang)	una/un	desgraciada/o
cricket	el	críquet
cross (religious)	la	cruz
cross (angry)		enojada/o; enfadada/o
cross-country trail	el	camino
a cuddle	un	abrazo
cup	una	copa
cupboard	el	armario
current affairs	un	informativo; noticiero
customs	la	aduana
to cut		cortar
cyber art	el	arte cibernético
to cycle		andar en bicicleta
cycling	el	ciclismo
cyclist	una/un	ciclista
cystitis	la	cistitis

D

dad		papá
dag; bozo		hortera
daily		diariamente
dairy products	los	productos lácteos
to dance		bailar
dancing	el	bailar
dangerous		peligrosa/o
dark		oscura/o
date (appointment)	una	cita
date (time)	la	fecha
to date		citarse
date of birth	la	fecha de nacimiento
daughter	la	hija
dawn	la	madrugada
day	el	día
day after tomorrow		pasado mañana
day before yesterday		anteayer

English		Spanish
in (six) days		dentro de [seis] días
dead		muerta/o
deaf		sorda/o
to deal		repartir
death	la	muerte
December		diciembre
to decide		decidir
deck (of cards)	una	baraja;
	un	mazo (de cartas)
deep		profunda/o
deer	el	ciervo; corzo; gamo
deforestation	la	deforestación
degree	el	título
delay	una	demora
delicatessen	la	charcutería
delirious		delirante
democracy	la	democracia
demonstration	una	manifestación; demonstración
dental floss	el	hilo dental
dentist	el	dentista
to deny		negar
deodorant	el	desodorante
to depart (leave)		partir; salir de
department store	un	grande almacene;
	una	tienda departmental (Mex)
departure	la	salida
descendent	el	descendiente
desert	el	desierto
design	el	diseño
destination	el	destino
to destroy		destruir
detail	un	detalle
deuce		iguales
diabetic		diabética/o
dial tone	el	tono
diaphragm	el	diafragma
diarrhoea	la	diarrea
diary	la	agenda
dice; die	los	dados
dictionary	el	diccionario
different		diferente
difficult		difícil
dining car	el	vagón restaurante
dinner	la	cena
direct		directa/o
director	la	directora;
	el	director
dirty		sucia/o
disabled		minusválida/o
disadvantage	una	desventaja
discount	un	descuento;
	una	rebaja
to discover		descubrir
discrimination	la	discriminación
disease	la	enfermedad
dismissal	el	despido
distributor	la	distribuidora;
	el	distribuidor
diving	el	submarinismo; bucear (Mex)
diving equipment	el	equipo de inmersión/ buceo (Mex)
dizzy		mareada/o
to do		hacer

What are you doing?
¿Qué haces?
I didn't do it.
No lo hice.

doctor	la	doctora;
	el	doctor;
	la/el	médica/o
a documentary	un	documental
dog	la/el	perra/o
dole	el	paro
dolls	las	muñecas

donkey	el	burro
door	la	puerta
dope	la	droga
double		doble
a double bed	una	cama de matrimonio
a double room	una	habitación doble
a dozen	una	docena
drama	el	drama
dramatic		dramática/o
draughts	las	damas
to draw		dibujar; pintar
to dream		soñar
dress	el	vestido
a drink	una	copa
to drink		beber; tomar
to drive		conducir
driver's licence	el	carnet; permiso de conducir;
	la	licencia de manejo (Mex)
drug	la	medicina; droga (Arg)
drug addiction	la	toxicomanía
drug dealer	el	traficante de drogas
drugs	las	drogas
drums	la	batería
to be drunk		emborracharse
to dry (clothes)		secar
duck	el	pato
dummy (baby's)	un	chupete

E

each		cada
eagle	el	águila
ear	la	oreja
early		temprano
It's early.		
Es temprano.		
to earn		ganar

earrings	los	pendientes
ears	las	orejas
Earth	la	Tierra
earth	la	tierra
earthquake	un	terremoto
east		este
Easter		Pascua; Semana Santa
easy		fácil
to eat		comer
economy	la	economía
ecstasy (drug)	el	éxtasis
editor	la	editora
	el	editor
education	la	educación
eight		ocho
eighteen		dieciocho
eighth		octava/o
eighty		ochenta
elections	las	elecciones
electorate	el	electorado
electricity	la	electricidad
elevator	el	ascensor
eleven		once
embarrassed		avergonzada/o; apenada/o (Mex)
embarrassment	la	vergüenza
embassy	la	embajada …
emergency exit	la	salida de emergencia
employee	la/el	empleada/o
employer	la/el	jefa/e
empty		vacía/o
end	el	fin
to end		acabar; terminar
endangered species	las	especies en peligro de extinción
engagement	el	compromiso
engine	el	motor
engineer	la/el	ingeniera/o

engineering	la	ingeniería
England		Inglaterra
English		inglés
to enjoy (oneself)		divertirse
enough		bastante; suficiente

Enough!
Basta!

to enter		entrar
entertaining		entretenido
envelope	el	sobre
environment	el	medio ambiente
epileptic		epiléptica/o
Epiphany	el	día de los reyes magos
epoch	la	época
equal opportunity	la	igualdad de oportunidades
equality	la	igualdad
equipment	el	equipo
erection	la	erección
erotic literature	la	literatura erótica
etching	el	aguafuerte
european	una/un	europea/o
euthanasia	la	eutanasia
evening	la	noche
every day		todas los días
example	el	ejemplo

For example, ...
Por ejemplo, ...

excellent		excelente; fantástica/o
exchange (money)	el	cambio
to exchange; give gifts		regalar
exchange rate	el	tipo de cambio
excluded		excluida/o

Excuse me.
Perdón.

to exhibit		exponer
exhibition	la	exposición
exit	la	salida
expensive		cara/o
exploitation	la	explotación
express		expreso
express mail	el	correo urgente/ expreso
eye	el	ojo

F

face	la	cara
factory	la	fábrica
factory worker	una/un	obrera/o
fall (autumn)	el	otoño
family	la	familia
famous		conocida/o; famosa/o
fan (hand held)	el	abanico
fan (machine)	el	ventilador
fans (of a team)	la	afición; aficionados

Fantastic!
¡Fantastico!

far		lejos
farm	la	granja
farmer	la	agricultora;
	el	agricultor;
	la/el	granjera/o
fast		rápida/o
fat		gorda/o
father	el	padre; papá
father-in-law	el	suegro
fault (in manufacture)	un	desperfecto
fault (someone's)	la	culpa
faulty		defectuosa/o
fear	el	miedo
February		febrero
to feel		sentir
feelings	los	sentimientos
fence	la	cerca
fencing	la	esgrima
festival	el	festival
fever	la	fiebre

few		pocos
fiancée/fiancé	la/el	novia/o; prometida/o (Mex)
fiction	la	ficción
field	el	campo
fifteen		quince
fifth		quinta/o
fifty		cincuenta
fight	la	lucha; pelea
to fight		luchar; combatir
figures	las	cifras
to fill		llenar
a film (negatives)	la	película
film (cinema)	el	cine
film (for camera)	un	carrete; rollo
film speed	la	sensibilidad
film noir	el	cine negro
films	el	cine
filtered		con filtro
to find		encontrar
a fine	una	multa
finger	el	dedo
fir	el	abeto
fire (controlled)	el	fuego
fire (uncontrolled)	un	incendio
firewood	la	leña
first (1st)		primera/o (1r)
first-aid kit	el	maletín de primeros auxilios
fish (alive)	el	pez
fish (as food)	el	pescado
fish shop	la	pescadería
five		cinco
flag	la	bandera
flat (land, etc)		plana/o
flea	la	pulga
flashlight	una	linterna
flight	el	vuelo
domestic flight	un	vuelo doméstico

floor	el	suelo
floor (storey)	el	piso
flour	la	harina
flower	la	flor
flower seller	la/el	vendedora; vendedor de flores
fly	una	mosca

It's foggy.
Hay niebla.

to follow		seguir
food	la	comida
foot	el	pie
football	el	fútbol
footpath	el	camino
foreign		extranjera/o
forest	el	bosque
forever		[para] siempre
to forget		olvidar

I forget.
Me olvido.
Forget about it!; Don't worry!
¡No te preocupes!!

to forgive		perdonar
fortnight	la	quincena
fortune teller	una	adivinadora
	un	adivinador
forty		cuarenta
four		cuatro
fourteen		catorce
fourth		cuarta/o
fox	el	zorro
foyer	el	vestíbulo
free (not bound)		libre
free (of charge)		gratis
to freeze		helar; congelar
Friday		viernes
friend		una/un amiga/o; una/un colega

It's frosty.
Está helando

frozen foods	los	productos congelados
fruit picking	la	recolección de fruta
to fuck		follar; coger; echar un polvo; joder
full		llena/o
fun	la	diversión;
	el	ocio
for fun		en broma
to have fun		divertirse
to make fun of		burlarse de
funeral	el	funeral
future	el	futuro

G

gallop	el	galope
game (games)	el	juego
game (sport)	la	partida;
	el	partido
a game show	un	concurso
garage (mechanic's)	el	taller
garbage	la	basura
gardening	la	jardinería
gardens	los	jardines
gas cartridge	el	cartucho;
	la	garrafa de gas
gate	la	puerta
gear stick	el	cambio de marchas
general		general
genet	una	gineta/burra

Get lost!
¡Hasta nunca!

gift	el	regalo
gig	un	bolo
girl	la	chica; niña
girlfriend	la	novia
to give		dar

Could you give me ...?
¿Podría darme ...?

glacier	el	glaciar
glandular fever	la	fiebre glandular
glass	el	vidrio
gloves	los	guantes
to go		ir; partir

Let's go.
Vamos; Vámonos.
We'd like to go to ...
Queremos ir a ...
Go straight ahead.
Vaya derecho.

to go out with		salir con
goal	el	gol
goalkeeper	la/el	portera/o; arquera/o (Arg)
goat	la	cabra
God		Dios
of gold		de oro

Good afternoon. (until about 8pm)
Buenas tardes.
Good evening/night.
Buenas noches.
Good health!; Cheers!
¡Salud!

| good hotel | un | buen hotel |

Good luck!
¡Buena suerte!
Good morning.
Buenos días.
Goodbye.
¡Adiós!

goose	el	ganso
gorilla	el	gorila
gorse	la	aulaga
government	el	gobierno
gram	un	gramo
grandchild	una/un	nieta/o
grandfather	el	abuelo
grandmother	la	abuela
grapes	las	uvas
graphic art	el	arte gráfico

grass	la	hierba
grave	la	tumba
great		fantástica/o
Great!		
¡Genial!		
green		verde
greengrocer	la	verdulería; frutería
grey		gris
to guess		adivinar
guide(person)	la/el	guía
guide (audio)	la	audioguía
guidebook	la	guía
guide dog	el	perro lazarillo
guided trek	una	excursión guiada
guinea pig	el	conejillo de indias; cobayo (Arg)
guitar	la	guitarra
gums	las	encías
gym	el	gimnasio
gymnastics	la	gimnasia rítmica

H

hair	el	pelo
hairbrush	el	cepillo (para el cabello; pelo)
half		media/o
half a litre	un	medio litro
to hallucinate		alucinar
ham	el	jamón
hammer	el	martillo
hammock	la	hamaca
hand	la	mano
handbag	el	bolso
handicrafts	la	artesanía
handlebars	el	manubrio
handmade		hecho a mano
handsome		hermoso; guapo

happy		feliz
Happy birthday!		
¡Feliz cumpleaños!		
Happy saint's day!		
¡Feliz santo!		
harbour	la	ensenada
hard		dura/o
hare	la	liebre
harness	el	arnés
harrassment	el	acoso
hash	el	hachís; chocolate (slang)
to have		tener; haber *see page 33.*
Do you have ...?		
¿Tiene usted ...?		
I have ...		
Tengo ...		
hayfever	la	alergia al polen
he		él
head	la	cabeza
a headache	un	dolor de cabeza
health	la	salud
to hear		oír
hearing aid	el	audífono
heart	el	corazón
heat	el	calor
heater	una	estufa
heather	el	brezo
heavy		pesada/o
Hello.		
¡Hola!		
Hello! (answering a call)		
¿Diga?;		
Hola (Arg)		
helmet	el	casco
to help		ayudar
Help!		
¡Ayuda!		
Can you help me?		
¿Puede ayudarme?		

hen	la	gallina
hepatitis	la	hepatitis
herbs	las	hierbas
herbalist	la/el	herborista
here		aquí
heroin	la	heroína;
		jaco;
		caballo (slang)
heroin addict	una/un	
		heroinómana/o;
		yonki (slang)
high		alta/o
high school	el	instituto; liceo
to hike		ir de excursión
hiking	el	excursionismo;
		senderismo
hiking boots	las	botas de
		montaña
hiking routes	los	caminos
		rurales
hill	la	colina
Hindu		hindú
to hire		alquilar

Where can I hire a bicycle?
¿Dónde puedo alquilar una bicicleta?

to hitchhike		hacer dedo;
		hacer auto stop;
		ir de aventón
		(Mex)
HIV positive		seropositiva/o
holiday	un	día festivo
holidays	las	vacaciones
Holy Week	la	Semana santa
homelessness	los	sin hogar
homeopathy	la	homeopatía
homosexual	la/el	homosexual
honey	la	miel
honeymoon	la	luna de miel
horns	los	cuernos
horrible		horrible

horse	el	caballo
horse riding	la	equitación
hospital	el	hospital
hot		caliente

It's hot.
Hace/Hará calor.

to be hot		tener calor
hot water	el	agua caliente
house	la	casa
housework	el	trabajo de casa
how		cómo

How do I get to ...?
¿Cómo puedo llegar a ...?
How do you say ...?
¿Cómo se dice ...?

hug	un	abrazo
human rights	los	derechos
		humanos
a hundred		cien
to be hungry		tener hambre
husband	el	esposo;
		marido

I

I		yo
ibex	una	cabra montés
ice	el	hielo
ice axe	un	piolet;
		picahielo
icecream	un	helado
identification	el	carnet;
card	la	tarjeta de
		identidad
identification	la	identificación
idiot	una/un	idiota
if		si
ill		enferma/o
immigration	la	inmigración
important		importante

It's important.
Es importante.
It's not important.
No importa.

in a hurry	prisa
in front of	enfrente de; delante de
included	incluido
income tax	el impuesto sobre la renta
incomprehensible	incomprensible
indicator	el intermitente
indigestion	la indigestión
industry	la industria
inequality	la desigualdad
an infection	una infección
an inflammation	una inflamación
influenza	la gripe
inhaler	el inhalador
to inject	sinyectarse; chutarse (coll)
injection	una inyección
injury	una herida
inside	adentro/dentro
instructor	la profesora el profesor
insurance	el seguro
intense	intensa/o
interesting	interesante
intermission	el descanso; intervalo; media parte
international	internacional
interview	una entrevista
Ireland	Irlanda
iris	el lirio
island	la isla
itch	una comezón; picazón
itinerary	el itinerario
IUD	un DIU

J

jack (for car)		un gato
jacket		una chaqueta; una chupa; chamorra (Mex)
jail	la	cárcel;
January		enero
jar	una	jarra
jaw	la	mandíbula
jealous		celosa/o
jeans	los	tejanos; vaqueros
jeep	un	yip
jewellery	la	joyería
Jewish		judía/o
job	el	trabajo
job advertisement	un	anuncio de trabajo
job centre	el	INEM
job description	una	descripción del trabajo
jockey	un	jockey
joke	una	broma
to joke		bromear
journalist	una/un	periodista
journey	el	viaje
judge	una/un	juez
judo	el	judo
juice	el	zumo; jugo
July		julio
to jump		saltar
jumper (sweater)	el	jersey; pullover; suéter
June		junio
justice	la	justicia

K

kestrel	el	cernícalo; mastuerzo

key	la	llave
keyboard	el	teclado
kick	un	chute;
	una	patada
kick off	el	saque
kidney	un	riñón
to kill		matar
kilogram	un	quilo
kilometre	un	kilómetro
kind		amable
kindergarten	la	escuela de párvulos;
	el	jardín de infantes (Arg)
king	el	rey
kiss	un	beso
to kiss		besar
Kiss me.		Bésame.
kitchen	la	cocina
kite (bird)	el	milano
kitten	la/el	gatita/o
knapsack	la	mochila
knee	la	rodilla
knife	un	cuchillo
to know (someone)		conocer
to know (something)		saber
I don't know.		
No lo sé.		

L

lace	el	encaje
lake	el	lago
lamb	el	cordero
land	la	tierra
languages	los	idiomas;
	las	lenguas
large		grande
last	la/el	última/o
last month	el	mes pasado
last night		anoche
last week	la	semana pasada
last year	el	año pasado
late		tarde
It's late.		
Es tarde.		
laugh		reírse; reír
launderette	la	lavandería
lavender	la	lavanda
law	la	ley
	el	derecho
lawyer	una/un	abogada/o
laxatives	los	laxantes
laziness	la	pereza
lazy		perezosa/o
leaded(petrol; gas)	la	gasolina con plomo
leader	una	jefa
	un	jefe; líder
league	la	liga
to learn		aprender
leather	el	cuero
leathergoods	los	artículos de cuero
ledge	el	saliente
to be left (behind; over)		quedar
left (not right)		izquierda
left luggage	la	consigna
left-wing		de izquierda; izquierdista
left-winger (inf)	una/un	mamerto
leg	la	pierna
leg (in race)	una	etapa
legalisation	la	legalización
legislation	la	legislación
lens	el	objetivo;
	la	lente
Lent	la	Cuaresma
Leo		leo
lesbian	una	lesbiana
less		menos

letter	una	carta
liar	una/un	mentirosa/o
library	la	biblioteca
lice	los	piojos
to lie		mentir
life	la	vida
lift (elevator)	el	ascensor; elevador (Mex)
light (n)	la	luz
light (adj)		liviano; leve; ligera/o
light (blonde)		rubia/o
light (clear)		clara/o
light bulb	la	bombilla;
	el	foco
light meter	el	fotómetro
lighter	el	encendedor; mechero
to like		gustar(le); apreciar
line	la	línea
lips	los	labios
lipstick	el	lápiz de labios
to listen		escuchar
little (small)		pequeña/o; poca/o
a little (amount)	un	poquito
a little bit	un	poco;
	un	poquito
to live (life)		vivir
to live (somewhere)		vivir; ocupar
Long live ...!		¡Arriba ...!; ¡Viva!
local		local
local; city bus	el	autobús
location	el	terreno para rodaje de exteriores
lock	la	cerradura
to lock		cerrar
long		larga/o
long distance		de larga distancia

long-distance bus; coach		autocar; autobús
to look		mirar
to look after		cuidar
to look for		buscar
looking after children		hacer de niñera
lookout point	un	mirador
to lose		perder
loser	la/el	perdedora/ perdedor
loss	la	pérdida
a lot		mucho
lottery ticket seller	el	vendedor de lotería
loud		ruidosa/o
to love		amar; querer
lover	la/el	amante
low		baja/o
low/high blood pressure	la	presión baja/ alta
loyal		leal
luck	la	suerte
lucky		afortunada/o
ludo	el	parchís; ludo
luggage	el	equipaje
luggage lockers	la	consigna automática; lockers para equipaje (Mex)
lump	un	bulto
lunch	el	almuerzo;
	la	comida
lunchtime	la	hora de comer
luxury	el	lujo
lynx	un	lince

M

machine	una	máquina
mad		loca/o
made (of)		estar hecho de
magazine	una	revista

magician	la/el maga/o	It doesn't matter.	
mail	el correo	No importa.	
mailbox	el buzón	What's the matter?	
main road	la carretera;	¿Qué pasa?	
	ruta (Arg)	mattress	el colchón
main square	la Plaza Mayor	May	mayo
majority	la mayoría	mayor	la/el alcalde
to make	hacer;	mechanic	una mecánica
	fabricar		un mecánico
make-up	el maquillaje	medal	una medalla
man	un hombre	medicine	la medicina;
manager	la/el jefa/e de		el medicamento
	sección;	meditation	la meditación
	manager;	to meet	encontrar
	gerente	member	el miembro
	la directora	menstruation	la menstruación;
	el director		regla
manual worker	la/el obrera/o;	menthol (cigarettes)	los (cigarrillos)
	trabajadora/		mentolados
	trabajador		
many	muchas/os	menu	un menú;
Many happy returns!			la carta
¡Que cumplas muchos más!		message	un mensaje
map	un mapa	metal	el metal
Can you show me on the map?		meteor	el meteorito
¿Lo puede mostrar en el mapa?		metre	el metro
March	marzo	midnight	la medianoche
mare	la yegua	migraine	una migraña;
margarine	la margarina		jaqueca
marijuana	la marihuana;	military service	el servicio militar
	maría (slang)	milk	la leche
marital status	el estado civil	millimetre	un milímetro
market	el mercado	million	un millón
marriage	el matrimonio	mind	la mente
to marry	casarse	mineral water	el agua mineral
marvellous	maravillosa/o	a minute	un minuto
mass	la misa	Just a minute.	
massage	el masaje	Espera un segundo.	
mat	la esterilla	In [five] minutes.	
match	el partido	Dentro de [cinco] minutos	
matches	los fósforos;	mirror	el espejo
	las cerillas	miscarriage	un aborto natural
		to miss (feel absence)	extrañar

mistake	un	error
to mix		mezclar
mobile breath testing unit	el	control de alcoholemia
mobile phone	el	teléfono móbil
modem	un	módem
Modernism	el	modernismo
moisturising cream	la	crema hidratante
monastery	el	monasterio
Monday		lunes
money	el	dinero
mongoose	la	mangosta
monk	el	monje
monkey	el	mono
month	el	mes
this month		este mes
monument	el	monumento
moon	la	luna
more		más
morning (6am - 1pm)		de la mañana
this morning		esta mañana; madrugada
mosque	la	mezquita
mother	la	madre; mamá
mother-in-law	la	suegra
motorboat	una	motora; lancha a motor
motorcycle	una	motocicleta; moto
motorway (tollway)	una	autopista
mountain	la	montaña
mountain bike	una	mountain bike; bicicleta de montaña
mountain hut	un	refugio de montaña;
	una	cabaña (Mex)
mountain path	el	sendero
mountain range	la	cordillera
mountaineering	el	alpinismo
mouse	el	ratón
mouth	la	boca

movie	la	película
mud	el	lodo
Mum		Mamá
muscle	el	músculo
museum	el	museo
music	la	música
musician	una/un	música/o
Muslim	una	musulmana
	un	musulmán
mute		muda/o

N

name	el	nombre
nappy	un	pañal
nappy rash cream	la	crema para la irritación de los pañales
national park	el	parque nacional
nationality	la	nacionalidad
nature	la	naturaleza
naturopath	la/el	naturópata
nausea	la	náusea
near		cerca
nearby hotel	un	hotel cercano
nebula	la	nebulosa
necessary		necesaria/o
necklace	un	collar
to need		necesitar
needle (sewing)	una	aguja
needle (syringe)	la	jeringa
neither		tampoco
net	la	red
never		nunca
new		nueva/o
news	las	noticias
newsagency	el	quiosco
newspaper	un	periódico
newspaper in English	un	periódico en inglés
newspapers	los	periódicos
New Year's Day	el	año nuevo

New Year's Eve	la	Nochevieja	ocean	el	océano
New Zealand		Nueva Zelanda	October		octubre
next		próxima/o	offence	una	ofensa;
next month	el	mes que viene			infracción (traffic)
next to		al lado de	office	la	oficina
next week	la	semana que viene	office work	el	trabajo de oficina
next year	el	año que viene	office worker	una/un	oficinista; empleada/o
nice		simpática/o; agradable	offside		fuera de juego
nickname	un	apodo	often		a menudo
night	la	noche	oil (cooking)	el	aceite
nine		nueve	oil (crude)	el	petróleo
nineteen		diecinueve	OK		regular; de acuerdo
ninety		noventa			
ninth		novena/o	old		vieja/o
noise	el	ruido	old city	la	ciudad antigua;
noisy		ruidosa/o		el	barrio viejo;
non-direct		semidirecto		el	casco antiguo
non-fiction	el	ensayo	olive oil	el	aceite de oliva
none		nada	olives	las	aceitunas
noon	el	mediodía	Olympic Games	los	juegos olímpicos
north	el	norte			
nose	la	nariz	omelette	la	tortilla;
notebook	un	cuaderno	on		en; sobre
nothing		nada	on time		a tiempo
It's nothing.			once; one time	una	vez
No es nada.			one		uno; una; un
not yet		todavía no	one million	un	millón
novel	la	novela	one-way (ticket)	un	(billete/boleto) sencillo
November		noviembre			
now		ahora	only		sola/o; solamente
nuclear energy	la	energía nuclear			
nuclear testing	las	pruebas nucleares	open		abierta/o
nun	una	monja	to open		abrir
nurse	una/un	enfermera/o	opening	la	inauguración
			opera	la	ópera
			opera house	el	teatro de la ópera
O					
oak	el	roble	operation	una	operación
obvious		obvia/o; evidente	operator	una/un	operadora

257

P

opinion	la	opinión
opposite		opuesta/o
optician	una/un	óptica/o
or		o
oral		oral
orange	una	naranja
orchestra	la	orquesta
orchid	una	orquídea
order	el	orden
to order		ordenar
ordinary		corriente; normal
organise		organizar
orgasm	el	orgasmo
original	el	original
other		otra/o
otter	la	nutria
outgoing		abiertos
outside	el	exterior; fuera
over		sobre
overcoat	un	abrigo
overdose	una	sobredosis
to owe		deber
owl	un	búho
owner	la/el	dueña/o
ox	el	buey
oxygen	el	oxígeno
ozone layer	la	capa de ozono

P

pacifier	un	chupete; chupón
package	un	paquete
packet (cigarettes)	un	paquete; una cajetilla
padlock	el	candado
page	una	página
a pain	un	dolor
painful		dolorosa/o

pain in the neck (bore)	una/un	plasta; pesada/o
painkillers	los	analgésicos
to paint		pintar
painter	una/un	pintora/pintor
painting (the art)	la	pintura
paintings	los	cuadros
pair [of gloves]	un	par [de guantes]
pair (a couple)	una	pareja
palace	el	palacio
pan	una	cazuela; cacerola
panty liners	el	salva slip
pap smear	un	papanicolau; una citología
paper	el	papel
paraplegic	una/un	parapléjica/o
parcel	un	paquete; una encomienda
parents	los	padres
a park	un	parque
to park		estacionar
parliament	el	parlamento
parrot	el	loro
part	una	parte
party	la	fiesta
party politics	los	partidos políticos
pass	un	pase
passenger	un	pasajero
passive		pasiva/o
passport	el	pasaporte
passport number	el	número de pasaporte
past	el	pasado
path	el	sendero
patient (adj)		paciente
to pay		pagar
payment	un	pago
peace	la	paz

peak	la	cumbre; cima
pedestrian	una/un	peatón
pen (ballpoint)	el	bolígrafo; birome
pencil	un	lápiz
penicillin	la	penicilina
penis	el	pene
penknife	la	navaja
pensioner	una/un	pensionada/o
people	la	gente
pepper	la	pimienta
percent		por ciento
performance	la	actuación
performance art	la	interpretación
period pain	el	dolor menstrual
permanent		permanente
permanent collection	una	exposición permanente
permission; permit	el	permiso
person	una	persona
personality	la	personalidad
to perspire		sudar; transpirar
petition	una	petición
petrol	la	gasolina; bencina
pharmacy	la	farmacia
phone book	una	guía telefónica
phone box	la	cabina telefónica
phonecard	la	tarjeta de teléfono
photo	una	fotografía; foto

Can (May) I take a photo?
¿Puedo sacar una foto?

photographer	una/un	fotógrafa/o
photography	la	fotografía
pick; pickaxe	una	piqueta
to pick up		ligar; levantar

pie	un	pastel
piece	el	pedazo; trozo
pig	el	cerdo
pill	una	pastilla
the Pill	la	píldora
pillow	la	almohada
pillowcase	una	funda (de almohada)
pinball	el	millón
pine	el	pino
pink		rosa
pipe	una	pipa
place	el	lugar; sitio
place of birth	el	lugar de nacimiento
plain	la	llanura
plane	el	avión
planet	el	planeta
plant	una	planta
to plant		sembrar
plastic	el	plástico
plate	un	plato
plateau	la	meseta
platform	el	andén
play	la	obra; pieza
to play (sport/games)		jugar
to play (music)		tocar
player (sports)	una	jugadora
	un	jugador
player	una/un	música/o
playing cards	los	naipes
	una	baraja (deck)
to play cards		jugar a cartas
plug (bath)	el	tapón
plug (electricity)	un	enchufe
pocket	el	bolsillo
poetry	la	poesía
point (tip)	el	punto
point (games)	un	tanto
to point		apuntar
poker	el	póquer

police	la	policía
politics	la	política
political speech	el	discurso
politicians	los	políticos
pollen	el	polen
polls	los	sondeos
pollution	la	contaminación
pool (swimming)	la	piscina; alberca
pool (game)	el	billar pool
poor		pobre
popcorn	las	palomitas (de maíz)
Pope	el	Papa
popular magazines	las	revistas del corazón
port	el	puerto
portrait sketcher	la/el	retratista; caricaturista
possible		posible
It's (not) possible.		(No) es posible.
postcard	la	postal
post code	el	código postal
postage	el	franqueo
poster	un	póster
post office		Correos
pot (ceramic)	la	olla
pot (dope)	el	costo
pottery	la	alfarería; cerámica
poverty	la	pobreza
power	el	poder
prayer	una	oración
prayer book	un	devocionario
to prefer		preferir
pregnant		embarazada
prehistoric art	el	arte prehistórico
pre-menstrual tension	la	tensión premenstrual
to prepare		preparar

present (gift)	un	regalo
present (time)	el	presente
presentation	la	presentación
presenter	una	presentadora;
	un	presentador
president	la/el	presidenta/e
pressure	la	presión
pretty		bonita/o
prevent		prevenir
price	el	precio
pride	el	orgullo
priest	un	sacerdote
prime minister	la	primera ministra
	el	primer ministro
a print (artwork)	un	grabado
prison	la	cárcel; prisión
prisoner	una/un	prisionera/o
private		privada/o
private hospital	la	clínica;
	el	hospital privado
privatisation	la	privatización
to produce		producir
producer	una	productora
	un	productor
profession	una	profesión
profit	el	beneficio
profitability	la	rentabilidad
programme	el	programa
projector	el	proyector
promise	una	promesa
proposal	una	propuesta
to protect		proteger
protected forest	el	bosque protegido
protected species	las	especies protegidos
protest	una	protesta
to protest		protestar
public toilet	los	servicios; baños públicos

to pull		jalar; tirar
pump	la	bomba
puncture	un	pinchazo
to punish		castigar
puppy	un	cachorro
pure		pura/o
purple		púrpura
to push		empujar
to put		poner

Q

qualifications	las	calificaciones
quality	la	calidad
quarrel	una	pelea; riña
quarter	un	cuarto
queen	la	reina
question	una	pregunta
to question		preguntar
question (topic)	el	asunto;
	la	cuestión
queue	una	cola
quick		rápida/o
quiet (adj)		tranquila/o
quiet (adj)		silenciosa/o
	la	tranquilidad
to quit		dejar

R

rabbit	el	conejo
race (breed)	la	raza
race (sport)	la	carrera
racing bike	la	bicicleta de carreras
racism	el	racismo
racquet	una	raqueta
radiator	el	radiador
railroad	el	ferrocarril
railway station	la	estación
rain	la	lluvia

It's raining.
Llueve.

rally	una	concentración
rape	la	violación
rare		rara/o
a rash	la	irritación
rat	una	rata
rate of pay	el	salario; sueldo
raw		cruda/o
razor	la	afeitadora
razor blades	las	cuchillas/hojas de afeitar
to read		leer
ready		lista/o

Are you ready?
¿Estás lista/o?
I'm ready.
Estoy lista/o.

to realise		darse cuenta de
realism (movies)	el	cine realista
Realism	el	realismo
reason	la	razón;
	el	motivo
receipt	el	recibo
to receive		recibir
recent		reciente
recently		recientemente
to recognise		reconocer
to recommend		recomendar
record	un	disco
record shop	la	tienda de discos; disquería
recording	una	grabación
recyclable		reciclable
recycling	el	reciclaje
recycling bin	el	contenedor de reciclaje
red		roja/o
referee	el	árbitro
reference	las	referencias
reflection (mirror)	el	reflejo
reflection (thinking)	la	reflexión
reflexology	la	reflexología

R

refrigerator	una	nevera; heladera (Arg); refrigerador (Mex)	return (ticket)	un	(billete/boleto) de ida y vuelta
refugee	una/un	refugiada/o	review	la	crítica
refund	un	reembolso	rhythm	el	ritmo
to refund		reembolsar	ribs	las	costillas
to refuse		negar(se)	rich (wealthy)		rica/o
regional		regional	to ride (a horse)		montar (a caballo)
registered mail	el	correo certificado	right (correct)		correcta/o; exacta/o
to regret		lamentar	right (not left)		derecha
relationship	la	relación	to be right		tener razón
to relax		relajar	You're right.		tienes razón
religion	la	religión	civil rights		derechos civiles
religious procession	la	procesión religiosa	right now		en este momento
to remember		recordar			
remote		remota/o	right-wing		derechista
remote control	el	mando a distancia; control remoto (Mex)	ring (on finger)	el	anillo
			ring (of phone)	la	llamada
			I'll give you a ring.		
			Te llamaré.		
rent	el	alquiler	ring (sound)	el	sonido
to rent		alquilar	ring-road	el	cinturón
to repeat		repetir		la	carretera de circunvalación
Could you repeat that please?					
¿Puede repetirlo, por favor?			rip-off	una	estafa
republic	una	república	risk	un	riesgo
reservation	una	reserva	river	el	río
to reserve		reservar	road (main)	la	carretera
resignation	la	dimisión; renuncia	road map	el	mapa de carreteras
respect	el	respeto	roadie	un	transportista
rest (relaxation)	el	descanso	to rob		robar
rest (what's left)	el	resto	rock	la	roca
to rest		descansar	rock climbing	la	escalada
restaurant	un	restaurante	[wall of] rock; crag	un	peñón
resumé	el	curriculum			
retired		jubilada/o	rock group	un	grupo de rock
to return		volver; regresar	rolling		de liar
			romance	el	amor

room (in hotel)	una	habitación
room (in any building)	un	cuarto
room number	el	número de la habitación
rope	la	cuerda
rosemary	el	romero
round		redonda/o
[at the] roundabout		[en la] rotonda
rowing	el	remo
rubbish	la	basura
rug	una	alfombra;
	un	tapete
ruins	las	ruinas
rules	las	reglas
to run		correr

S

sad		triste
saddle	el	sillín; silla para montar (Mex)
safe (adj)		segura/o
safe (n)	una	caja fuerte
safe sex	el	sexo seguro
saint		santa/o;
(when followed by a saint's name)		san
saint's day	el	santo
salary	el	salario
[on] sale		estar en venta
sales department	el	departamento de ventas
salt	la	sal
same	la/el	misma/o
sand	la	arena
sanitary napkins	las	compresas; toallas femeninas
Saturday		sábado
to save		salvar; ahorrar (money)

to say		decir
to scale/climb		trepar; escalar
scarves	los	pañuelos
	las	bufandas
school	la	escuela
science	las	ciencias
science-fiction	la	ciencia ficción
sci-fi movies	el	cine de ciencia ficción
scientist	una/un	científica/o
scissors	las	tijeras
to score		marcar
scoreboard	el	marcador
Scotland		Escocia
screen	la	pantalla
script	el	guión
scriptwriter	una/un	guionista
sculptor	una/un	escultora/escultor
sculpture	la	escultura
sea	el	mar
seasick		mareada/o
seaside	la	costa
seat	un	asiento
seatbelt	el	cinturón de seguridad
second (n)	un	segundo
second		segunda/o
secretary	una/un	secretaria/o
to see		ver

We'll see! Ya veremos!
I see. [understand] Ya entiendo.
See you later. Hasta luego.
See you tomorrow. Hasta mañana.

self-employed	una	trabajadora autónoma/
	un	trabajador autónomo
selfish		egoísta

self-service	el	autoservicio
to sell		vender
to send		enviar
sensible		sensata/o; juiciosa/o
sentence (grammatical)	una	frase
sentence (judiciary)	una	sentencia
to separate		separar
September		setiembre/ septiembre
series	una	serie
serious		seria/o
service (assistence)	el	servicio
service (religious)	el	oficio
seven		siete
seventeen		diecisiete
seventh		séptima/o
seventy		setenta
several		varias/os
to sew		coser
sex	el	sexo
sexism	el	sexismo
shade; shadow	la	sombra
shampoo	el	champú
shape	la	forma
to share (with)		compartir
to share a dorm		compartir un dormitorio
to shave		afeitarse
shaving foam	la	espuma de afeitar
she		ella
sheep	una	oveja
sheet (bed)	la	sábana
sheet (of paper)	una	hoja
shell	una	concha
shelves	las	estanterías
ship	un	barco
to ship		enviar; transportar por vía marítima

shirt	una	camisa
shoe shop	la	zapatería
shoes	los	zapatos
to shoot		disparar
shop	una	tienda
to go shopping		ir de compras
short (length)		corta/o
short (height)		baja/o
short films	los	cortos
short stories	los	cuentos
shortage	una	escasez
shorts	los	pantalones cortos
shoulders	los	hombros
to shout		gritar
a show	un	espectáculo
to show		mostrar
Can you show me on the map?		
¿Me puede mostrar en el mapa?		
shower	la	ducha
shrine	la	capilla (in a church);
	el	altar
to shut		cerrar
shuttle	la	lanzadera espacial
shy		tímida/o
sick		enferma/o
a sickness	una	enfermedad
side	el	lado
a sign	la	señal
to sign		firmar
signature	la	firma
silk	la	seda
of silver		de plata
similar		similar
simple		sencilla/o
sin	un	pecado
since (May)		desde (mayo)
to sing		cantar
singer	una/un	cantante
singer-songwriter	una	cantautora
	un	cantautor
single (person)		soltera/o

S

single (unique)		sola/o; única/o	social-democratic	social demócrata
single room	una	habitación individual	social sciences las	ciencias sociales
sister	una	hermana	social security la	seguridad social
to sit		sentarse	social welfare el	bienestar social
six		seis	socialist una/un	socialista
sixteen		dieciséis	socks los	calcetines
sixth		sexta/o	solid	sólida/o
sixty		sesenta	some	algún; algunas/os
size (of anything) el		tamaño	somebody	alguien
size (clothes)	la	talla	something	algo
size (shoes)	el	número	sometimes	a veces; de vez en cuando
ski slope	la	pista	son el	hijo
ski-boots	las	botas	song la	canción
ski-lift	el	tele-arrastre	soon	pronto
ski-pass	el	forfait; pase (Mex)	sore throat un	dolor de garganta
ski-suit	el	traje de esquí	I'm sorry.	
skiing	el	esquí	Lo siento.	
to ski		esquiar	sound el	sonido
skin	la	piel	south	sur
skirt	una	pollera	South America	América del Sur/ Sudamérica
skis	los	esquíes	souvenir un	recuerdo
sky	el	cielo	souvenir shop la	tienda de recuerdos
to sleep		dormir	space el	espacio
sleeping bag	un	saco;	space la	exploración espacial
	una	bolsa de dormir	exploration	
sleeping car	el	coche cama	Spanish	española/ español
sleeping pills	las	pastillas para dormir	sparrowhawk un	gavilán
sleepy		tener sueño	to speak	hablar
slide (film)	la	diapositiva	special	especial
slow; slowly		despacio	specialist una/un	especialista
small		pequeña/o	speed la	velocidad
a smell	un	olor	speed limit el	límite de velocidad
to smell		oler	spicy	picante; condimentada/o
to smile		sonreír		
to smoke		fumar		
snake	la	serpiente; víbora		
snow	la	nieve		
soap	el	jabón		
soap opera	una	telenovelón		
soccer	el	fútbol		

spider	una	araña
spine	la	columna (vertebral)
sport	los	deportes
sportsperson	una/un	deportista
a sprain	una	torcedura
spring (season)	la	primavera
spring (coil)	el	muelle; resorte
square (shape)	un	cuadro; cuadrado
square (town)	la	plaza
stables	la	cuadra;
	el	establo
stadium	el	estadio
stage	el	escenario
stainless steel	el	acero inoxidable
stairway	la	escalera
stallion	el	semental
stamps	los	sellos
standard (usual)		normal
standard of living	el	nivel de vida
stars	las	estrellas
to start		comenzar
station	la	estación
stationers	la	papelería
statue	la	estatua
to stay (remain)		quedarse
to stay (somewhere)		alojarse; hospedarse
an STD (sexually transmitted disease)	una	enfermedad de transmisión sexual
to steal		robar
steam	el	vapor
steep		escarpada/o; inclinado/a
step	un	paso
stepbrother	el	hermanastro
stepfather	el	padrastro
stepmother	la	madrastra
stepsister	la	hermanastra

stockings; pantyhose	las	medias
stomach	el	estómago
stomachache	un	dolor de estómago
stone	una	piedra
stoned		ciega/o
stop	una	parada
to stop		parar
Stop!		¡Parada!
stork	la	cigüeña
storm	una	tormenta
story	un	cuento
stove	la	estufa; cocina
straight		recta/o; derecho
strange		extraña/o
stranger	una/un	extranjera/o
stream	un	arroyo
street	la	calle
	el	paseo
street demonstration	una	manifestación
street-seller	una	vendedora callejera/
	un	vendedor callejero
strength	la	fuerza
a strike (stop work)	la	huelga
on strike		en huelga
string	la	cuerda
stroll; walk	el	paseo
strong		fuerte
stubborn		testaruda/o
student	una/un	estudiante
studio	un	estudio
stupid		estúpida/o
style	el	estilo
subtitles	los	subtítulos
suburb	el	barrio
suburbs of ...	las	afueras de ...

subway station	la	parada de metro; subte (Arg)
success	el	éxito
to suffer		sufrir
sugar	el	azúcar
suitcase	la	maleta; valija
summer	el	verano
sun	el	sol
sunblock	la	crema solar;
	el	bloqueador solar (Mex)
sunburn	una	quemadura de sol
Sunday		domingo
sunflower oil	el	aceite de girasol
sunglasses	las	gafas/lentes/anteojas de sol
sunny		Hace sol; Hará sol; soleado (Mex)
sunrise	el	amanecer
sunset	la	puesta del sol;
	el	atardecer
sunstroke	una	insolación
supermarket	el	supermercado
supporters	las/los	hinchas; fanaticos (CAm)
Sure.		Claro.
surface mail		por vía terrestre
surfboard	la	tabla de surf
surname	el	apellido
a surprise	una	sorpresa
to survive		sobrevivir
sweet		dulce
to swim		nadar
swimming	la	natación
swimming pool	la	piscina
swimsuit	el	bañador; traje de baño

sword	la	espada
sympathetic		comprensiva/o
synagogue	la	sinagoga
synthetic		sintética/o
syringe	la	jeringa; (chuta)

T

table	la	mesa
table football	el	futbolín
table tennis	el	ping pong
tackle	el	placaje
tail	el	rabo
	la	cola
to take (away)		llevar
to take (food; the train)		tomar
to take photographs		hacer/tomar fotos
to talk		hablar
tall		alta/o
tampons	los	tampones
tasty		sabrosa/o
tax	los	impuestos
taxi stand	la	parada de taxis
teacher	una	profesora
	un	profesor
teaching	la	enseñanza
team	el	equipo
tear (crying)	una	lágrima
technique	la	técnica
teeth	los	dientes
telegram	un	telegrama
telephone	el	teléfono
to telephone		llamar (por teléfono)
telephone office	la	central telefonica;
	la	central de teléfonos (Arg)
telescope	el	telescopio
television	la	televisión

temperature (fever)	la	fiebre
temperature	la	temperatura
temple	un	templo
ten		diez
tennis	el	tenis
tennis court	la	cancha de tenis
tent	una	carpa
tent pegs	las	piquetas
tenth		décima/o
term of office (political)	un	mandato
terrible		terrible; de pena
test	una	prueba
to thank		dar gracias
Thank you. Gracias.		
theatre	el	teatro
theme park	un	parque de atracciones
they		ellas/ellos
thick		gruesa/o
thief	un	ladrón
thin		delgada/o
to think		pensar
third	un	tercio
third (adj)		tercera/o
thirsty	la	sed
I'm thirsty. Tengo sed.		
thirteen		trece
thirty		treinta
thought	un	pensamiento
thousand		mil
three		tres
three of a kind	un	trío
three-quarters		tres cuartos
thrillers (movie)	el	cine de suspenso
throat	la	garganta

thrush (bird)	el	zorzal
thrush (illness)	la	afta
Thursday		jueves
thyme	el	tomillo
ticket	un	billete; boleto (Mex)
ticket (theatre)	la	entrada
ticket collector	la/el	revisora/revisor
ticket machine	la	venta automática de billetes
ticket office	la	taquilla; boletería
ticket scalping	la	reventa
tide	la	marea
tight		apretada/o
time	el	tiempo
What time is it? ¿Qué hora es?		
timetable	el	horario
tin (can)	la	lata
tin opener	el	abrelatas
tip (gratuity)	una	propina
tired		cansada/o
tissues	los	pañuelos de papel; papel tisú (Arg)
toad	el	sapo
toast	la	tostada
tobacco	el	tabaco
tobacco kiosk	el	quiosco de tabaco;
	la	tabaquería (Mex)
today		hoy
together		juntas/os
toilet paper	el	papel higiénico
toilets	los	servicios
toll-free motorway	la	autovía; autopista (Arg)
tomorrow		mañana
tomorrow afternoon; evening mañana por la tarde; noche		

tomorrow morning			trail; route	el	camino; sendero
mañana por la mañana			train	el	tren
tonight		esta noche	train station	la	estación de tren
too (as well)		también	tram	el	tranvía
too expensive		demasiado cara/o	transit lounge	el	tránsito
			to translate		traducir
too much; many		demasiado/s	to travel		viajar
tooth (front)	el	diente	travel agency	la	agencia de viajes
tooth (back)	la	muela			
toothache		el dolor de muelas	travel sickness	el	mareo
			travel (books)	los	libros de viajes
toothbrush	el	cepillo de dientes	traveller	una/un	viajera/o
			traveller's cheques	los	cheques de viajero
toothpaste	la	pasta dentífrica/ de dentes (Mex)			
			tree	un	árbol
			trek	una	excursión
torch (flashlight)	una	linterna	trendy (person)		moderna/o
tortoise	una	tortuga	trip	un	viaje
to touch		tocar	trousers	los	pantalones
tour	una	excursión; un viaje	truck	un	camión
			It's true.		
tourist	una/un	turista	Es verdad.		
tourist	el	guiri (slang)	trust	la	confianza
tourist information office			to trust		confiar
la oficina de turismo			truth	la	verdad
tournament	el	torneo	to try		intentar; probar
towards		hacia			
towel	una	toalla	to try [to do something]		intentar [hacer algo]
tower	una	torre			
town (large, city)	una	ciudad	T-shirt	una	camiseta; remera (Arg)
town (small, village)	un	pueblo			
			Tuesday		martes
toxic waste	los	residuos tóxicos	tune	una	melodía
			Turn left …		
track (car-racing)	el	autódromo	Doble/Vuelta (Mex) a la izquierda …		
track (footprints)	el	rastro;			
	las	huellas (Arg)	Turn right …		
track (sports)	la	pista	Doble/Vuelta (Mex) a la derecha …		
track (path)	el	sendero	TV	la	tele
trade union	los	sindicatos	TV set	el	televisor
traffic	el	tráfico			
traffic lights	los	semáforos			

twelve		doce	urgent		urgente
twenty		veinte	USA	Los	Estados Unidos
twice		dos veces	useful		útil
twin beds		dos camas; camas gemelas (Mex)	usher	una	acomodadora
				un	acomodador
twins	los	gemelos			
two		dos	**V**		
two pairs		doble pareja; para doble	vacant		vacante; libre
			vacation	las	vacaciones
two tickets		dos billetes/ boletos (Mex)	vaccination	una	vacunación
			valley	el	valle
to type		escribir a máquina	valuable		preciosa/o
			value (price)	el	precio
typical		típica/o	van	una	caravana; furgoneta
tyres	los	neumáticos;			
	las	llantas (Mex)	vegetable	una	legumbre
			vegetarian	una/un	vegetariana/o
U					
ultrasound	un	ultrasonido	vegetation	la	vegetación
umbrella	el	paraguas	vein	la	vena
underpants (men)	los	calzoncillos	venereal disease	una	enfermedad venérea
underpants (women)	las	bragas; interiores; bombaches (Arg)	venue	un	local
			very		muy
			video tape	la	cinta de vídeo
to understand		entender; comprender	view	una	vista
			view of the sea; mountain		
unemployed		desempleada/o; en el paro	las vistas al mar; a la montaña		
			village	un	pueblo; pueblecito
unemployment	el	desempleo; paro	vine	la	vid
unions	los	sindicatos	vineyard	un	viñedo
universe	el	universo	virus	un	virus
university	la	universidad	visa	un	visado;
unleaded		sin plomo		una	visa
unsafe		insegura/o	to visit		visitar
until (June)		hasta (junio)	vitamins	las	vitaminas
unusual		extraña/o; inusual (Mex)	voice	la	voz
			volume	el	volumen
up		arriba	to vote		votar
uphill		cuesta arriba	vulture	el	buitre

W

Wait!
Espera!

waiter	la/el	camarera/o; mozo (Arg)
waiting room	la	sala de espera
to walk		caminar
wall (inside)	la	pared
wall (outside)	el	muro
want		querer;
desear		
war	la	guerra
wardrobe	el	vestuario
warm		caliente
to warn		advertir
to wash (something)		lavar
to wash (oneself)		lavarse
washing machine	una un	lavadora; lavarropas (Arg)
watch	el	reloj
to watch		mirar
water	el	agua
mineral water	el	agua mineral
water bottle	la	cantimplora
waterfall	una	cascada
waterskiing	el	esquí acuático
waterskis	los	esquís para el agua
wave	la	ola
way	el	camino

Please tell me the way to …
¿Por favor, cómo llego a …
Which way?
¿Por dónde?;
¿En qué dirección?

Way Out		Salida
we		nosotras/ nosotros
weak		débil
wealthy		rica/o
to wear		llevar
weather	el	tiempo

wedding	la	boda
wedding anniversary	el	aniversario de bodas
wedding cake	la el	tarta nupcial; pastel de boda
wedding present	el	regalo de bodas
Wednesday		miércoles
week	la	semana
this week		esta semana
weekend	el	fin de semana
to weigh		pesar
weight	el	peso
welcome		bienvenida
welfare	el	bienestar social
well		bien
west		oeste
wet		mojada/o
what		qué

What is he saying?
¿Qué está diciendo?
What time is it?
¿Qué hora es?

wheel	la	rueda
wheelchair	la	silla de ruedas
when		cuándo

When does it leave?
¿Cuándo sale?

where		dónde

Where is the bank?
¿Dónde está el banco?

white		blanca/o
who		quién

Who is it?
¿Quién es?
Who are they?
¿Quiénes son?

whole		todo
why		por qué

Why is the museum closed?
¿Por qué está cerrado el museo?

wide		ancha/o	worried		preocupada/o
wife	la	esposa, mujer	worship	la	adoración
wild animal	un	animal salvaje	worth	el	valor
to win		ganar	wound	una	herida
wind	el	viento	to write		escribir
window	la	ventana	writer	una/un escritora/ escritor
window (car; ticket office)	la	ventanilla	wrong		falsa/o

window (shop) el escaparate
to [go] window-shopping
mirar los escaparates

windscreen; windshield	el	parabrisas
wine	el	vino
winery	la	bodega
wing	el	ala
winner	la/el	ganadora/ ganador
winter	el	invierno
wire	el	alambre
wise		sabia/o
with		con
within		dentro de
within an hour/ month		dentro de una hora/un mes
without		sin
without filter		sin filtro
wolf	el	lobo
woman	una	mujer
wonderful		maravillosa/o
wood	la	madera
woodpecker	el	pico; pajaro carpinter (Arg)
wool	la	lana
word	una	palabra
work	el	trabajo
to work		trabajar
workout	el	entrenamiento
work permit	el	permiso de trabajo
workshop	un	taller
world	el	mundo
worms	las	lombrices

I'm wrong. (my fault)
Tengo la culpa
I'm wrong. (not right)
No tengo razón.

Y

year	el	año
this year	este	año
yellow		amarilla/o
yesterday		ayer

yesterday afternoon; evening
ayer por la tarde; noche
yesterday morning
ayer por la mañana; madrugada

yet		todavía
you (pol)		usted
(inf)		tú
(pl)		ustedes
(pl, inf)		vosotras/os
young		joven
youth (collective)	la	juventud
youth hostel	un	albergue juvenil; de juventud

Z

zebra	la	cebra
zero	el	cero
zodiac	el	zodíaco

In this dictionary we have included the definite (la or el, corresponding to 'the' in English) or indefinite article (una or un, corresponding to 'a' or 'one' in English) with each noun. We have chosen either the definite or indefinite article according to the way the word is most likely to be used. However, note that in most cases the articles are interchangeable. Thus un abanico, 'a fan' may also be el abanico, 'the fan'. La abuela, 'the grandmother', may also be una abuela, 'a grandmother'. Just remember, el becomes un, while la becomes una.

Note that the letter 'll' is listed within the 'l' listing. This is because contemporary Spanish no longer has the 'll' listed as a separate letter. If you are using an older dictionary as well, you'll probably find it still listed separately.

The letters 'ch' are considered one letter in Spanish, and therefore come between the letter 'C' and 'D'. When looking for anything with 'ch' in it, remember that it will be listed after the alphabetical listings containing 'c'. For example, enchufe (plug) will be after encontrar (to meet), *not* between encendedor (electricity) and encima (above).

The letter 'ñ' is always listed after the letter 'n'. Thus you will find año (year) *after* all words beginning with 'an'.

A

	abajo	below
un	abanico	fan
las	abejas	bees
el	abeto	fir
	abierta/o	open
una/un	abogada/o	lawyer
	a bordo	aboard
el	aborto	abortion
un	aborto natural	miscarriage
un	abrazo	cuddle
el	abrebotellas	bottle opener
el	abrelatas	can opener
el	abrigo	coat
	abril	April
	abrir	to open

la	abuela	grandmother
el	abuelo	grandfather
	aburrida/o	boring
	acabar	to end
	acampar	to camp

¿Está permitido acampar aquí?
Can we camp here?

el	acantilado	cliff
un	accidente	accident
el	aceite	oil
el	aceite de girasol	sunflower oil
el	aceite de oliva	olive oil
las	aceitunas	olives
el	acero inoxidable	stainless steel
una	acomodadora;	usher
un	acomodador	

el	acoso	arrassment
una/un	activista	activist
la	adicción	addiction
una	actriz	actor
un	actor	
una	actuación	performance
	adentro	inside
una/un	adicta/o	addict
	¡Adiós!	
	Goodbye!	
una/un	adivina/o	fortune teller
	adivinar	to guess
la	adoración	worship
la	aduana	customs
una/un	adulta/o	adult
un	aerograma	aerogram
la	afeitadora	razor
	afeitarse	to shave
la	afición	fans
una/un	aficionada/o	amateur; enthusiast
	afortunada/o	lucky
la	afta	thrush (illness)
las	afueras de …	suburbs of …
la	agencia de viajes	travel agency
la	agenda	diary
	agosto	August
	agradable	nice
	agresiva/o	aggressive
una	agricultora	farmer
un	agricultor	
la	agricultura	agriculture
el	agua	water
el	agua caliente	hot water
el	agua fría	cold water
un	aguafuerte	etching
el	agua mineral	mineral water
el	águila	eagle
una	aguja	needle (sewing)
	ahogar	to drown
	ahora	now

el	aire	air
el	sajedrez	chess
	al lado de	next to
la/el	alcalde	mayor
un	alcornoque	cork oak
una	alergia	an allergy
la	alergia al polen	hayfever
la	alfarería	pottery
una	alfombra	rug
	algo	something
el	algodón	cotton
	alguien	somebody
	algunas/os	some
el	almacén	general store; shop
la	almohada	pillow
el	almuerzo	lunch
	alojarse	to stay (somewhere)
el	alpinismo	mountaineering
	alquilar	to rent; hire

¿Dónde puedo alquilar una bicicleta?

Where can I hire a bicycle?

el	alquiler	the rent
	alta/o	high
la	altura	altitude
	alucinar	to hallucinate
	amable	kind
el	amanecer	sunrise
la/el	amante	lover
una	amapola	poppy
	amar	to love
	amarilla/o	yellow
	a menudo	often
	América del Sur	South America
	amiga/o	friend
una	ampolla	blister
los	analgésicos	painkillers
un	análisis de sangre	blood test

una/un	anarquista	anarchist
	andar en bicicleta	to cycle
la	anemia	anaemia
el	anillo	ring (on finger)
un	animal salvaje	wild animal
el	aniversario de bodas	wedding anniversary
	anoche	last night
	anteayer	day before yesterday
la	antena	antenna
la	antena parabólica	satellite dish
	antes	before
los	anticonceptivos	contraceptives
	antigua/o	ancient
los	antigüedades	antiques
las	antologías	anthologies
	anual	annual
un	anuncio de trabajo	job advertisement
el	año	year
el	año nuevo	New Year's Day
el	año pasado	last year
el	año que viene	next year
un	aparato de transparencias	overhead projector
el	apellido	surname
el	apéndice	appendix
un	apodo	nickname
	apreciar	to like
	aprender	to learn
una	apuesta	a bet
	aquí	here
una	araña	spider
el	árbitro	referee
la	ardilla	squirrel
la	arena	sand
el	armario	cupboard
el	arnés	harness

	arriba	above
	¡Arriba ...!	Long live ...!
un	arroyo	stream
el	arte cibernético	cyber art
el	arte gótico	Gothic art
el	arte prehistórico	prehistoric art
el	arte renacentista	Renaissance art
la	artesanía	handicrafts
los	artículos de cuero	leathergoods
una/un	artista callejera/o	busker; performing artist
la	ASA; sensibilidad	ASA; film speed
el	ascensor	lift (elevator)
un	asiento	seat
el	asunto	question
el	atardecer	sunset
	a tiempo	on time
el	atletismo	athletics
el	audífono	hearing aid
	autocar	long-distance bus; coach
una/un	autónoma/o	self-employed
una	autopista	motorway (with tolls)
el	autoservicio	self-service
la	autovía	toll-free motorway
la	avenida	avenue
	avergonzada/o	embarrassed
el	avión	plane
	ayer	yesterday
	ayer por la mañana; madrugada	yesterday morning
	ayer por la tarde; noche	yesterday afternoon; evening

la	ayuda	aid (help)	
	ayudar	to help	
	¡Ayuda!		
	Help!		
el	azúcar	sugar	
	azul	blue	

B

el	babero	bib
	bailar	to dance
el	baile	dancing
	baja/o	low; short (height)
un	balde	bucket
el	balonmano	handball
la	bandera	flag
el	bañador	swimsuit
el	baño	bathroom
una	baraja	deck (of cards)
el	barco	boat
el	barrio	suburb
el	barrio viejo	old city
	¡Basta!	
	Enough!	
	bastante	enough
la	basura	garbage
el	bate	bat
la	batería	battery; drums
el	bautizo	baptism
un	bebé	baby
	beber	to drink
	bendecir	to bless
el	beneficio	profit
	besar	to kiss
	Bésame.	
	Kiss me.	
un	beso	kiss
el	biberón	feeding bottle
la	Biblia	the Bible
la	biblioteca	library
una	bici	bike

la	bicicleta aeroestática	exercise bicycle
la	bicicleta de carreras	racing bike
una	bicicleta de montaña	mountain bike
un	bicho	bug
	bien	well
	bien escrita/o	well-written
el	bienestar social	welfare
el	billar	billiards/pool
los	billetes (de banco)	banknotes
la	biografía	biography
	blanca/o	white
	blanco y negro	B&W (film)
la	boca	mouth
la	boda	wedding
el	boleto (Mex)	ticket
el	bolígrafo	pen (ball point)
un	bolo	gig
la	bolsa	carrier bag
el	bolsillo	pocket
el	bolso	handbag
la	bomba	pump
la	bombilla	flashlight; light bulb; torch
	bondadosa/o	caring
	bonito	beautiful
	bordar	to embroider
el	bosque	forest
el	bosque protegido	protected forest
las	botas (de montaña)	(hiking) boots
una	bota de vino	leather wine bottle
la	botella	bottle
los	botones	buttons
el	boxeo	boxing
	brava/o	brave
el	brezo	heather
	brillante	brilliant
una	broma	joke

	bromear	to joke
la	bronquitis	bronchitis
la	brújula	compass
una/un	budista	Buddhist
	buena/o	good
	¡Buena suerte!	
	Good luck!	
	Buenas noches.	
	Good evening/night.	
	Buenas tardes.	
	Good afternoon.	
	Buenos días.	
	Good morning.	
	¡Buen provecho!	
	Bon apetit!	
	¡Buen viaje!	
	Bon voyage!	
el	buey	ox
la	bufanda	scarf
el	búho	owl
el	buitre	vulture
un	bulto	lump
	burlarse de	to make fun of
el	burro	donkey
	buscar	to look for
el	buzón	mail box

C

el	canario	canary
el	caballo	horse; heroin (slang)
la	cabeza	head
la	cabina telefónica	phone box
el	cable	cable TV
la	cabra	goat
una	cabra montés	ibex
	cabronaza/o	bastard
una/un	cachorra/o	puppy
un	cacto; cactus	cactus
	cada	each
	cada día	every day

la	caja	box; cashier
una	caja fuerte	safe (n)
la	caja registradora	cash register
el	cajero automático	automatic teller
una	cajetilla	packet
los	calcetines	socks
el	calendario	calendar
la	calidad	quality
	caliente	hot
la	calle	street
el	calor	heat
los	calzoncillos	underpants (men)
los	calzones (Mex)	underpants (women)
la	cama	bed
una	cama de matrimonio	double bed
la	cámara	room; camera
la/el	camarera/o	waiter
	cambiar	to change
el	cambio	exchange; change (coins)
	caminar	to walk
el	camino	trail; route
los	caminos rurales	hiking routes
el	camión de catering	catering truck
una	camioneta (mex)	van
una	camisa	shirt
una	camiseta	T-shirt
los	campeonatos	championships
el	camping	campsite
el	campo	countryside; field
el	canal	canal; channel
la	canasta	basket
	cancelar	to cancel

C

la	canción	song	el	castillo	castle
la	cancha	court	un	catarro	cold
el	candado	padlock		catorce	fourteen
	cansada/o	tired	el	cava	champagne
	cantar	to sing	una	cazuela	pan
una	cantautora	singer-song writer		celebrar	to celebrate (an event)
un	cantautor			celosa/o	jealous
la	cantimplora	water bottle	la	cena	dinner
la	capa	cape	el	cenicero	ashtray
la	capa de ozono	ozone layer	la	Central Teléfonica (Mex)	telephone office
	ser capaz de	to be able to do (can)	el	centro de la ciudad	city centre
la	capilla	shrine; altar	el	cepillo de dientes	toothbrush
el	capote	cloak	el	cepillo (para el cabello; pelo)	hairbrush
	cara/o	expensive		cerca	near
la	cara	face	la	cerca	fence
una	caravana	van	el	cerdo	pig
la	cárcel	jail	el	cernícalo	kestrel
un	cardenal	bruise	el	cero	zero
el	carnet de conducir	driver's licence		cerrado/o	closed
el	carnet de identidad	identification card	la	cerradura	lock (n)
la	carrera	race (sport)		cerrar	to close; lock
un	carrete	film (camera)	la	cesta	basket
la	carretera	main road		ch	see separate list after 'C'
un	carro	trolley		ciega/o	blind; stoned (slang)
una	carta	letter; menu	el	cielo	sky
la	carta astral	chart (astrological)		cien	hundred
las	cartas	cards	la	ciencia ficción	science fiction
el	cartón	carton	las	ciencias	science
el	cartucho de gas	gas cartridge	las	ciencias sociales	social sciences
la	casa	house	una/un	científica/o	scientist
	casarse	to marry	el	ciervo	deer
una	cascada	waterfall	una	cifra aproximada	ballpark figure
el	casco	helmet	las	cifras	figures
el	casco antiguo	old city			
el	casete	cassette			
	casi	almost			
	castigar	to punish			

los	cigarrillos	cigarettes
un	cigarro	a cigarette
la	cigüeña	stork
	cinco	five
	cincuenta	fifty
el	cine	film (cinema)
el	cine arte	art films
el	cine negro	film-noir
el	cine realista	realism
la	cinta de video	video tape
el	cinturón	ring-road
el	cinturón de seguridad	seatbelt
el	circo	circus
una	cita	date; appointment
	citarse	to date
una	citología	pap smear
la	ciudad	city
la	ciudad antigua	old city
la	ciudadanía	citizenship
	clara/o	light

Claro.
Sure.

la	clínica	private hospital
el	cobrador	conductor (bus)
una/uncocainómana/o		cocaine addict
la	cocina	kitchen; stove
	cocinar	to cook
el	coche	car
el	coche cama	sleeping car
el	código postal	post code
	coger	to fuck
la	cola	bum; ass
una	cola	queue
el	colchón	mattress
la	colina	hill
un	collar	necklace
la	columna (vertebral)	spine
	combatir	to fight

la	comedia	comedy
la	comedia negra	black comedy
	comenzar	to start
	comer	to eat
el	comerciante	business person
una	comezón	itch
la	comida	food
la	comida de bebé	baby food
	cómo	how

¿Cómo puedo llegar a …?
How do I get to …?
¿Cómo se dice …?
How do you say …?

	cómoda/o	comfortable
el	compact	CD
una/un	compañera/o	companion
	compartir (un dormitorio)	to share (a dorm)
	comprender	to understand
	comprensiva/o	sympathetic
las	compresas	sanitary napkins
el	compromiso (appointment;	engagement
		to marry)
	con aire acondicionado	airconditioned
una	concentración	rally
un	concierto	concert
un	concurso	game show
una	concha	shell
un	condón	condom
	conducir	to drive
el	conductor	driver
el	conejillo de indias	guinea pig
el	conejo	rabbit
una	confesión	confession
	con filtro	filtered
	confirmar	to confirm
	congelar	to freeze
	conocer	to know (someone)

C

	conocida/o	famous
el	consejo	advice
	conservador	
la/el	conservadora/ conservador	conservative; curator
la	consigna	left luggage
	estar constipada/o	to have a cold
la	construcción	construction work
	construir	to build
la	contaminación	pollution
	contar	to count
el	contenedor de reciclaje	recycling bin
el	contestador automático	answering machine
la	contrarreloj	race against the clock
el	contrato	contract
el	control de alcoholemia	mobile breath testing unit
una	copa	drink; cup
el	corazón	heart
el	cordero	lamb
la	cordillera	mountain range
el	corredor de apuestas	bookmaker
el	correo	mail
el	correo certificado	registered mail
	Correos	post office
el	correo urgente	express mail
	correr	to run
la	corrida	bullfight
	corriente	ordinary
	corrupta/o	corrupt
	corta/o	short
	cortar	to cut
los	cortos	short films
el	corzo	deer

	coser	to sew
la	costa	seaside; coast
	costar	to cost
	Cuesta bastante.	It costs a lot.
	¿Cuánto cuesta?	How much is it?
las	costillas	ribs
el	costo	pot (dope)
la	crema hidratante	moisturising cream
la	crema solar	sunblock
la	crítica	review
	cruda/o	raw
la	cruz	cross (religious)
un	cuaderno	notebook
la	cuadra	stables
un	cuadrado; cuadro	square (shape)
los	cuadros	paintings
	¿Cuánto?	How much; many?
	¿Cuánto cuesta?	How much is it?
	cuarenta	forty
la	Cuaresma	Lent
	cuarta/o	fourth
un	cuarto	room
un	cuarto	quarter
	cuatro	four
una	cubeta (Mex)	bucket
un	cubo	bucket
una	cucaracha	cockroach
las	cuchillas de afeitar	razor blades
un	cuchillo	knife
la	cuenta	bill
el	cuento	story
la	cuerda	rope
los	cuernos	horns

el	cuero	leather
el	cuerpo	body
	cuesta arriba	uphill
las	cuevas	caves
	¡Cuidado!	
	Careful!	
	cuidar	to look after
	cuidar de	to care (someone)
la	culpa	fault; blame; guilt
la	cumbre	peak
el	cumpleaños	birthday
	¡Que cumplas muchos más!	
	Many happy returns!	
un	cupón	coupon
el	curriculum	resumé

CH

	chachi	great
la	chamarra (Mex)	jacket
el	champán (Mex)	champagne
una	chaqueta	jacket
la	charcutería	delicatessen
los	cheques de viaje	travellers' cheques
	chévere (slang)	cool
la	chica	girl
el	chicle	chewing gum
el	chico	boy
el	chupete/ chopón (Mex)	dummy; pacifier
la	chuta (slang)	syringe
un	chute	kick

D

los	dados	dice; die
	dar	to give
	darse cuenta (de)	to realise

un	dato	piece of information
	De acuerdo.	
	OK.	
	deber	to owe
	débil	weak
	décima/o	tenth
	decidir	to decide
	decir	to say
	¿Cómo se dice ...?	
	How do you say ...?	
un	decorado	prop
el	dedo	finger
	defectuosa/o	faulty
	de izquierda/ izquierdista	left-wing
	delante de	in front of
	delantero	forward
	de larga distancia	long distance
	delirante	delirious; crazy (coll, Arg)
	demasiado cara/o	too expensive
	demasiada (s)	too much; many
	demasiado (s)	
una	demora	a delay
	dentro de (seis) días	in (six) days
	dentro de una hora/un mes	in an hour/ month
el	departamento de ventas	sales department
la	dependencia	dependence
los	deportes	sport
una/un	deportista	sportsperson
	derechista	right-wing
	derecha	right (not left)
el	derecho	law
el	desayuno	breakfast

D

	descansar	to rest
el	descanso	intermission
	descompuesta/o	broken (out of order); sick (person-Arg)
una	descripción del trabajo	job description
	descubrir	to discover
un	descuento	discount
	desde (mayo)	since (May)
	desear	to want
el	desempleo; paro	unemployment
una/un	desgraciada/o	creep (coll)
el	desierto	desert
la	desigualdad	inequality
el	desodorante	deodorant
	despacio	slow; slowly
un	despertador	alarm clock
el	despido	dismissal
	después (de)	after
el	destapador (Mex)	bottle opener
	destemplada/o	shivery
el	destino	destination; destiny
	destruir	to destroy
una	desventaja	disadvantage
	detrás de	behind
	de vez en cuando	sometimes
un	devocionario	prayer book
el	día	day
el	día de los reyes magos	Epiphany
un	día festivo	holiday
la	diapositiva	slide
	diariamente	daily
	dibujar	to draw
los	dibujos animados	animation; comics
el	diccionario	dictionary
	diciembre	December
los	dientes	teeth

	diez	ten
	¿Diga?	
	Hello! (answering a call)	
la	dimisión	resignation
el	dinero	money
la	dirección	address
	directo	direct
la/el	directora/director	director
un	disco	record
una	discoteca	discoteque
	discutir	to argue
el	diseño	design
	disparar	to shoot
un	DIU	IUD
la	diversión	fun
	divertirse	to have fun
	dividir (entre)	to share (with); to divide

Doble a la derecha …
Turn right …
Doble a la izquierda …
Turn left …

el	doble	double
	doce	twelve
una	docena	dozen
el	dolor	pain
un	dolor de cabeza	headache
un	dolor de estómago	stomach ache
un	dolor de garganta	sore throat
	dolor de muela	toothache
el	dolor menstrual	period pain
	dolorosa/o	painful
	domingo	Sunday
	dormir	to sleep
	dónde	where

¿Dónde está …?
Where is …?
¿Dónde puedo alquilar una bicicleta?
Where can I hire a bicycle?

	dos	two

282

	dos veces	twice
la	drogadicción	addiction
las	drogas	drugs
la	ducha	shower
la/el	dueña/o	owner

E

la	economía	business; economy
la	edad	age
el	edificio	building
un	ejemplo	example
	él	he
	ella	she
	ellas/ellos	they
	embarcarse	to board (a ship)
la	embajada …	embassy
	embarazada	pregnant
el	embrague	clutch
la/el	empleada/o	employee
	empujar	to push
	en	on; in
	en broma	for fun; joking
el	encaje	lace
	encantadora	charming
	encantador	charming
	encargada/o de luces	lighting operator
el	encendedor	lighter
las	encías	gums
	encima de	above; on top of
	encontrar	to meet
un	enchufe	plug (electricity)
	en el paro	unemployed
	enero	January
	enferma/o	sick
	enfadada/o	angry
la	enfermedad	disease
una/un	enfermera/o	nurse

	enfrente de	in front of
el	ensayo	non-fiction
la	enseñanza	teaching
	entender	understand
	[Ya] entiendo. I see. (understand)	
la	entrada	ticket (theatre)
	entrar	to enter
	entre	between
la	entrenadora	coach; trainer
el	entrenador	
el	entrenamiento	workout
	entretenido	entertaining
una	entrevista	interview
	enviar	to send
	epiléptica/o	epilectic
el	equipaje	luggage
el	equipo	team; equipment
el	equipo de inmersión	diving equipment
la	equitación	horseriding
la	escalada	rock climbing
la	escalera	staircase
el	escaparate	window (shop)
	escarpada/o	steep
una	escasez	shortage
el	escenario	stage
	Escocia	Scotland
	escoger	to choose
	escribir	to write
	escribir a maquina	to type
una	escritora;	writer
un	escritor	
el	escrutinio	counting of votes
	escuchar	to listen
la	escuela	school
la	escuela de párvulos	kindergarten
una	escultora/	sculptor
un	escultor	

el	esgrima	fencing
el	espacio	space
la	espada	sword
la	espalda	back
	española/ español	Spanish (adj)
los	especies en peligro de extinción	endangered species
las	especies protegidas	protected species
un	espectáculo	show
el	espejo	mirror
	¡Espera!	Wait!
la	esposa; mujer	wife
el	esposo; marido	husband
la	espuma de afeitar	shaving foam
el	esquí	skiing
el	esquí acuático	waterskiing
	esquiar	to ski
la	esquina	corner
	esta mañana; madrugada	this morning
	esta noche	tonight
	esta semana	this week
	esta tarde	this afternoon
	Está helando.	It's frosty.
	Está nublado.	It's cloudy.
el	establo (Mex)	stable
la	estación	station
	estacionar	to park
el	estadio	stadium
el	estado civil	marital status
Los	Estados Unidos	USA
una	estafa	rip-off
las	estanterías	shelves
	este	east
	este año	this year
	este mes	this month

la	esterilla	mat
el	estilo	style
el	estómago	stomach
las	estrellas	stars
el	estreñimiento	constipation
	estropeada/o	broken
la	estufa	stove; heater
una	etapa	leg (in race)
	europea/o	european
la	eutanasia	euthanasia
una	excursión	trek
una	excursión	tour group
una	excursión guiada	guided trek
el	excursionismo	hiking
el	éxito	success
la	exploración espacial	space exploration
la	explotación	exploitation
	exponer	to exhibit
una	exposición	exhibition
una	expresa/o	express
una	expulsión	send-off
el	éxtasis	ecstasy (drug)
el	exterior	outside
	extranjera/o	foreign
una	extranjera	stranger
un	extranjero	
	extraña/o	unusual
	extrañar	to miss (feel the absence of)

F

la	fábrica	factory
	fabricar	to make
	fácil	easy
una	falda	skirt
una	falta	fault; foul
	fantástico	Fantastic!
	farandulera/o	flash; nouveau-riche type
	febrero	February

la	fecha	date
la	fecha de nacimiento	date of birth
	¡Felicidades!; ¡Felicitaciones! (Arg)	
	¡Congratulations!	
	feliz	happy
	¡Feliz cumpleaños!	
	Happy birthday!	
	¡Feliz santo!	
	Happy saint's day!	
el	ferrocarril	railway
	festejar	to celebrate
la	ficción	fiction
la	fiebre	fever
la	fiebre glandular	glandular fever
la	fiesta	party
el	fin	end
el	fin de semana	weekend
la	firma	signature
la	flor	flower
el	foco (Mex)	flashlight, bulb
	[en el] fondo	[at the] bottom
el	forfait	ski-pass
la	forma	shape
los	fósforos	matches
el	fotómetro	light meter
el	franqueo	postage
los	frenos	brakes
	frente a	opposite
	fría/o	cold (adj)
la	frontera	border
la	frutería	greengrocer
el	fuego	fire (controlled)
	fuera	outside
	fuera de juego	offside
	fuerte	strong
la	fuerza	strength
	fumar	to smoke
una	funda de .	pillowcase

	almohada	
una	furgoneta	van
el	fútbol sala	indoor soccer
el	futbolín	table soccer

G

las	gafas de sol	sunglasses
la	gallina	hen
el	gallito	cockerel
el	gamo	deer
el	ganadora	winner
el	ganador	
	ganar	to earn
el	ganso	goose
la	garganta	throat
la/el	gata/o	cat
un	gato	jack (for car)
la/el	gatita/o	kitten
los	gauchos (Mex)	tent pegs
un	gavilán	sparrowhawk
el	gel de baño	shower gel
los	gemelos	twins
la	gente	people
una	gineta	genet
el	glaciar	glacier
el	gobierno	government
	gorda/o	fat
un	grabado	print
una	grabación	recording
	grande	big
los	grandes almacenes	department stores
la	granja	farm
la/el	granjera/o	farmer
el	gringo (slang)	tourist
la	gripe	influenza
	gris	grey
	gritar	to shout
una	grulla	crane (bird)
el	grupo sanguíneo	blood group
los	guantes	gloves

el	guardarropa	cloakroom
la	guardería	childminding service
las	guarniciones	harness
la	guía	guidebook; guide (f)
el	guía	guide(m)
el	guión	script
una/un	guionista	scriptwriter
	gustar(le)	to like (it)

H

	haber	to have *see page 33.*
	habilidosa/o	crafty
la	habitación	room
una	habitación doble	double room
una	habitación individual	single room
una	habitación sencilla (Mex)	single room
	hablar	to talk

Hace calor.
It's hot.
Hace frío.
It's cold
Hace sol.
It's sunny

	hace un rato	[a while] ago
	hace [media hora]	[half hour] ago
	hace [tres días]	[three days] ago
	hacer	to do
	hacer dedo; hacer auto stop	to hitchhike
	hacer fotos	to take photographs
	hacer	to make
el	hachís	hash

la	hamaca	hammock
el	hambre	hunger
la	harina	flour

Hasta luego.
See you later.
¡Hasta nunca!
Get lost!

	hasta (junio)	until (June)

Hay niebla.
It's foggy.

	hecho a mano	handmade

¡Hecho!
Agreed!

un	helado	icecream
	helar	to freeze
el	hermanastro	stepbrother
una	herida	wound
la	hermana	sister
la	hermanastra	stepsister
el	hermano	brother
	hermosa/o	handsome
la	heroína	heroin
una/un	heroinómana/o	heroin addict
el	hielo	ice
la	hija	daughter
el	hijo	son
los	hijos/niños	children
el	hilo dental	dental floss
los	hinchas	supporters
una	hoja	sheet (paper); leaf
las	hojas de afeitar	razor blades

¡Hola!
Hello.

un	hombre	man
los	hombros	shoulders
la	hora de comer	lunchtime
la	hormiga	ant
	hospedarse	to stay (somewhere)
un	hotel barato	cheap hotel
un	hotel cercano	nearby hotel

un	hotel limpio	clean hotel
	hoy	today
la	huelga	strike (work)
	en huelga	on strike
el	hueso	bone
los	huevos	eggs
los	huevos de chocolate	chocolate eggs
las	humanidades (Mex)	humanities

I

los	idiomas	languages
una	iglesia	church
la	igualdad	equality
la	igualdad de oportunidades	equal opportunity
	iguales	deuce
	No importa.	It doesn't matter.
el	impuesto sobre la renta	income tax
los	impuestos	tax
la	inauguración	opening
un	incendio	fire (uncontrolled)
	no incluido	not included
el	INEM	job centre
	infantil	child's
un	informativo	news bulletin
la/el	ingeniera/o	engineer
la	ingeniería	engineering
	ingeniosa/o	crafty
la	Inglaterra	England
el	inhalador	inhaler
una	injuria	an insult
la	insolación	sunstroke
el	instituto	high school
	intentar [hacer algo]	to try [to do something]
	intentar; probar	to try
los	interiores	underpants

		(women)
el	intermitente	indicator (car)
la	interpretación	interpretation; performance art
el	invierno	winter
una	inyección	injection
	inyectarse	to inject oneself
	ir de compras	to go shopping
	ir de excursión	to hike
	ir; partir	to go
la	Irlanda	Ireland
una	irritación	a rash
	irse de aventón (Mex)	to hitchhike
la	isla	island
	de izquierda; izquierdista	left-wing
	izquierda	left (not right)

J

un	jabalí	boar
el	jabón	soap
	jalar	to pull
el	jamón	ham
la	jardinería	gardening
el	jardín	garden
una	jarra	jar
la/el	jefa/e	employer
la/el	jefa/e de sección	manager
la	jeringa	syringe
una/un	jíbaro	drug dealer (slang)
	joder	to fuck (Arg) to trick; to bother
la	joyería	jewellery
	jubilada/o	retired
	judía/o	Jewish

el	judo	judo
el	juego	game
los	juegos de computador	computer games
los	juegos olímpicos	Olympic Games
	jueves	Thursday
una/un	juez	judge
una	jugadora	player (sports)
un	jugador	
	jugar	to play (sport; games)
	jugar cartas	to play cards
el	jugo (Mex)	juice
	juicioso/o	sensible
	julio	July
	junio	June
el	juzgado	court (legal)
	¡Jesús!	
	Bless you! (sneezing)	

K

un	kilo	kilogram

L

los	labios	lips
el	lado	side
el	lago	lake
	lamentar	to regret
la	lana	wool
la	lanzadera espacial	shuttle
un	lápiz	pencil
el	lápiz de labios	lipstick
	larga/o	long
	de larga distancia	long-distance
la	lata	can (tin; aluminium)
el	latón	brass
la	lavandería	launderette

los	laxantes	laxatives
	leal	loyal
la	leche	milk
	leer	to read
	lejos	far
la	leña	firewood
los	lentes de contacto	contact lenses
las	letras	humanities
el	levantamiento de pesas	weightlifting
	leve	light (not heavy)
	libre	free (not bound)
la	librería	bookshop
un	libre de rejos (Mex)	prayer book
los	libros	books
los	libros de viajes	travel books
la	licencia de manejo (Mex)	driver's licence
la	liebre	hare
el	lienzo	canvas
	ligar	to chat up
	ligera/o	light; fast
	lila	lilac; purple
el	límite de velocidad	speed limit
	limpia/o	clean
un	lince	lynx
la	línea	line
una	linterna	torch (flashlight)
el	lirio	iris
	lista/o	ready
	¿Estás lista/o?	
	Are you ready?	
	Estoy lista/o.	
	I'm ready.	
la	llamada	ring (of phone); phonecall
la	llanura	plain
la	llave	key

	llegadas	arrivals
	llegar	to come; arrive

¿Cómo puedo llegar a …?
How do I get to …?

	llena/o	full
	llenar	to fill
	llevar	to take (away); carry

Llueve.
It's raining.

la	lluvia	rain
el	lobo	wolf
	loca/o	crazy
	local	local
un	local	venue
el	lodo	mud
las	lombrices	worms
el	loro	parrot
los	sin hogar	homeless
las	luces	lights
la	lucha	fight
	luchar contra	to fight
el	lugar	place
el	lugar de nacimiento	place of birth
el	lujo	luxury
	luminosa/o	light
la	luna	moon
la	luna de miel	honeymoon
	lunes	Monday

Readers looking for a word beginning with 'll' should look in the previous listing. In contemporary Spanish, the 'll' is no longer listed as a separate letter.

M

el	machismo	sexism
la	madera	wood
la	madrastra	stepmother
la	madre; mamá	mother
la	madrugada	dawn
la/el	maga/o	magician
	mala/o	bad
la	maleta	suitcase
el	maletín de primeros auxilios	first-aid kit
una/un	mamerto	lefty
un	mandato	term of office; order
la	mandíbula	jaw
el	mando a distancia	remote control
el	manillar	handlebars
la	mano	hand
la	manta	blanket
la	mantequilla	butter
	mañana	tomorrow
la	mañana	morning
	mañana por la manana	tomorrow morning
	mañana por la tarde; noche	tomorrow afternoon; evening
la	mangosta	mongoose
el	mapa de carreteras	road map

¿Me puede mostrar en el mapa?
Can you show me on the map?

una	máquina	machine
la	máquina de tabaco	cigarette machine
el	mar	sea
	maravillosa/o	marvellous
el	marcador	scoreboard
	marcar	to score
la	marea	tide
	mareada/o	dizzy; seasick
el	mareo	travel sickness
la	mariposa	butterfly
	por vía	by sea;

	marítima	sea mail
	marrón	brown
	martes	Tuesday
el	martillo	hammer
	marzo	March
	más	more
el	masaje	massage
la/el	masajista	massage therapist
	matar	to kill
la	matrícula	car registration
el	matrimonio	marriage
	mayo	May
la	mayoría	majority
el	mechero	lighter
la	media parte	halftime
	media/o	half
la	medianoche	midnight
las	medias	stockings; pantyhose
la	medicina	medicine
la	médica	doctor
el	médico	doctor
un	medio galope	canter
	medio litro	half a litre
el	mediodía	noon
la/el	mejor	best
la	melé	scrum
la/el	mendiga/o	beggar
	menos	less
un	mensaje	message
la	mente	mind
	mentir	to lie
una	mentirosa	liar
un	mentiroso	
los	(cigarillos) mentolados	menthol (cigarettes)
el	mercado	market
el	mes	month
el	mes pasado	last month
el	mes que viene	next month
la	mesa	table

la	mesa de ping pong	table tennis table
la	meseta	plateau
el	metro	metre
	mezclar	to mix
la	mezquita	mosque
el	miedo	fear
la	miel	honey
el	miembro	member
	miércoles	Wednesday
	mil	thousand
el	milano	kite (bird)
un	millón	one million
el	millón	pinball
	minusválida/o	disabled
	mirar los escaparates	window-shopping
un	mirador	lookout point
	mirar	to look
la	misa	mass
la/el	misma/o	same
el	mitin	political meeting
la	mochila	backpack
las	monedas	coins
las	monedas sueltas	loose change
una	monja	nun
un	monje	monk
la/el	mona/o	monkey
la	montaña	mountain
	montar a caballo	to ride a horse
una	mordedura	bite (dog)
la	mosca	fly
	mostrar	to show
	¿Me puede mostrar en el mapa?	
	Can you show me on the map?	
el	motivo del viaje	reason for travel
	muchas/os	many
	muda/o	mute
el	muelle	spring (coil)

	muerta/o	dead
la	muerte	death
una	multa	a fine
las	muñecas	dolls
las	murallas	city walls
el	músculo	muscle
el	museo	museum; art gallery
una	musulmana	Muslim
un	musulmán	

N

	nada	none
	No es nada.	
	It's nothing.	
	nadar	to swim
una	naranja	orange
la	nariz	nose
la	natación	swimming
la	naturaleza	nature
la	navaja	penknife
la	Navidad	Christmas Day
	nebulosa	nebula
	necesitar	to need
	negar	to deny
	negarse	to refuse
	negra/o	black
los	neumáticos	tyres
una	nevera	refrigerator
una/un	nieta/o	grandchild
la	nieve	snow
la	niña	girl
la	niñera	babysitter
el	niño	boy
un	nivel	a level; standard
el	nivel de vida	standard of living
la	noche	evening; night
la	Nochebuena	Christmas Eve

la	Nochevieja	New Year's Eve
el	nombre	name
el	nombre de pila	christian name
el	norte	north
	nosotras/os	we
las	noticias	news
la	novela negra	crime; detective novels
las	novelas	novels
	novena/o	ninth
	noventa	ninety
la	novia	girlfriend; bride
el	novio	boyfriend; groom
la	nube	cloud
	nueva/o	new
	nueve	nine
el	número de andén	platform number
el	número de la habitación	room number
el	número de pasaporte	passport number
	nunca	never
la	nutria	otter

O

	o	or
el	objetivo	lens
una	obra de arte	artwork
	obrera/o	factory worker
	obvia/o	obvious
	octava/o	eighth
	octubre	October
	ocupar	to live (somewhere)
	ochenta	eighty
	ocho	eight

	oeste	west
la	oficina central	head office
la	oficina de teléfonos de larga distancia; telecom	telephone office
una/un	oficinista; empleada/o	office worker
el	oficio religioso	service (religious)
	oír	to hear
el	ojo	eye
	¡Ojo!	Careful!
la	ola	wave
	oler	to smell
la	olla	pot; pan
un	olor	a smell
	olvidar	to forget
	once	eleven
la	ópera	opera; opera house
una	oración	prayer
la	orden	order (command)
el	orden	order (placement)
	ordenar	to order
la	oreja	ear
el	orgullo	pride
el	oro	gold
	oscura/o	dark
el	oso	bear
	otoño	autumn
	otra/o	other
una	oveja	sheep

P

el	padrastro	stepfather
el	padre	father
	¡Padre! (Mex)	Great!; Cool!

los	padres	parents
	pagar	to pay
una	página	page
un	pago	payment
un	país	country
el	País de Gales	Wales
el	pájaro	bird
la	pala	table tennis bat
las	palomitas de maíz	popcorn
la	palanca de cambios	gear stick
el	pan	bread
la	panadería	bakery
la	pantalla	screen
los	pantalones	trousers
los	pantalones cortos	shorts
un	pañal	nappy
los	pañales descartables	disposable nappies
los	pañuelos de papel	tissues
el	Papa	Pope
	papá	dad
el	papel	paper
el	papel de fumar	cigarette papers
el	papel higiénico	toilet paper
la	papelería	stationers
un	par [de guantes]	pair [of gloves]
el	parabrisas	windscreen; windshield
una	parada	a stop
el	paraguas	umbrella
una/un	parapléjica/o	paraplegic
el	parchís	ludo
una	pareja	pair (a couple)
los	parientes	relations
el	paro	dole; short strike (Arg)

un	parque de atracciones	theme park
la	partida	game (sport)
la	partida de nacimiento	birth certificate
el	partido	match
los	partidos políticos	political parties
	partir	to depart; leave
	partir de	to leave from
	pasado	past
	pasado mañana	day after tomorrow
un	pasajero	passenger
un	pase	pass
un	paseo	a stroll
un	paso	step
la	pasta dentífrica	toothpaste
un	pastel	pie
el	pastel de cumpleaños	birthday cake
la	pastelería	cake shop
una	pastilla	pill
las	pastillas para dormir	sleeping pills
una	patada (Mex)	kick
el	pato	duck
la/el	payasa/o	clown
la	paz	peace
una/un	peatón	pedestrian
un	pecado	sin
el	pecho	chest; breast
un	pedazo	piece
	pedir	to ask (for something); borrow
un	peine	comb
una	pelea	a quarrel
una	película	film
el	pelo	hair
la	pelota de juego	game ball
la	pelota de partido	match ball

la	pelota de ping pong	ping pong ball
la	pelota vasca	pelota
el	pelotari	pelota player
los	pendientes	earrings
el	pene	penis
el	peñón	[wall of] rock; crag
	pequeña/o	small
la	perdedora	loser
el	perdedor	
	perder	to lose
	perdonar	to forgive
la	pereza	laziness
	perezosa/o	lazy
un	periódico	newspaper
un	periódico en inglés	newspaper in English
una/un	periodista	journalist
el	permiso de conducir	driver's licence
el	permiso de trabajo	work permit
	pero	but
la/el	perra/o	dog
el	perro lazarillo	guide dog
	pesada/o	heavy
las	pesas	weights
el	pescado	fish (as food)
el	pez	fish
	picante	spicy
una	picazón	itch
un	pico	beak; pick-axe (Mex)
el	pie	foot
la	piedra	stone
la	piel	skin
la	pierna	leg
la	pila	battery
la	píldora	the Pill
la	pimienta	pepper
un	pinchazo	puncture
el	pino	pine

	pintar	to paint
una/un	pintora/pintor	painter
la	pintura	painting (art of)
los	piojos	lice
el	piolet	ice axe
una	pipa	pipe
una	piqueta	pick; pickaxe
las	piquetas	tent pegs
la	piscina	swimming pool
el	piso	floor (storey)
la	pista	race track; tennis court; ski slope
el	placaje	tackle
	plana/o	flat (land, etc)
una	planta	plant
una/un	plasta	pain in the neck; a bore
el	plástico	plastic
la	plata	silver
un	plato	plate
la	playa	beach
la	Plaza Mayor	main square
la	plaza	square (in town)
la	plaza de toros	bullring
	pobre	poor
la	pobreza	poverty
un	poco; poquito	a little bit
	pocos	few
el	poder	power
	poder	to be able to do; can

¿Podría darme …?
Could you give me …?
¿Puede ayudarme?
Can you help me?
¿Puedo sacar una foto?
Can (May) I take a photo?

el	pollo	chicken
	poner	to put
un	poquito	a little (amount)

	por	for
	por ciento	percent
	Por ejemplo, …	For example, …
	porque	because
los	portales	arcades
	por vía terrestre; marítima	surface; sea mail
una	postal	a postcard
las	postales	postcards
el	precio	price
una	pregunta	a question
	preguntar	to ask (question)
	preocupada/o	worried
	preocuparse por	to care (about something)

¡No te preocupes!
Forget about it!; Don't worry.

	preparar	to prepare
los	preservativos	condoms
la	presión arterial	blood pressure
la	presión baja/ alta	low/high blood pressure
	prevenir	to prevent
la	primavera	spring (season)
el	primer	first
la	primera ministra	prime minister
el	primer ministro	
los	prismáticos	binoculars
	privada/o	private
	probar	to try
la	procesión religiosa	religious procession
los	productos congelados	frozen foods
los	productos lácteos	dairy products
	profunda/o	deep
una	promesa	promise
	pronto	soon
una	propuesta	proposal
la	prórroga	extra time

	proteger	to protect
	próxima/o	next
el	proyector	projector
una	prueba de embarazo	pregnancy test kit
las	pruebas nucleares	nuclear testing
un	pueblo; pueblecito	a village
el	puente	bridge
la	puerta	gate
el	puerto	harbour; port
la	puesta del sol	sunset
la	pulga	flea
el	punto	point (tip)

Q

	¿Qué?	
	What?	
	¿Qué hace/es?	
	What are you doing?	
	¿Qué pasa?	
	What's the matter?	
	quedar	to be left (behind)
	quedarse	to stay (remain)
una	quemadura	a burn
una	quemadura de sol	sunburn
	querer	to want; to love
	Queremos ir a …	
	We'd like to go to …	
el	queso	cheese
	quince	fifteen
la	quincena	fortnight
	quinta/o	fifth
el	quiosco	newsagency
el	quiosco de tabaco	tobacco kiosk

	quitar	to take away
R		
el	rabo	tail
una	rata	rat
el	ratón	mouse
el	ratonero	buzzard
la	raza	race (breed)
la	razón	reason
	realizar	to carry out
una	rebaja	discount
	recibir	to receive
el	recibo	receipt
	reciente	recent
	recientemente	recently
la	recogida de equipajes	baggage claim
	reconocer	to recognise
	recordar	to remember
	de largo recorrido	long-distance
un	recuerdo	souvenir
la	red	net
	redonda/o	round
	reembolsar	to refund
un	reembolso	refund
el	reflejo	reflection (mirror)
la	reflexión	reflection (thinking)
una/un	refugiada/o	refugee
un	refugio de montaña	mountain hut
	regalar	to exchange; give gifts
un	regalo	present (gift)
el	regalo de bodas	wedding present
la	regla	menstruation
las	reglas	rules
	regresar	to return
	Regular	OK

la	reina	queen
	reírse	laugh
la	relación	relationship
	relajar	to relax
el	reloj	watch; clock
el	remo	rowing
la	rentabilidad	profitability
	repartir	to deal
	repartir (entre)	to share (with)
un	resfriado	a cold
la	residencia de estudiantes	college
los	residuos tóxicos	toxic waste
	respirar	to breathe
una	respuesta	answer
el	retablo	altarpiece
la/el	retratista	portrait sketcher
la	reventa	ticket scalping
	revisar	to check
la/el	revisora/ revisor	ticket collector
una	revista	magazine
las	revistas del corazón	popular magazines
el	rey	king
	rica/o	rich (wealthy)
un	riesgo	risk
el	rincón	corner (interior)
el	río	river
una	riña	a quarrel
el	riñón	kidney
el	ritmo	rhythm
	robar	to rob; steal
el	roble	oak
la	rodilla	knee
	roja/o	red
el	romero	rosemary
la	ropa	clothing
	rosa	pink
el	roscón de pascua	easter cake
	rota/o	broken (out of order)

[en la]	rotonda	[at the] roundabout
	rubia/o	blonde
la	rueda	wheel
el	ruido	noise
	ruidosa/o	loud

S

[para]	siempre	forever
el	sexo siguro	safe sex
	sábado	Saturday
la	sábana	sheet
	saber	to know (something)
un	saco de dormir	sleeping bag
la	sal	salt
la	sala	salon
la	sala de espera	waiting room
la	sala de fiestas	ballroom
	Salida	Way Out
la	salida	exit
la	salida de emergencia	emergency exit
las	salidas	departures
el	saliente	ledge
	salir con	to go out with
	salir de	to depart (leave)
	saltar	to jump
la	salud	health
	¡Salud! Bless you! (sneezing)	
el	salva slip	panty liners
	salvar	to save
	san	saint
	sangrar	to bleed
la	sangre	blood
	santa/o	saint
el	sapo	toad
	secar	to dry

	sencilla/o	simple
la	sed	thirst
la	seda	silk
	seguir	to follow
	segura/o	safe
el	seguro	insurance
	seis	six
los	sellos	stamps
[en el] semáforo	[at the] traffic lights
la	Semana santa	Holy Week
la	semana	week
la	semana pasada	last week
la	semana que viene	next week
	sembrar	to plant
el	semental	stallion
el	senderismo	hiking
el	sendero	trail; mountain path
los	senos	breasts
la	sensibilidad; ASA	film speed; ASA
	sensible	sensitive
	sentarse	to sit
	sentir	to feel
	séptima/o	seventh
	ser	to be
	(estar see page 34)	
	seria/o	serious
	seropositiva/o	HIV positive
la	serpiente	snake
los	servicios	toilets
	sesenta	sixty
	setenta	seventy
	setiembre/ septiembre	September
el	sexo seguro	safe sex
	sexta/o	sixth
una	señal	a sign
el	SIDA	AIDS
	siempre	always
	Lo siento.	
	I'm sorry.	
	siete	seven

la	silla	chair
la	silla de ruedas	wheelchair
el	sillín	saddle
	simpática/o	nice; friendly
	sin filtro	without filter
	sin plomo	unleaded
los	sindicatos	trade unions
el	síndrome de abstinencia	cold turkey (mono)
el	sitio	place
	sobornar	to bribe
un	soborno	a bribe
	sobre	above; on
el	sobre	envelope
una	sobredosis	overdose
un	sobretodo	coat
el	sol	sun
	sola/o	alone
	sólo	only
	solamente	
	sola/o	single (unique)
	soltera/o	single (person)
la	sombra	shade
los	sondeos	polls
el	sonido	sound
	sonreír	to smile
	sorda/o	deaf
	soñar	to dream
	subir	to climb
el	submarinismo	diving
	sucia/o	dirty
la	sucursal	branch office
	Sudamérica	South America
	sudar	to perspire
la	suegra	mother-in-law
el	suegro	father-in-law
el	suelo	ground; floor
la	suerte	luck
	sufrir	suffer
el	sujetador	bra
	¡Por supuesto!	
	Great!; Of course!	
	sur	south

	sufrir	suffer
el	sujetador	bra
	¡Por supuesto!	
	Great!	
	sur	south

T

la	tabla de surf	surfboard
el	tablero de ajedrez	chess board
el	talco	baby powder
la	talla	size (clothes)
el	taller	garage
el	tamaño	size (of anything)
	también	also
	tampoco	neither
	tan grande como	as big as
un	tanto	point (games)
un	tapete	rug
la	taquilla	ticket office
	tarde	late
	[de la] tarde	[in the] afternoon
una	tarjeta de crédito	credit card
la	tarjeta de embarque	boarding pass
la	tarjeta de teléfono	phonecard
una	tarjeta postal	postcard
la	tarta nupcial	wedding cake
la	tasa del aeropuerto	airport tax
el	teclado	keyboard
los	tejanos	jeans
el	tejón	badger
la	tele	TV
el	tele-arrastre	ski-lift
el	teleférico	cable car
una	telenovela	soap opera
el	telescopio	telescope

el	televisor	TV set
un	templo	temple
	temprano	early
	tener prisa	to be in a hurry
	tener razón	to be right
	tener	to have
	see page 33.	
	¿Tiene usted ...?	
	Do you have ...?	
	tercera/o	third (adj)
un	tercio	a third
	terminar	to end
el	ternero	calf
un	terremoto	earthquake
el	terreno para rodaje de exteriores	location
	terrible	terrible
	por vía terrestre	surface mail
	testaruda/o	stubborn
el	tiempo	weather; time
una	tienda (de campaña)	tent
la	tienda de alimentación	general store; shop
una	tienda de artesanía	craft shop
la	tienda de discos	record shop
la	tienda de fotografía	camera shop
la	tienda de recuerdos	souvenir shop
la	Tierra	Earth
la	tierra	earth
las	tijeras	scissors
el	tipo de cambio	exchange rate
	tirar	to fuck
el	tiro	hit; shot
el	título	degree; title
un	tiquete	ticket
un	tiquete de ida y vuelta	return ticket

el	tomillo	thyme
una	torcedura	sprain
el	tordo	thrush (bird)
el	torneo	tournament
el	toro	bull
el	toro bravo	fighting bull
los	toros	bullfighting
la	torre	tower
una	tortuga	tortoise; turtle
un	tos	a cough
la	toxicomanía	drug addiction
una/un	trabajador	manual worker
una	trabajadora autónoma/	self-employed
un	trabajador autónomo	
el	trabajo	job
el	trabajo de oficina	office work
	traer	to bring
el	traficante de drogas (camello)	drug dealer
el	traje de esquí	ski-suit
una/un	tramposa/o	a cheat
el	tranvía	tram
	trece	thirteen
	treinta	thirty
el	tren	train
	trepar	to scale; climb
	tres	three
	tres cuartos	three-quarters
	tres en raya	noughts & crosses
el	tribunal	court (legal)
un	trío	three of a kind
	triste	sad
un	trozo	piece
	tú	you (inf)
la	tumba	grave

U

la/el	última/o	last
un	ultrasonido	ultrasound
	única/o	single (unique)
	una/o	one
	usted	you (pol)
	ustedes	you (pl)
las	uvas	grapes

V

	va	he/she/it goes
la	vaca	cow
	vacía/o	empty
el	vagón restaurante	dining car
	valer	to cost

¿Cuánto vale ir a ...?
How much is it to go to ...?

el	valle	valley

Vámonos.
Let's go.

el	vapor	steam
los	vaqueros	jeans
	varias/os	several
	veinte	twenty
la	vela	candle
la	vena	vein
la/el	vencedora/ vencedor	winner
un	vendaje	bandage
	vender	to sell
	venir	to come
la	venta automática de billetes	ticket machine
	[estar en] venta	[to be on] sale
una	ventaja	advantage
la	ventana	window
la	ventanilla	window (car; ticket office)
el	ventilador	fan
	ver	to see

¡Ya veremos!
We'll see!

	venir	to come
la	venta automática de billetes	ticket machine
	[estar en] venta	[to be on] sale
una	ventaja	advantage
la	ventana	window
la	ventanilla	window (car; ticket office)
el	ventilador	fan
	ver	to see
	¡Ya veremos! We'll see!	
el	verano	summer
	verde	green
la	verdulería	greengrocer
el	vestíbulo	foyer
el	vestido	dress
el	vestuario	wardrobe
los	vestuarios	changing rooms
una	vez	once
	viajar	to travel
el	viaje	journey
la	vida	life
el	vidrio	glass
	vieja/o	old
el	viento	wind
	viernes	Friday
un	viñedo	vineyard
la	violación	rape

una	visa/	visa
un	visado	
la	vista	view
	vivir	to live (life & somewhere)
el	volumen	volume
	volver	to return
	vosotras/os	you (pl, inf)
la	voz	voice
el	vuelo	flight
el	vuelo doméstico	domestic flight

Y

	y	and
	ya	already
la	yegua	mare
un	yip	jeep
	yo	I
una/un	yonki	junkie

Z

la	zapatería	shoe shop
los	zapatos	shoes
el	zorro	fox
el	zorzal	thrush (bird)
el	zumo	juice

INDEX

Phrasebooks

L onely Planet phrasebooks are packed with essential words and phrases to help travellers communicate with the locals. With colour tabs for quick reference, an extensive vocabulary and use of script, these handy pocket-sized language guides cover day-to-day travel situations.

- handy pocket-sized books
- easy to understand pronunciation chapter
- clear & comprehensive grammar chapter
- romanisation alongside script for ease of pronunciation
- script throughout so users can point to phrases for every situation
- full of cultural information and tips for the traveller

'...vital for a real DIY spirit and attitude in language learning'
– *Backpacker*
'the phrasebooks have good cultural backgrounders and offer solid advice for challenging situations in remote locations'
– *San Francisco Examiner*

Arabic (*Egyptian*) • Arabic (*Moroccan*) • Australian (*Australian English, Aboriginal and Torres Strait languages*) • Baltic States (*Estonian, Latvian, Lithuanian*) • Bengali • Brazilian • British • Burmese • Cantonese • Central Asia • Central Europe (*Czech, French, German, Hungarian, Italian, Slovak*) • Costa Rica Spanish • Eastern Europe (*Bulgarian, Czech, Hungarian, Polish, Romanian, Slovak*) • Ethiopian (*Amharic*) • Fijian • French • German • Greek • Hebrew • Hill Tribes • Hindi & Urdu • Indonesian • Italian • Japanese • Korean • Lao • Latin American Spanish • Malay • Mandarin • Mediterranean Europe (*Albanian, Croatian, Greek, Italian, Macedonian, Maltese, Serbian, Slovene*) • Mongolian • Nepali • Pidgin • Pilipino (*Tagalog*) • Portuguese • Quechua • Russian • Scandinavian Europe (*Danish, Finnish, Icelandic, Norwegian, Swedish*) • South-East Asia (*Burmese, Indonesian, Khmer, Lao, Malay, Tagalog Pilipino, Thai, Vietnamese*) • South Pacific (*Fijian, Fijian Hindi, Hawaiian, Kanak, Maori, Niuean, Pacific French, Pacific Englishes, Rapanui, Rarotongan Maori, Samoan, Spanish, Tahitian, Tongan*) • Spanish (*Castilian; also includes Catalan, Galician and Basque*) • Sri Lanka • Swahili • Thai • Tibetan • Turkish • Ukrainian • USA (*US English, Vernacular, Native American languages, Hawaiian*) • Vietnamese • Western Europe (*Basque, Catalan, Dutch, French, German, Greek, Irish*)

COMPLETE LIST OF LONELY PLANET BOOKS

AFRICA Africa – the South • Africa on a shoestring • Arabic (Egyptian) phrasebook • Arabic (Moroccan) phrasebook • Cairo • Cape Town • Central Africa • East Africa • Egypt • Egypt travel atlas • Ethiopian (Amharic) phrasebook • The Gambia & Senegal • Kenya • Kenya travel atlas • Malawi, Mozambique & Zambia • Morocco • North Africa • South Africa, Lesotho & Swaziland • South Africa, Lesotho & Swaziland travel atlas • Swahili phrasebook • Trekking in East Africa • Tunisia • West Africa • Zimbabwe, Botswana & Namibia • Zimbabwe, Botswana & Namibia travel atlas
Travel Literature: The Rainbird: A Central African Journey • Songs to an African Sunset: A Zimbabwean Story • Mali Blues: Traveling to an African Beat

AUSTRALIA & THE PACIFIC Australia • Australian phrasebook • Bushwalking in Australia • Bushwalking in Papua New Guinea • Fiji • Fijian phrasebook • Islands of Australia's Great Barrier Reef • Melbourne • Micronesia • New Caledonia • New South Wales & the ACT • New Zealand • Northern Territory • Outback Australia • Papua New Guinea • Papua New Guinea (Pidgin) phrasebook • Queensland • Rarotonga & the Cook Islands • Samoa • Solomon Islands • South Australia • Sydney • Tahiti & French Polynesia • Tasmania • Tonga • Tramping in New Zealand • Vanuatu • Victoria • Western Australia
Travel Literature: Islands in the Clouds • Sean & David's Long Drive

CENTRAL AMERICA & THE CARIBBEAN Bahamas and Turks & Caicos • Barcelona • Bermuda • Central America on a shoestring • Costa Rica • Cuba • Dominican Republic & Haiti • Eastern Caribbean • Guatemala, Belize & Yucatán: La Ruta Maya • Jamaica • Mexico • Mexico City • Panama
Travel Literature: Green Dreams: Travels in Central America

EUROPE Amsterdam • Andalucía • Austria • Baltic States phrasebook • Berlin • Britain • British phrasebook • Central Europe • Central Europe phrasebook • Croatia • Czech & Slovak Republics • Denmark • Dublin • Eastern Europe • Eastern Europe phrasebook • Edinburgh • Estonia, Latvia & Lithuania • Europe • Finland • France • French phrasebook • Germany • German phrasebook • Greece • Greek phrasebook • Hungary • Iceland, Greenland & the Faroe Islands • Ireland • Italian phrasebook • Italy • Lisbon • London • Mediterranean Europe • Mediterranean Europe phrasebook • Paris • Poland • Portugal • Portugal travel atlas • Prague • Provence & the Côte D'Azur • Romania & Moldova • Russia, Ukraine & Belarus • Russian phrasebook • Scandinavian & Baltic Europe • Scandinavian Europe phrasebook • Scotland • Slovenia • Spain • Spanish phrasebook • St Petersburg • Switzerland • Trekking in Spain • Ukrainian phrasebook • Vienna • Walking in Britain • Walking in Italy • Walking in Ireland • Walking in Switzerland • Western Europe • Western Europe phrasebook
Travel Literature: The Olive Grove: Travels in Greece

INDIAN SUBCONTINENT Bangladesh • Bengali phrasebook • Bhutan • Delhi • Goa • Hindi/Urdu phrasebook • India • India & Bangladesh travel atlas • Indian Himalaya • Karakoram Highway • Nepal • Nepali phrasebook • Pakistan • Rajasthan • South India • Sri Lanka • Sri Lanka phrasebook • Trekking in the Indian Himalaya • Trekking in the Karakoram & Hindukush • Trekking in the Nepal Himalaya

COMPLETE LIST OF LONELY PLANET BOOKS

Travel Literature: In Rajasthan • Shopping for Buddhas

ISLANDS OF THE INDIAN OCEAN Madagascar & Comoros • Maldives • Mauritius, Réunion & Seychelles

MIDDLE EAST & CENTRAL ASIA Arab Gulf States • Central Asia • Central Asia phrasebook • Iran • Israel & the Palestinian Territories • Israel & the Palestinian Territories travel atlas • Istanbul • Jerusalem • Jordan & Syria • Jordan, Syria & Lebanon travel atlas • Lebanon • Middle East on a shoestring • Turkey • Turkish phrasebook • Turkey travel atlas • Yemen
Travel Literature: The Gates of Damascus • Kingdom of the Film Stars: Journey into Jordan

NORTH AMERICA Alaska • Backpacking in Alaska • Baja California • California & Nevada • Canada • Florida • Hawaii • Honolulu • Los Angeles • Miami • New England USA • New Orleans • New York City • New York, New Jersey & Pennsylvania • Pacific Northwest USA • Rocky Mountain States • San Francisco • Seattle • Southwest USA • USA • USA phrasebook • Vancouver • Washington, DC & the Capital Region
Travel Literature: Drive Thru America

NORTH-EAST ASIA Beijing • Cantonese phrasebook • China • Hong Kong • Hong Kong, Macau & Guangzhou • Japan • Japanese phrasebook • Japanese audio pack • Korea • Korean phrasebook • Kyoto • Mandarin phrasebook • Mongolia • Mongolian phrasebook • North-East Asia on a shoestring • Seoul • South-West China • Taiwan • Tibet • Tibetan phrasebook • Tokyo
Travel Literature: Lost Japan

SOUTH AMERICA Argentina, Uruguay & Paraguay % Bolivia • Brazil • Brazilian phrasebook • Buenos Aires • Chile & Easter Island • Chile & Easter Island travel atlas • Colombia • Ecuador & the Galapagos Islands • Latin American Spanish phrasebook • Peru • Quechua phrasebook • Rio de Janeiro • South America on a shoestring • Trekking in the Patagonian Andes • Venezuela
Travel Literature: Full Circle: A South American Journey

SOUTH-EAST ASIA Bali & Lombok • Bangkok • Burmese phrasebook • Cambodia • Hill Tribes phrasebook • Ho Chi Minh City • Indonesia • Indonesian phrasebook • Indonesian audio pack • Jakarta • Java • Laos • Lao phrasebook • Laos travel atlas • Malay phrasebook • Malaysia, Singapore & Brunei • Myanmar (Burma) • Philippines • Pilipino (Tagalog) phrasebook • Singapore • South-East Asia on a shoestring • South-East Asia phrasebook • Thailand • Thailand's Islands & Beaches • Thailand travel atlas • Thai phrasebook • Thai audio pack • Vietnam • Vietnamese phrasebook • Vietnam travel atlas

ALSO AVAILABLE: Antarctica • Brief Encounters: Stories of Love, Sex & Travel • Chasing Rickshaws • Not the Only Planet: Travel Stories from Science Fiction • Travel with Children • Traveller's Tales

LONELY PLANET

Series Description

travel guidebooks	in depth coverage with background and recommendations
	download selected guidebook Upgrades at www.lonelyplanet.com
shoestring guides	for travellers with more time than money
condensed guides	highlights the best a destination has to offer
citySync	digital city guides for Palm TM OS
outdoor guides	walking, cycling, diving and watching wildlife
phrasebooks	just don't stand there, say something!
city maps and road atlases	essential navigation tools
world food	for people who live to eat, drink & travel
out to eat	a city's best places to eat and drink
read this first	invaluable pre-departure guides
healthy travel	practical advice for staying well on the road
journeys	travel stories for armchair explorers
pictorial	lavishly illustrated pictorial books
ekno	low-cost international phonecard with e-services
TV series and videos	on the road docos
web site	for chat, Upgrades, destination facts
lonely planet images	on line photo library

LONELY PLANET OFFICES

Australia
PO Box 617, Hawthorn,
Victoria 3122
☎ (03) 9819 1877
fax (03) 9819 6459
email: talk2us@lonelyplanet.com.au

USA
150 Linden St, Oakland,
CA 94607
☎ (510) 893 8555
TOLL FREE: 800 275 8555
fax (510) 893 8572
email: info@lonelyplanet.com

UK
10a Spring Place,
London NW5 3BH
☎ (020) 7428 4800
fax (020) 7428 4828
email: go@lonelyplanet.co.uk

France
1 rue du Dahomey,
75011 Paris
☎ 01 55 25 33 00
fax 01 55 25 33 01
email: bip@lonelyplanet.fr
website: www.lonelyplanet.fr

**World Wide Web: www.lonelyplanet.com _or_ AOL keyword: lp
Lonely Planet Images: lpi@lonelyplanet.com.au**